Sasha Swire is the author of the l
She was born and brought up in v
Sir John Nott, was MP for the S
journalist on national and regiona
working as her husband Hugo Swire's political researcher from
2001 to 2019. She divides her time between Devon and London.

'A meditation on language and journeys – knowing, alert to the
politics and history of landscape – to the mundane within the
transcendental. A real achievement – unexpectedly moving with
every beat and turn of its taut, precise prose' Rory Stewart

'Beautifully written ... In the contemplative, Paul Theroux-like
exploration of our most stunning coastline, Swire escapes the
stifling Lilliputian world of Westminster to follow the path from
Minehead in Somerset to Land's End in Cornwall ... A lively
mix of history, botany, philosophy, poetry and personal family
memories' Celia Walden, *Daily Telegraph*

'Swire is an amiable companion, who ingeniously evokes the landscapes, famous people who lived here and, especially, the flora and
fauna' Simon Worrall, *Guardian*

'A glorious historical ramble along a favourite coastline' Robin
Hanbury-Tenison

'Swire, brought up in Cornwall, has given free rein to her considerable literary talents and pondered places and prospects with
fascinating details and soulful observations' Rory Knight Bruce

'Such range and surprise – every turn she makes on the South-West
Coast Path, Sasha Swire turns up another story, another glimpse
of history or archaeology or local lore. *Edgeland* is itself like the
best days out on the cliffs – deeply rewarding and enjoyable'
Philip Marsden

Also by Sasha Swire
Diary of an MP's Wife

EDGELAND

A Slow Walk West

Sasha Swire

abacus
books

ABACUS

First published in Great Britain in 2023 by Abacus
This paperback edition published in Great Britain in 2024 by Abacus

1 3 5 7 9 10 8 6 4 2

A CIP catalogue record for this book
is available from the British Library.

ISBN 978-0-349-14519-8

Typeset in Baskerville by M Rules
Printed and bound in Great Britain by Clays Ltd, Elcograf S.p.A.

Papers used by Abacus are from well-managed forests
and other responsible sources.

Abacus
An imprint of
Little, Brown Book Group
Carmelite House
50 Victoria Embankment
London EC4Y 0DZ

An Hachette UK Company
www.hachette.co.uk

www.littlebrown.co.uk

To my parents, who brought me west.

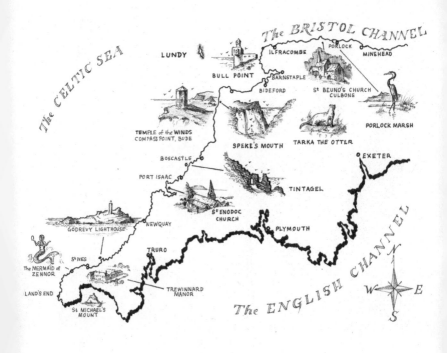

The BRISTOL CHANNEL

The CELTIC SEA

LUNDY

ILFRACOMBE
PORLOCK
MINEHEAD

BULL POINT

BARNSTAPLE

BIDEFORD

St BEUNO'S CHURCH
CULBONE

PORLOCK MARSH

TEMPLE of the WINDS
COMPASS POINT, BUDE

SPEKE'S MOUTH

TARKA THE OTTER

BOSCASTLE

EXETER

PORT ISAAC

TINTAGEL

GODREVY LIGHTHOUSE

NEWQUAY

St ENODOC
CHURCH

PLYMOUTH

The MERMAID of
ZENNOR

St IVES

TRURO

LAND'S END

TREWINNARD
MANOR

St MICHAEL'S
MOUNT

The ENGLISH CHANNEL

N
W   E
S

Contents

Edge

According to the *Oxford English Dictionary* (abbreviated):

NOUN

The outside limit of an object.

An area next to a steep drop: *'the cliff edge'*.

The point immediately before something unpleasant or
momentous occurs.

The sharpened side of the blade of a cutting implement
or weapon.

The line along which two surfaces of a solid meet.

An intense, sharp, or striking quality.

A quality or factor which gives superiority over
close rivals.

VERB

Provide with a border or edge.

Move or cause to move gradually or furtively in a particular direction.

Give an intense or sharp quality to.

PHRASES

On the edge of one's seat.

Set someone's teeth on edge.

Take the edge off.

On edge.

Edge someone out.

Almost at the most westerly point of England, on a bony ridge of land stretching far out into the Atlantic Ocean, there is a church called St Senara's. In it, a small oak panel, formerly the end of a bench, stands lonely and apart. But it's not the panel so much as the character it portrays that is of interest: half woman, half fish, an ancestor of storm demons and ancient goddesses and sirens, a creature that has been hauled up and stranded in a human world. She is the Mermaid of Zennor, and her carving is medieval and simple, no fuss; she kneels upright on her tail alongside her crook, and she is holding up a mirror and a large rectangular comb. There are streaks in her hair where she has combed it, but her face is lost, as is a quatrefoil upon which woodworm have feasted.

But why here? Zennor sits on the metaphorical high-water mark, its arrangement with nature and prehistory making it a beguiling place, imbued with story and myth. It is a land ready furnished to nurture a creature such as she, with its swirling sea mist; its trees bearded and bent in lichens, huddled together like Macbeth's witches; the vomitus of granite boulders between the bracken and gorse; the rainless gales from the west. For old communities, the mermaid represented danger, being one thing and not quite another. Her ambiguous, hybrid form makes her a creature from the edge, just like Zennor is; she is from a place where one world ends and another begins.

Eight hundred years before Christ, a new people arrived on the natural edges of the South West Peninsula and created artificial ones. They started to throw up ramparts across the necks of the headlands, cutting them off from the mainland. Although they had wells from which water could be obtained, they did not live in these fortresses: they used them as places of retreat in time of war, and with their huge walls of earth and stone, and their deep ditches, they provided a retreat in which to hold out against almost any besieger and any abuse from the raging sea.

For thousands of years miners have broken the surface of this earth in order to excavate its depths. They have long known about the rich mineral wealth to be found. The mine shafts are a rim over and into the underland and its matter. The miners stand at the top of the shaft, waiting to go down. Their clothes are stained and tattered. They wear hardened felt hats with a candle stuck into a lump of sticky clay. The cage comes up to the surface, the miners step into it and a moment later drop, with terrifying speed, into the darkness below. After a while the cage halts, and the men get out and make their way along a tunnel which brings them to the lode. Here, in this cave, the creases and folds enclose inner edges, natural ones, like ribs in a vertebrate body; they enclose the miners as if protecting them – or sometimes, if the mine collapses, endangering them. Later in time, and in this same space, they will pick up their compressed-air drills and start blasting. The roar of the drills resounds to the very edge of the workings, making the rocks tremble. The air is hot and smoky, water is dripping down the dark walls of granite, the only natural light is from pinpricks far above them. Holes are drilled and carefully filled with cartridges of blasting gelignite. The men pull back. The last man lights a fuse that sizzles its way to the edge of the rock and a few minutes later there is a deafening roar of pain from the rock. The men wait for the smoke to clear, then go in and load the broken lumps of ore into little trucks. They are singing now. These men know all there is to know about edges and rims. For them it is more than work: it is a feeling, it is crossing over into something that feels forbidden, unspoken, a place beyond the ordinary.

In a seaside town, a drug addict is injecting himself with heroin;

he needs to take the edge off his craving. He is at the very brink of doom, the extreme; he is at a point of exhaustion. He came to this end-of-the-line destination guided by the sun. He wanted to sit in the golden glow of its evening light and find himself again. What he found instead was dingy bedsits and guest houses and small hotels occupied by people on benefits and part-time foreign workers with overflowing rubbish outside and scavenging seagulls bombing over a single half-eaten burger. Living here is like being trapped in someone else's dream. He watches it as if he is a ghost – is he biologically dead or is he socially dead? He doesn't know any more. What he does know was the ride west was a mistake. A big mistake. West is where you go to die, it is the direction of the setting sun, west symbolises the end.

He is high now. He goes down to the water's edge and sits on the rocks and watches the sea. It is night and the town's lights sprinkle glitter on the surface of the water. His phone wriggles in his pocket but he ignores it. He likes it when the tide stretches its slack; it is how he is feeling now: calm, the gentle whack of waves against his bare feet. Most people are waiting to get older. He knows he is waiting to die. He takes his clothes off and eases his naked body down into the water, clinging to a rock, hanging for a moment before he lets himself fall, slowly, as if in his own sonata, then seaweed and warmth, seaweed and warmth, and then a sun, at last. In the morning they find him face-down at the water's edge, as if he is looking for something.

Most people understand the word edge as being the outermost part of an object or the end of something, but that understanding dismisses the multeity of edges; they can also be existences, actualities even. Often, they are dynamic places, transitory, they can enclose an object, a place or an event. They can mark the disappearance of something and the start of something. As the American philosopher Edward S. Casey states, 'Where and when edges harden and sharpen, people gather, resistance is generated, creativity is sparked, and new ways of being with one another emerge.'

We live in a crowded edge world without really knowing or understanding it; our lives are replete with verges of every description: not only the harsh and the physical, but everyday edges that we have to navigate with our bodies and our minds. Edges can enact or establish not only what we understand of the world, but the places and events we find ourselves in. They do more than demarcate or delimit; they can be the very foundation of experience: perceptual, practical, aesthetic, emotional. So much emanates from them and begins with them, whether in art, in politics, in industry, in geography, in the natural world, and everything ends in them.

The journey I describe here is through an edgeland, one that is deeply familiar to me: the South West Coast Path. It is a linear journey, that blows westward then turns east following, for 630 miles, the contours of natural borders. It started at Minehead in Somerset, clambering up North Hill to a gorse-tangled plateau, and from there travelled through three counties, finishing in Poole in Dorset. It passed through big towns, small towns, villages and hamlets, even wilderness; it wove between gone worlds that have risen and dissolved; it offered artistic associations and rocks that are more durable than the gathering of heavens; it gave me freedom on blond beaches under blue skies and God over saint-wooed ground.

When I started walking, I was not seeking a lucid understanding of an edge world, just ecotherapy, as respite from the stresses of my job in an urban existence. I came where many people come, to the line between land and sea. I just wanted to add my feet to the current of a coastal path looking seaward. As I sauntered along, on and off over a ten-year period, I became increasingly charmed, even enthralled, by the sheer level of expressive forces at work on the fringes. It felt as if each edge had a creation story attached to it, and every one of those stories epitomised ingenuity over the hardships of geography. It applied not only to the flora and fauna but to humans as well, those who had chosen to make their place here. I found many of their methods and their manners of adaptation have been precursors to whole movements and industries, more often than not culturally transmitted to the demurer and more unadventurous and settled members of their species further inland. But edges can also expose us to risk: they can lead us astray or bring us to an unwelcome fate. I found that too.

What I discovered was the edge is where the action is, not the surface. That it is a whole philosophy of the way we have lived and how we are living now. What was needed was a phenomenology, a particular form of sensitivity, a process of learning how to be more attentive and more responsive to what we casually pass by. Because, by looking at parts that negotiate and express the whole, one can find a voice in the things themselves and in so doing discover an altogether different dominion. For me it happened in the insistent presence of edges; an ambiguous, transitory, often ephemeral and elusive zone with an identity all of its own. One that tells us a profound story about our island nation, its history, its nature and its people.

Home and Away

Minehead to Porlock

The hills have eyes. What must they have seen from this pro-
trusion of Exmoor that rises beside a town looking out to
sea? The English seaside as its port declines: quaytown houses
turned to boarding houses; steamships, bathing machines, a
steam train, ice-cream parlours run by Italian immigrants.
There are amusement arcades, a theatre, a cinema and concert
hall, and a pier. In the nineteenth century, polo ponies were
exercised on the beach. In 1874, the railway brought even more
summer visitors. Hotels were built and more shops opened. Then,
in the twentieth century, stiff competition from resorts abroad
meant a chill wind blew on seaside resorts like these. Poor transport links, an ageing population and low expectations ensured
that Minehead will spend the next decades running to stand
still. It is another story about the near and the far away. Of other
places and other worlds.

I am on North Hill, at the start of my walk. Rising nine
hundred feet from the sea, the hill hovers over the town in a
friendly fashion. I am on rare coastal heathland. Among gorse
and bracken, bell heather and ling, I have clear views across the
Bristol Channel. Somewhere below me, although I cannot see it
from here, spread out before the sea, lies that which Minehead

is reliant on for its economic health: Butlin's holiday camp, the largest employer in this small coastal town.

Its founder was a rogue called Billy Butlin. Billy looked like a diminutive Rhett Butler and behaved like one, particularly with the women; he was an archetypal edgeland character. Born of fairground stock, he acquired his business acumen ducking and diving between the gingerbread stalls and toffee-apple barrels, flirting with the punters and learning where and when to use his animal charm. His first pitch was a hoopla stall, his prizes cheap rewards, chocolate and dyed wrens passed off as canaries. From there he moved on to operate a string of arcades, amusement parks and fairground pitches and zoos all over the country. For one who bobbed and weaved, it is appropriate that his early fortune came from importing dodgem cars. A natural gambler, he borrowed heavily to set up his first holiday camp in Skegness in 1936, and many more would follow as his business boomed after the war. The camp in Minehead opened in 1962, and flooded the area with thirty thousand people in its first year alone.

The Minehead camp was built on former grazing marshes, with a trench around the perimeter to keep the sea out. It is a story of enclosure: enclosing the British holidaying public in their masses. As a painting exists within a frame, the same could be said of a holiday camp. The frame is not a limit for pleasure, but shelters and supports it; it makes the pursuit of pleasure containable. Billy Butlin pinpointed this containment as a huge financial opportunity. Escape from the boredom of the post-war years was ripe for exploitation. Billy Butlin became Britain's seaside ringmaster, the significant performer in his own big-tent show, directing the audience's attention and producing a seamless performance. He was bigger and better than anyone else in the pleasure-dome world. Billy would present new visions of what happiness should be. In his own unique way, he taught people how to live and love again.

Billy came to an edge in the natural world and created another artificial one, a cultural one, and in doing so changed the coastal topography of Britain for good. He created a place of transcend-ence, fixed it into place, introduced new boundaries and borders. He closed the windows and caged the wounded birds inside until they were nursed back to health. He grounded them. They didn't mind: Butlin's was a place where they could leave the world behind, literally, and where nothing but emptiness lay ahead, a sea, just like a desert. The horizon was where the landscape ended; it would be an end of reflectiveness, of incidence, of avail-ability. But the barriers didn't work for ever: when the campers finally pressed their foreheads against the glass, watching the white trails of aeroplanes make pathways in the sky above them, they opened the windows and flew away looking for new hori-zons. Time had moved on and Billy could no longer contain his flock; the edges had moved outwards and something else had to be created in the mud of disintegration.

On this, my first day of walking, Hurlstone Point. There is a birdwatcher with his binoculars raised, standing lonely at the sharpness of the edge.

'What can you see?'

He reels off a list: falcons and wheatears, stonechats, ring ouzels and black redstart. He tells me a wide array of birds hover over this point and adds that it's an excellent time of year to watch them, because the migrants are flying overhead on their journey to Africa.

The birdwatcher comes to this location because it is where the earth retreats and he has room to move outwards, further and further away from the near space in which he resides. And it is not an uncommon sight, solitary men obsessed by birds, in this border territory. It gets me thinking: J. A. Baker's *The Peregrine*, Paul Gallico's *The Snow Goose*, T. H. White's obsession with fal-conry. *Kes.* Ted Hughes *is* 'Hawk Roosting'. William Faulkner said, 'If I were reincarnated, I'd want to come back as a buzzard. Nothing hates him or envies him or wants him or needs him. He is never bothered or in danger, and he can eat anything.' Faulkner never much liked women. Are birds like ghosts to these men? Their real selves coming and going?

I have a theory: that birdwatching in men comes from the dark corners where the conflicts with hunting and hurting reside. Man's whole narrative has been of escaping the wild, supressing his savage and primal instincts; one of moving towards civilisation, away from caveman conditions towards hearth and home, but I wonder if there is still something beating in his heart from that time, some residue? This intense viewing of species and behaviours, understanding the intricacies of their world, is like any great hunting or military operation; it takes careful planning and thinking. Between that plan and operation is a void, the unknown; this is the zone the birdwatcher inhabits, the zone that defines weakness or victory, success or failure. It is important to understand your opponent, even though sometimes one can get tangled up with admiration for it. Of course, the pursuit of power is difficult to confess to; difficult to classify. But it can run deep in a man; it can drive him in even the smallest of interests such as birdwatching. If you drew a map of the male mind, I'm sure it would all be there, a cartography marked by nature: power, vison, competition, killing. He is not owned by anything or anyone other than his primal being. It's about being fit for war.

I look at the birdwatcher again, and him looking out to sea, and yes, this is his default state, this is the savage mind at play, and as I turn away I remember D. H. Lawrence's words about the tribal mysteries his blood had lived: 'every drop of me trembles still alive to the old sound, every thread in my body quivers to the frenzy of the old mystery. I know my derivation.'

We are at the autumn equinox. England is at the fulcrum of manic migration activity; headlands such as this are hubs, as frantic and intense as international airports filled with sun-seeking tourists. Just as an airport is an area of transition, so it could be said is the ecotone: that space where two biological communities meet and integrate. It is a place made up of no places, a between place, if you like: between land and sea, forest and plain, between destinations, between cities, between futures to be made and pasts left behind; a place where stories are easily spun because everything is in such an uncertain state and open to interpretation. In nature, the intermingling is known as the edge effect. It occurs where two different communities or creatures crash up against each other with an intensity not otherwise possible: a raptor, let's say, coming out of a forest to the hunting grounds of a field, or the tiny souls of birds confronting big oceans. It offers a greater variety and density of experience, a proliferation of perspectives. Still, it's not always for the good; bad stuff happens as well: the colonisation of habitat by an invasive species, a terrorist boarding a plane with a bomb in the sole of his shoe, logging in areas impacted by human development.

The word ecotone, like all good etymology, tells you how it really is: a marriage of eco ('ecology') and tone, from the Greek *tonos*, or 'tension'. And it is this tension which makes it so interesting, because although we are dealing with boundaries, they are endlessly porous, leaving us, and the natural world, forever passing through them.

Coastal erosion on Porlock Beach has led to the exposure of Mesolithic lands. On the western side of the bay, near Porlock Weir, a petrified forest is visible at low tide, preserved like Damien Hirst's pickled animal corpses in a subaqueous silence. For over six thousand years, before melting ice from the last Ice Age caused sea levels to rise and shift the shoreline inland, it was fish, not birds, that had woven in and out of the forest's trees and branches; now, that whole other existence is revealed in the blue clay of an old river channel: flints, the spines of aurochs, piddocks. And on the saltmarsh itself, a plantation of seemingly stunned skeletal trees, bleached silver by salt and wind, raising their bare branches heavenwards, turning history into elegy and as beautiful as any death poem can be.

Time is light over the world. A weakening of the ridge protecting the marsh, which was formed from the natural supply of stone from Culbone cliffs, means that it now no longer reaches the beach, while the shingle already there is being bullied by the sea to build up the eastern end, making the western end thinner. The submerged forest will soon be silent again in waters deep. Sometimes, if you are really unlucky, you can die again and again as Lazarus did.

I tread gingerly across paths and pontoons in land stolen by water. Travelling over a thick, gelatinous, glossy mud not known to me, where only those who come armed, with sharp or pointy beaks, are successful finding food: grey herons, little egrets and curlews among them. The ground is full of marsh samphire and sea-blite, Babington's leek and milkwort.

Every day these plants live with the salt, with the wind; they are dusted up by grey clay, the mud, they are waterboarded by the tides. One day the saltwater marsh will return to being a lagoon and everyone and everything will give up the fight. But not yet, not yet. The plants resist by trapping and binding the sediment, exporting nutrients to their enemy and providing support for migratory visitors. Some even show their optimism and love by formulating tiny flowers on their stems under the sea. The yellow horned poppy, for example, grows a coat of fine hairs to protect it from the salt. Subjecting something to a harsh or cruel form of domination often acts as a catalyst at the edge.

But the greatest hero of them all is *Salicornia europaea*, or samphire, the Spartacus of the marsh lands. Rough and ready, with an 'iodine-and-ozone tang' and a 'chimera from a medieval bestiary, half vegetable, half miniature sea monster' appearance, it has stripped itself of leaves and donned an armour of minute scales for protection. Nonetheless, its strategic supremacy is not based on its physicality but on its ability to colonise this glutinous mud, shoals of it carpeting the flats 'like bowling greens'. By anchoring itself into the cracks and awaiting the surging immensity of the waves, it creates a first line of defence. It does this by laying down its vast armies so other troops such as sea aster and lavender and other perennials can come in with their garrisons, establish themselves and join the fight, a fight which is all about raising land levels. Soon the perennials take over and the samphire is left with fewer and fewer patches for its own seeds. Like all power struggles, a single homogenous culture will eventually weaken and even die out. Why? Because evolution, as in politics, is a social activity where compromises have to be made. Samphire has a purpose: it may be able to create a pasture good enough for sheep to graze on at the very edge of possibilities, but in doing so it destroys itself. And yet it cannot be entirely written off as a victim; sometimes all it needs is a single storm surge, a weakened ridge, a new lagoon, a land that keeps shifting its edges, and it will rise up again as the hero of the wetlands.

Richard Mabey, one of our greatest nature writers, shares my enthusiasm for this plant and the lessons it teaches us: 'Samphire taught me that the divisions between plant as sustenance for the body and nourishment for the imagination, and between scientific fascination and romantic inspiration, were fluid. Everything I have written since has been influenced by the thought of its ephemeral life, in which opportunism, self-expression and utility are able to coexist.'

On 29 October 1942, a long-range bomber was flying low like a big fat homing pigeon over this swampland, having completed a mission against German U-boats in the Bay of Biscay. It was returning to its base at Holmsley South airfield in the New Forest, and like the bird itself was following the grooves and hollows of valleys and seas, flying low to evade hawks and harassers. Because of heavy rain and poor visibility, it clipped the top of Bossington Hill, which was in low cloud, and swung westward over Porlock, debris falling from the stricken plane. A wheel and part of the undercarriage plunged onto Sparkhayes Lane before its carcass dropped heavily into the marsh, killing eleven of its twelve American crew. The airmen's memorial, which has been moved from its original site onto the footpath so more people can see it, is made from the remains of the aircraft.

When people die like this, slipping between different realms, they become ghosts where they fall and that is how they stay alive with all that is already there. After all, what goes on here is otherworldly, ethereal, fluid; those native to the marsh already brave and longing to forget and smouldering through time. It truly is a land fit for heroes. A place of desperate reaching.

Contagions

Porlock Weir to Lynmouth Harbour

From Porlock Weir I walk up the wooded spiral to Culbone. It is scraggy all around, with green weaving tops, the path travelling through a passageway, passing alongside tumbling mossy walls that are occasionally bridged. I am being led as if I were a tradesman, unseen, up from the road in the only crevice that breaks the stubborn row of hills lining the shore between Minehead and the Valley of the Rocks, travelling through tunnels to the back entrance of a considerably larger house. Those who lived there clearly liked their privacy.

Here, in some of the most natural woodland left in England on the edge of Exmoor, rest the remains of Ashley Combe, a once-fabulous fantasy mansion twinkling with minarets and cloisters and alien architectural features; a dreamland hewn out of the escarpment by yodelling Swiss mountaineers laying carriageways and walkways through which its owners could move as secrets. Yearnor Wood has now reclaimed the land as its own, but it has been generous, it has left space for absences, absences equal in size to what it left behind, absences that are tangible and need to be sought out.

In that way you just know there is a presence. I feel it now.

It is the mid-nineteenth century. A sumptuous shifting of long skirts as Ada Lovelace, the daughter of Lord Byron, passes above us, no doubt on one of the wooded walks laid one above the other, backed by a row of alcoves and joined by spiral stairs. Maybe she is heading down towards the beach, where a bathhouse has been built into the rock by her adoring husband, William King, Earl of Lovelace, to enable her to bathe privately. Not a gleam of light in these woods, but I can see her now, the brim of her wide hat casting shadows on those dark and devilish poet's features.

She loves it here: the denseness of the wood, the rustling of the trees, the noises of hidden brooks, the echoes of literary ghosts, the absolute wildness of this place. It is somewhere where her deepest expressions can be liberated. Like the landscape that surrounds her, she is untameable, a creature cooked up by the rogue genetics of her poet father struggling with the formality of her mother Annabella, who passed on to Ada her gift for numbers and science.

When Ada roamed 'over hills, valleys, moors, downs and every variety of wild beautiful country', she was following in the footsteps of the Romantics, a movement that had reshaped the world in which she lived: artists and writers and scientists like herself who felt they were no longer beholden to God, King or Country, who needed to remove themselves from the trappings of modern civilisation. Ada would adopt their unruliness, come to believe that intuition and the freedom of the imagination to run wild were critical to the effective application of mathematical and scientific concepts. She would challenge the primacy of the edges they offered but she didn't dismiss them; she used them to connect and carry forward concepts rather than be confined by them. She would also cross over the boundaries of her sex in a time when fixed ideas of behaviour were imposed upon women. And she would learn to value metaphysics as much as mathematics, viewing both as tools for exploring the 'unseen worlds around us'. It would be the key motivation to her success as a scientist.

*

Ada, William Wordsworth, Samuel Taylor Coleridge: all trod the path I now walk in that ancient recognition of the close relationship between thinking and walking: *solvitur ambulando*, 'to be solved by walking'. Wordsworth and Coleridge, inspired by all that surrounded them, produced *Lyrical Ballads* in 1798, a pure and noble expression of Romantic ideals that found dignity in the commonplace. It was revolutionary, political even, and broke the boundaries of literary convention and heralded a new understanding of the world, of nature and our place in it. Coming to the wild edge, the Romantics enter an ever-new yet old place-world, where the wildness purifies them; it is as if they are entering the choric space of Plato's *Timaeus*, a place of dynamic changes which will lead to new social solutions. In many ways the Romantics entered one topography and in doing so came into another, that of their own reflective thinking. This coastline, this edge, became a crack from which light appeared and from which a new dawn could be created. In that way edges are not only the terminus of something, they are also where that something begins.

The trees eventually give way to a pool of light and Culbone church appears out of nowhere like a mirage, which is how religious apparitions should be; out of the dark, out of the sorrows of this world: small, tidy, to the point. If they want us to believe, they should set more things down in the wild like this, among the deer and the fern and the cranesbill, with nothing but a ceiling of birdsong above. They should make us journey to them like they do here.

Long before Christianity came to these shores, the hamlet of Culbone, whose other name is Kitnor, 'cave by the sea', was a centre for pagan worship. Then in the fifth century, following rumours that Joseph of Arimathea passed by on his way from Looe to Glastonbury with the infant Jesus in tow, a community of monks set up home here. The first church was built two centuries later, dedicated to the Welsh saint Beuno, a wandering preacher who is said to have led a solitary ascetic life here for a time. There is certainly evidence of an anchorite's cell on the north side of the building. An elective activity, granted, which could be terminated anytime, but still one where the body has nowhere to move or go. For me, an oppression of walls; for a Celtic saint, the most perfect of settings.

I walk on through these woods, through what would have once been the King estate, over brooks via which Exmoor expels its waters into the sea. It really is Xanadu: a lush utopia of streams cascading down paths, with ferns and yellow reindeer mosses and liverworts scenting the air, and sounds of wild deer, foxes, badgers, martens, squirrels and those seasonal waterfalls falling as ground lightning. Coleridge writes: 'But oh! that deep romantic chasm which slanted / Down the green hill athwart a cedarn cover!' This is ground that remembers him well. It might not be covered in cedar trees and the rivers not as violent and uncontrollable as in 'Kubla Khan', but all the lush and sensuous signals are present, the ones that transport you into the poet's vision of a great ruler's kingdom.

It is a well-worn tale, but I will repeat it for those who have not heard it before. Coleridge had come here to clear his writer's block, but he was also suffering from dysentery; he thought walks in these parts might prove a laxative for his clotted mind and ease his exhausted body. And he was right; lines for his verse drama *Osorio* started to flow fast like the brooks that surrounded him. After one of his walks through the tiny vale that embraces Culbone church, he returned to Ash Farm, where he was staying, took off his boots and resumed the book he was reading, a volume published in 1613 which went by the name of *Purchas his Pilgrimage*. Then, still feeling a little queasy, he took a few drops of opium to settle his stomach. Just as he reached a passage about Xanadu, where 'the Khan Kubla commanded a palace to be built, and a stately garden thereunto', he crossed over into a deep, drug-induced sleep that lifted him up to a different level of consciousness. Out of that dream would come one of the most beautiful poems in English, because in his reverie Coleridge travelled on a voyage of discovery to the limits of his imagination.

On waking, Coleridge immediately jotted down what he could remember of his Mongol emperor, the grandson of Genghis Khan, but he was interrupted by 'a person on business from Porlock, and detained by him above an hour'. On returning to his poem, Coleridge found 'to his no small surprise and mortification, that though he still retained some vague and dim recollection of the general purport of the vision, yet, with the exception of some eight or ten scattered lines and images, all the rest had passed away like the images on the surface of a stream into which a stone had been cast'. What was left was a work that deeply evokes the landscape from which its images are drawn, including the shoreline of the Bristol Channel, where cliffs and steep slopes and caves are cut into the rock face:

In Xanadu did Kubla Khan
A stately pleasure-dome decree:
Where Alph, the sacred river, ran
Through caverns measureless to man
    Down to a sunless sea.

It goes on, the fantastical faraway lands really a description of the place I am passing through:

A savage place! as holy and enchanted
As e'er beneath a waning moon was haunted
By woman wailing for her demon-lover!
And from this chasm, with ceaseless turmoil seething,
As if this earth in fast thick pants were breathing,
A mighty fountain momently was forced:
Amid whose swift half-intermitted burst

Huge fragments vaulted like rebounding hail,
Or chaffy grain beneath the thresher's flail:
And mid these dancing rocks at once and ever

Somehow it does not matter that Coleridge was interrupted
or that the poem was not longer, for in 'Kubla Khan' are all
the dreams we have lost to waking. But the poem also contrasts
a man-made, earthly paradise, which proves unable to resist
demonic forces and is doomed to be annihilated, with a true form
of paradise. This was Coleridge's whole world; he had grown up
in an era of industrialisation which he thought cut humanity off
from the wellsprings of creativity, from nature, so he and others
tried to pull it back. It was here, walking vast distances, sometimes absorbed by the moonlight, that he would try to make sense
of the world he found himself in.

On I walk, between the trees, and they are all there, the
Romantic revolutionaries and those still to come, silent presences
like clouds passing, without the rain falling, all telling me to
follow ideals rather than rules.

I now enter this broad belt of ancient woodland, the most extensive coastal forest in the country; woods that are thick with
bramble and whortleberry, and trees of rare mountain ash and
sweet chestnut and downy birch and hazel and, most signifi-
cantly, ancient sessile oak.

I become rather fascinated by the sessile oak springing from
the mossy and ferny nether regions of these damp combes. I
think it is because it has none of *Quercus robur*'s nationalistic
bombastic dominance; it is so much smaller, it does not wave its
acorns on the end of stalks like precious orbs but carries them
more discreetly, on outer twigs. Its heart is not our ships or our
men. It goes about its business all quiet and in the shade, clinging precariously to the steep hillside here; it has no hunger for

lands outside its boundaries. The colour of its leaves is not the green of England, but milkier; undersides downy with a silvery sheen which catches the light. It cannot be bothered with culture, so it has none. And its almost-empty larder does not court popularity. The sessile oaks here are weedy and thin, stunted, contorted into unusual and twisted forms by coppicing; they could never shelter kings, but unlike their pedunculate brothers they know how to cling on these edges, to dance with the wind – to transcend with their entire bodies as if in drug-induced delirium like Coleridge himself. What tree leaves behind life and enters a more spiritual realm than this one? How many trees, other than these ones, tell us where they have been in their dreams? How many poets?

Dor beetles cross my path as well. You think this is the centre of total blackness, then one upturns to reveal a bluey-green sheen and suddenly it's disco lights. I crouch down to look at it, but I'm distracted by a dark spot on my arm. I think it might be an embedded tick. Is everything and everyone out for a stroll in these woods? And how did it penetrate my own fleshy barriers? Did it feel my vibrations? My heat? Or was it the clouds of carbon dioxide from my breath? Certainly, a woodland ambush: it buried its hook-like limbs into my clothes and then went walkabout for moister, yielding ground. It's probably feeding now, its little body swelling like risen bread from gorging on all that sweet blood. I wonder whether it will leave behind Lyme's disease; its own scorched-earth policy in this interaction of bodily edges and surfaces. Note to self: go to the local hospital and have it removed. If a bull's eye forms around it, insist on going on a course of antibiotics.

Then a huge landslip yawns self-importantly, unpleasantly, in the open, interrupting the weave of this high and sheltered path through Culbone's hanging woods. Everything has been serene until now, untroubled in mind, lines and boundaries marked. The landslip comes upon me like the line in Jen Hadfield's poem about a dog: 'His tongue spools out his head like magma.' This is a fresh slippage; the torn, raw flesh of pink boulders, the uprooting of trees, a sieving of rocks, all tumbling over the edge of this steep place in a vertical stream to the sea. I tread warily over it, as if I am stepping through a door into the unknown. Parts of this ground are made up of some of the oldest rocks in the world, older than whole continents, and they are forever moving: having started life in the bottom half of the earth, they are due to arrive north of the Arctic Circle about a hundred million years from now. Progress, of the best kind, is usually slow. Step by step. For me as well, on my slow walk west.

It is high up here, and remote, this stretch between Glenthorne and Countisbury. Because of the steepness of the cliffs there is nothing below, no landward access, nowhere to moor a boat, no houses. They say that if you were to wait for tides low enough to walk between access points it would take five years to cover the thirty-four-mile length of shore. Even then some serious rock climbing would be involved. It feels rare, these days, to be excluded from any location. To be somewhere where God intended only nature to be.

But nature is not all good. Some of it is bad. Really bad. I am marching now with an invasive plant rather like the army in *Macbeth*; except the moving forest this time is made up of *Rhododendron ponticum*, which was first cultivated at Kew in the mid-eighteenth century and was later introduced by the Victorians to their coastal hunting estates to provide shelter for game. On the Glenthorne Estate some are even smiling; they are in flower – such is its confidence in its ability to conquer whole territories. *Ponticum* can, in suitable conditions, outcompete most native plants, and grow so tall it can completely block out the light. No one likes to live in the darkness for long, not even neighbourly animals.

We are so often fooled by flowers, are we not? Their delicate colouring, their innocence and vulnerability, when really they are like weeds, sheltering thousands of seeds, seeds that will eventually obstruct all our carefully laid plans for harmony and boundaries. Walking on, I can't help thinking of all the dynasties whose familial lines have ended, the veteran oaks and ash, the larches, so that one's eye becomes mournful and feels the need to seek out survivors: the sulphur-yellow growths of chicken-in-the-woods, hirsute branches of lichen, the hornet nesting in the hollow of an old oak ... and then in this dense shading I see a single whitebeam, down in mood from all this change, heroic at the edge and making a stand but knowing that as a tree, this hermaphrodite, with its male and female parts, will soon be vanquished as well. Your homeland, after all, never leaves your body until the very end, until the moment you die.

Now it feels as if everywhere something is calling to me from the hidden, from under the leaves, in dead and dying wood – Look at me, I'm here, try to see me, know me, I belong to you, I'm of you, rescue me – oak, ash, bat, bee, beetle, dormouse. It's the tensions that come with porous boundaries again. With this in mind, one can't help but see woods like these as soundless battlegrounds, full of clashes between groups of species for light and nutrients. The battle's character – its duration, number of participants, weapons and tactics employed, its fronts and strategies – markedly variable. Even the language assists: natives, aliens, colonisers, invaders. And just like all battles, this one is bound up with the social, economic and political features of its age.

This is usually how it starts. First comes the surprise attack, then the call for back-up. That will be for us, with our bipedalism and large, complex brains. Species: *H. Sapiens*. Class: *Mammalia*. Order: *Primates*. Genus: *Homo*. In we charge with our chainsaws, feeding the cuttings into the mulcher, treating the stumps and foliage with herbicide, burning piles of leftovers. Until the landscapes looks so scarred with fallen limbs and razed ground it brings on another melancholy all of its own, to do with messing around with the natural order of things. You can see this here, the interventionism, the obsession with driving the enemy from the battlefield in the name of a new ecological god we call Conservation. But it isn't really conservation, it's favouritism: it's red squirrels instead of grey, otters instead of fish; it's Robin Hood stealing from the rich to pay the poor, and ultimately I'm not sure any battle of this nature can ever be decisive.

There are other new and innovative weeds here as well: walkers. When Natural England promised to create 'the world's longest coastal footpath', it had not counted on the landed elite who consider such people equally invasive. The former owner of Glenthorne House, the philanthropist Sir Christopher Ondaatje, had offered part of his extensive gardens for a path but the new owner, a German fashion designer, subsequently decided not to allow this. The push and pull of boundaries goes on.

I stumble across a small spring beneath a cairn and rough-hewn slate cross. An elaborate structure, with splayed retaining walls, was erected over the spring in the nineteenth century and named Sister's Fountain because the young sisters of Glenthorne's then owner liked to play there. The actual spring is reputed to have gushed forth from the spot where Joseph of Arimathea struck the ground with his staff when he needed refreshment on his way to Glastonbury. It is a quiet, gladed place suitable for a distilled rumour or legend. Could it be possible? Maybe.

There is little in the Bible to say that Joseph of Arimathea was anyone other than the man who buried Jesus; certainly nothing about him being related to the Saviour. The connection might derive from the tradition that senior male relatives of a crucified person would often assist with the burial. Whatever the truth, the link sticks to the pervading legend in these parts: that Joseph visited Britain first with the young Jesus, then secondly after the crucifixion to bring the Holy Grail to Glastonbury in Somerset. A veritable forest has grown up around these stories and include the suggestion that Joseph was the first person to penetrate our shores and thereby bring Christianity to Britain; that he built the first church here; that he was Mary's uncle and thus Jesus's great-uncle; that he was a merchant who visited England to buy Cornish tin and on one trip brought with him his nephew. Questioning these claims extends even into our national pride. Every time we sing William Blake's stirring hymn 'Jerusalem', the question is posed: 'And was the holy lamb of God / On England's pleasant pastures seen?'

I like to compare the spread of Christianity, or any religion for that matter, to the life cycle of another invasive seed, the dandelion. The seeds are encased in tiny fruits and have their own special feathery parachutes to help them float through the air: the parachutes here being the disciples and the Bible. If the air is still, they stay on the flower head and are vulnerable to those who wish to halt their progress: seed-eating birds like goldfinches and officials like Pontius Pilate. If you – or the wind – blow on them, you start the seeds on a journey. They may fall close by, in and around the Roman Empire, but if there is enough updraught they can be carried for long distances, maybe to a dry point on the low-lying Somerset levels, a place called Glastonbury. When the fruit lands, it no longer needs the parachute that has carried it on its journey, and it breaks off. Over the coldness of the winter the seeds sink into the soil, waiting for the ground to warm, and then they begin to germinate and spread.

And so a small spring beneath a man-made cairn and rough-hewn slate cross rises in a faraway wood.

Devils and Gods

Lynmouth Harbour to Combe Martin

I leave behind Lynton's granny guest houses and stroll on along North Walk and around Hollerday Hill, which is a neat frill of a path. It happens unexpectedly, an encounter with a feral goat standing on a plinth, controlling passage through the Valley of the Rocks. The smell alone was a sign that something bad was coming. But it was staring into those elongated elliptical pupils that finally did it, those horizontal slits, which make you feel almost as if you are canyoning into his evil heart, falling into its cold and infinite depths. The inverted pentagram, the symbol used in Satanism, is said to be shaped like a goat's head, is it not?

What sort of place is this?

I am in a drain, a gutter in the crust, worn away by a river, possibly in an age of ice, but this valley is different, unique even: it runs parallel to the sea, not inland from it. Legend says it was the location of the Devil's Castle. While the Devil was away, his wives took part in a naked drunken orgy with a neighbour. On finding out what had happened, he turned the women into turrets of rock. Sharp formations of sandstone and shale, each with their own distinct characteristics, have been sword-fighting the wind ever since.

The locals have tried to gentrify the place: they introduced a cricket pitch and signage. After goats were found digging up the local graveyard, they even attempted murder, feeding the animals poisoned green peppers. But it didn't work; the Valley of the Rocks was determined not to lose its malevolent air, nor the Devil his minions.

And that is why writers and artists came and kept coming: it just has something; something dark and elemental. In 1799, the poet Robert Southey described it as 'covered with huge stones . . . the very bones and skeletons of the earth; rock reeling upon rock, stone piled upon stone, a huge terrific mass'. Seventy years later, R. D. Blackmore used the valley for Mother Meldrum's kitchen in *Lorna Doone*.

William Hazlitt, who visited the valley with Coleridge, wrote:

> There is a place called the *Valley of the Rocks* (I suspect this was only the poetical name for it) bedded among precipices overhanging the sea, with rocky caverns beneath, into which the waves dash, and where the sea-gull for ever wheels its screaming flight. On the tops of these are huge stones thrown transverse, as if an earthquake had tossed them there, and behind these is a fretwork of perpendicular rocks, something like the *Giant's Causeway*.
>
> A thunder-storm came on while we were at the inn, and Coleridge was running out bare-headed to enjoy the commotion of the elements in the *Valley of Rocks*, but as if in spite, the clouds only muttered a few angry sounds, and let fall a few refreshing drops. Coleridge told me that he and Wordsworth were to have made this place the scene of a prose-tale, which was to have been in the manner of, but far superior to, the 'Death of Abel', but they had relinquished the design.

I walk on, around Wringcliff Bay with the towering Castle Rock above, and look back on it; under a slanted rock, there is an outline of a white witch carrying a tray, silhouetted against a darker sky.

As if to try to counter all this darkness, the next big feature on the path is the Christian community of Lee Abbey. The house sits loudly, superciliously and messily over beautiful Lee Bay; the long, perfect sweep to the sea ruined by its fabricated benevolence. For some it might feel satisfyingly symmetrical, heaven to the previous hell.

Why does so much religion occur where water meets land: is it because we go out to sea in search of something from the shore? Or is it because we return to the shore after a long voyage? I'm wondering if we come to places like this to be tested by the earth's enduring elementary forces, by its stories, by its experiences of hardship, places reduced to bare rock, where everything is frayed and porous, just like us. Do we come to the wild edge, where anything can come towards us because we want things to happen to us?

On the other side of the bay I meet a retired couple, probably in their late sixties, walking as snails with their homes on their backs, all thrift and modesty and wild camping. Other than saying 'Hello', 'Where have you walked from?' and 'How long did it take?', I generally do not engage in conversation. But on this occasion, I stop the couple because they are very unusual-looking. The nursery rhyme, *There was a crooked man, and he walked a crooked mile* – that is him; thin and bent as a sessile oak with skin all wrinkled, with a long grey beard down to his knees tied in a ponytail. He looks like a druid. She is dormouse-squat, grey, her head shaved except for a tuft. They tell me they live in Poole and that this is the third time they have done the path. It has taken six weeks to walk non-stop, leaving at 5 a.m. and pitching their tent under a tree canopy at 7 p.m., eating wild whenever they can. I listen with a mixture of puzzlement and admiration. For a while afterwards, as I walk, I can't stop thinking about them, about their secure, self-reliant life, something

I could never emulate; about being 'Well satisfied to be his own / Whole treasure'. But I also wonder if they are looking for something – a cure, an illusion? Maybe they are pilgrims. Maybe I am one as well.

So why am I walking? What is my quest? Isn't that what travel writing is all about? The exterior and interior journey. I have no great illness to overcome, no inherent sense of adventure. I don't want to do anything silly like walk a tightrope between two mountains. The South West Coast Path just seemed a good idea at the time: it is on my doorstep, and it is my homeland.

I grew up in the West Country, in that long bony ridge of land which stretches far out into the Atlantic. My father, Sir John Nott, was Member of Parliament for St Ives from 1966 to 1983 and his constituency covered the south-west of Cornwall, taking in the most southerly and westerly points of England. Along with the Western Isles, it has to be one of the most romantic constituencies in the land. Today my father is mostly remembered for holding the post of Secretary of State for Defence during the Argentine invasion of the Falkland Islands.

Being the daughter of a politician was not enough; I then stupidly went and married one: Hugo Swire, who later became MP for East Devon. The constituency, where we raised our young family together, contains some of the most breathtaking coastal scenery in all of south-west England and is classified as an Area of Outstanding Natural Beauty. It takes in the sandy beaches of Exmouth, the pebbled coast at Budleigh Salterton, and the red cliffs at Sidmouth. My father's family are Devonian born and bred, and my husband's family live in Dorset. I have spent all my life in this leg of land, travelling up and down its length, through the flood plains of Somerset, crossing the River Tamar, over Brunel's bridge at Saltash and back again. I have roamed its two national parks and explored its World Heritage Sites; I have been to weddings and funerals in its churches; I have followed its folklore, its traditions and customs; I have been nourished by its bountiful larder and read its renowned writers. I have been buffeted and soothed by its climate.

I did not set off on this walk as a homage, but on account of politics, the other world that was my life: Whitehall and Westminster, where I was not only an MP's spouse but a political researcher. Westminster moves in a decidedly different and artificial rhythm from real time; so much there is determined by electoral cycles, opposition, scrutiny, data. It issues laws in times of crisis that embolden leaders, and which override everyday politics, which are slow, legislation rushed through to implement lockdowns during a pandemic a good example of this. At Westminster, you can speed things up, or slow them down. It is a place where tricks are played on us the whole time, tricks that can accelerate and decelerate political turmoil. The pace is sometimes so fast, so overworked, whole governments can spiral and crash. It's no surprise politicians always want to be setters of clocks, to determine pace, become chief timekeepers: it's how they maintain power. To a politician, time is everything.

I need to come to the wild edges because it is a natural dominion, a place where there is no plan, or if there is one it has nothing to do with human intelligence. Of course, as humans we do alter things: rivers, plants, flowers are manipulated to our benefit, land is cleared, trees are cut down, towns are built, but all these actions are relatively new in the history of the world. Change in the natural world is altogether different, it comes from the clocks within, in the matter, in the genomic patterns, crystalline formation, in volcanic activity. If politics happens here, it is autogenous, it is self-governing; if there is an impact of forces it is provisional, secondary even. I like that idea, I like it very much. As I walk along this path, I am walking out all the bossiness, all the debating, all the rivalries and the ambitions; mostly, the social media mania that drives the news cycle and worsens situations. I am being presented with the knowledge of how unimportant these things really are in the order of things.

I am walking to the different rhythms of my body, to the beat of my heart, to sunrise and sunset, to the changing of the seasons and the push and pull of the tides. I am learning to master the art of slowness. Not to calculate. Not to count. Thankfully, there is so much joy to be found in what we don't actually own or understand; there are still places that hold on to their secrets. Yes, we want to open the door, follow the rabbit down its hole, make the mountain welcome us, but even if we force ourselves in, over the edge of it, it is only an antechamber. *You are nothing to us*, it says, *you are unimportant, you are not native, you are alien.*

Because to go somewhere wild is really a state of becoming, like religion is. It is not located in any particular place or region. It can be found everywhere, even in cities, in back yards and motorway edges, underfoot, actually, it is even in *us*, in our meandering thoughts as well as in our unconscious mental life and our bottled-up emotions. To ask of my wild edges, *Why here?* I will tell you *why here*: because I am not being invited to join in, to organise, to be judged. In fact, there is much to prevent me: wind, rain, the hardness of terrain, the slowness of time; and that brings with it the most extraordinary sense of relief when you live or have lived a life of politics. The total disjunction from the land of decision-making. The removal from the bedlam of it all, the tumult of political life. I come here to remind myself that, although I live in a high-speed society, I don't live in a high-speed world. I come here to slow down.

Here, these wild edges start gently, returning to a theme of faith; as if you are entering a kingdom in the clouds, a land of sacred temples and pilgrimage, giant ferns and trickling streams and woods and the waterfall of Hollow Brook dropping more than six hundred feet to the sea, but you would be wise to stop to take in the views when a gap appears. The coast ahead, twenty miles or so of it, appears like a defensive building with battlements cutting its crenellations into the rock. To proceed I must see myself as a crusader, the rocks as huge as any Byzantine or Muslim fortification. This is another of nature's gifts, it presents worlds to us, each one of which has a distinctive character. Landscape is not only bucolic and beautiful, it is 'edgy' in the real sense of the word: it operates in a tension of clashing powers, and to be in the centre of that is to be conversant with it, to be challenged.

So, I stand here, looking at these high cliffs anchored into the sea, and find them daunting, frightening even. What I see is a silhouette of something I must conquer, and for a brief second I'm not sure if I have the stamina to take it on. But I know I must. The experience might well transform into something else later, who knows what – a memory? A page in a book? A painting? A religious conversion? – just like Mount Everest or Mount Rushmore might do for others. Mont Sainte-Victoire would have remained just a local landmark, had Cézanne not painted it so beautifully. Colin Thubron, in *To a Mountain in Tibet*, breathlessly ascends Mount Kailas along with many other pilgrims, a ritual of walking meditation as they head to a zone of 'charged sanctity' to find peace with their dead. 'A journey is not a cure,' he says. 'It brings an illusion only, of change, and becomes at least a Spartan comfort . . . To ask of a journey, Why? Is to hear only my silence.' His mountain might not offer redemption or a finale, even though he has reached its summit, but in its edges it has drawn an outline in his mind that needs exploring, an illusion of something else, something that might cure him. To look outwards is to look inwards as well.

Down I go to the Riverside Walk towards the Hunter's Inn, over a stone bridge then out of the woods into a steep dry valley balding with bracken and birch and hawthorn, up again 330 feet, turning seawards. Coastwards I go to Peter Rock, overlooking the mouth of the Heddon. This is a slate-surfaced rock staircase, up, level, up, it goes until you reach East Cleave, opening up cliffs to the west. Across the Bristol Channel, Wales is in view:

the Mumbles, with Swansea and Port Talbot steelworks to the right and the Gower Peninsula to the left. And so it goes on. I find there is no symmetry and balance in these edges either, these ups and downs. In fact, they are deeply asymmetrical in their patterns; to go up one side is different from coming down, each exploit is different. I also realise that not everything is found in the conquest of the whole – the mountain itself – but in the experiences of the journey: the places you sit down and catch your breath, next to the animals, trees and flowers, before setting off again. This is the near sphere, it is the surface up close, where the edges are more complex than the overall profile; this is where the multiplicity of activities take place. It is the place where Thubron writes of a wobbling tin bridge over a gush of water, the 'cathedral shadow' of trees, of crafty smugglers in bobble hats driving buffalo laden down with Chinese cigarettes. It is where the chapters occur, the events are organised, within the overall narrative; it is where the characters come into being. It is where the opener, the incident, the crisis, the climax, the ending happens. You cannot only look up at the mountain in the tall distance, you need to bow your head in order to understand the path that takes you there.

The significant mountain on this stretch of walk is Holdstone Down, a summit that has been commandeered by a religious movement called the Aetherius Society, whose activities are centred around the radiation of spiritual energy through prayer. This 'mountain' is of particular significance because it's where members believe an extra-terrestrial called the Cosmic Master transformed himself into a Jesus figure so he could appear before a former London cab driver, Dr George King, on 23 July 1958. The mission was called Operation Starlight, and King was used as a channel to place a powerful charge of cosmic energy into eighteen or nineteen other mountains scattered throughout the British Isles, and others again in America, Australia, New Zealand, Switzerland, France and Tanzania.

Every year on 23 July, hundreds of people make the pilgrimage to Holdstone to commune with their Cosmic Masters. Here they are charged up like car batteries with spiritual energy ready to be released when the Aetherians decide the world is in most dire need of it. Their representative on earth, Mark Bennett, explains: 'This is a real energy and because of the way we pray, people can feel this as a tangible, actual thing – like electricity. Anyone who goes up to Holdstone Down can invoke this energy, whether they believe in it or not. You could get an orthodox Christian going up there and if they are doing or thinking about something in a totally unselfish way, they will invoke this spiritual energy.'

I can't say I felt anything myself. No transference at all. But I can understand the concept, like standing at the edge of a heath at dusk when something beautiful falls from the sky, the song of a thrush maybe. One is keyed into something so different from one's own life that it can impregnate the mind, instil a spirit into a place, find a moment to walk out of one life and enter a different one.

Politicians have never liked cult leaders. Too often they fall into what Ralph Waldo Emerson termed the 'vulgar mistake of dreaming that [they] are persecuted whenever [they are] contradicted'. And being contradicted often brings on political paranoia. Equally, they get competitive when attention is pulled off them and all trussed up by the binds of jealousy. It is not surprising, therefore, that papers released by Scotland Yard in 2015 show that Special Branch had tailed George King for five years, and even infiltrated society meetings, following his confession that he had been in telepathic contact with aliens. Extraordinarily the decision was made from high command amid dark Cold War fears that George King was a Soviet puppet. You would have thought, as soon as he pronounced he could communicate with an alien called Aetherius, or that space travellers from Venus had made it through the foggy clouds and sulphuric acid of their homeland and were now integrating harmoniously into our communities, that the guy was a bit kooky but no, this man was considered a very real threat. You wonder who was the madder? But then King did go out of his way to taunt the establishment. His most memorable moment came in 1959, when he was interviewed on a BBC programme called *Mars and Venus Speak to Earth*. In it, a consultant psychiatrist explained to the audience that King was actually a conduit for Aetherius, who was speaking through him in order to pass on messages from Mars Sector 6. The audience was gripped by the tension, particularly when King emerged exhaustedly from his trance and came over all political, saying the atom bomb should be outlawed and that he had been told when World War Three was due to start. You can see how the spooks got spooked.

On, again, down to sea level, into the valley of Sherrycombe and over a stream, and then you rise towards its west side. Eventually a cairn of loose stones will signify the summit of the Great Hangman, at 1,043 feet (318 metres) the highest point on the whole of the South West Path, the highest cliff in south England. And there you will sit, gasping from your exertions, among the glowing magenta and yellow sweep of cross-leaved heath, of ling and bell heather and western gorse, where the stonechats, whinchats, meadow pipits and yellowhammers sing. And in your tiredness, in that moment when you cross over and have lost all sensation, when only your feet are doing the walking, when nothing exists except a renunciation of a bodily and material world, your walk ends as if in a forgiving and lightness of dream. It is then you have arrived at your own wild edge.

Silver

Combe Martin to Croyde Bay

Combe Martin. Under this calm civil parish on the North Devon coast, silver threads run its miraculous length like eels in the wet darkness of an underworld.

For an element, silver has no real biological role – it irritates the skin and causes death in lesser creatures if ingested – but here, at least, it has reached mythical status. In 1292 Edward III came west to dig, and his shafts continued to fund the whims of monarchs after him, including Henry V, who used the silver found here to advance his military campaigns in France. They say that the battles of Crécy, Poitiers and Agincourt were won in the mines of Combe Martin. There was even a royal mint on this site during the Civil War.

But, as with all wealth, fluctuations will occur, discoveries are rare, and their effects, though powerful, are limited to periods of comparatively short duration. There was renewed activity during the eighteenth century, but in the 1880s the mines eventually closed. Here and now, it's quite a test of the imagination to think it was once such a noisy, smoky, industrial place, its inhabitants rudely labelled shammickits, or slum-dwellers.

I am thinking, as I follow the coast road west up the hill and around the corner above the beach, about silver's long association with war: the points of swords, flying bullets, inside electromagnets used for enriching uranium during the Second World War. Today, it helps us rid the world of stockpiles of vile chemical weapons, reducing them to harmless salts that can then be safely disposed of, as if it is finally paying for its sins.

But to be honest, usefulness is not really where my interests lie. I'm thinking instead of hues, thinking in terms of colour. Silver: the light that tells you all about dying, the colour of the obituary, a colour of purity, clarity, vision and truth. How clouds often have bright silver edges where the sun reflects. The way it casts spiritual light on problems. The guanine crystals in the skin of a fish that camouflage them as they swim near the surface, bouncing the light away. The colour of the future: of space rockets and men who walked on a silver moon for the first time. Of sixties metal minidresses generating their own radiations of space on a dancefloor. The glitter of falling rain. An element that contains mystical powers, from a cross held high to ward off a vampire to the making of magic mirrors. How silver is integrated into the story as a good ending, a happy ending. Silver has always been used to express light, not only in what we see but in what we can create from it.

Away from the caravans at Hele Bay, which sit as army encampments do – determined, bull-headed, ugly and always in the most strategic of positions (were thirty pieces of silver exchanged for this location?) – the path winds up through a steep wood fringed by stranglers and dog tooth ferns until you are in open ground again, overlooking the harbour at Ilfracombe.

It was the Victorians that developed Ilfracombe into a top seaside resort. Holidaymakers would arrive by paddle steamer from Bristol and Cardiff. In 1874, the Barnstaple and Ilfracombe Railway brought more visitors, and so successful was it that in 1888 work began on doubling the track, which later carried direct trains from both Waterloo and Paddington, eventually handling some ten thousand passengers on summer Saturdays until its closure in 1970.

You have to seek out the old Victorian resort now; it is there, distressed and washed out. The town, like so many coastal holiday destinations, suffered when the tourism market faltered with the arrival of cheap foreign package holidays in the 1960s. Subsequently, it became the last option for many benefit claimants who were moved into unoccupied holiday accommodation, the result of government-sponsored social development schemes covering rural areas. It has also become a place where upwardly mobile transient families nudge up against its less affluent and more permanent residents. Another ecotone, this time a human one.

Silver waxes and wanes in alternate cycles of polishing and tarnishing, which can also be said of many towns along this coast. It frequently needs to be mixed with other elements to make it shine.

When Damien Hirst arrived in Ilfracombe, it was as though a whole town was looking up to the sky and seeing a new full moon, luminous in its shine. For a while the town basked in his reflection, danced under it, held hands as he promised the earth: huge eco-housing developments, a restaurant and a 65-foot statue of a girl with her insides exposed, standing in a Degas *Little Dancer*-style pose with a raised silver sword, an allegory, apparently, of truth and justice. Its sheer size still dominates the town today, like a mountain looming over a landscape.

Hirst, the UK's richest artist, is a silver Midas; he has always been good at giving things a metallic lustre. *For the Love of God*, his platinum cast of a human skull encrusted with more than eight thousand diamonds, was said to have been sold for fifty million pounds. It blinded everyone with its starry brilliance. The art historian Rudi Fuchs described the work as 'a glorious intense victory over death – at least over the temporal, physical and ugly aspect of it: rotting decay. The piece expresses a wonderful pride of vision, putting melancholy at a distance.' And the skull does feel like an embodiment of Dylan Thomas's poem 'Do not go gentle into that good night'. But it also reflects the confidence of youth, of that sense of immortality, its light; you can see it in the pale teeth, which is almost smiling at you in contempt. Hirst is trying to subvert the emotions that death brings, which is what he valiantly tried to do with Ilfracombe.

There is another, less assertive, hero connected to this town, and one no less brilliant. He is Henry Williamson, author of *Tarka the Otter*, and I have just passed his modest terraced house. Williamson's book has never been out of print. Time will tell whether Hirst's shimmer and shine are eternal like his diamonds, or whether he is merely from the money-grubbing sensational world of conceptual art and, as some critics suggest, he is nothing more than a showman and a salesman of genius. A streak of silver lightning.

Reeling in disillusion from the First World War, Williamson came to this area and turned feral. He strode out alone to that great hunk of moor detained between the rivers Taw and Torridge and minutely followed the trail of the otter up and down and round this coast of the Severn Sea, from Lynton to the estuary, and along Braunton Sands. From the 'high country of the winds' to lying low in sycamore holts under the 'eve-star shining above the hill', moving with the mist in which 'cattle stood on unseen legs', watching bubbles rise in river pools, scrambling through hawthorn by the mill-leat, listening out for their 'flute-like whistles', wading the tonnage of mud in the tide-head pool, Williamson was determined to see the world through an otter's eye and ear. Like all good detectives he put together a case built from small clues, with no detail too insignificant. Effort and attention were all that were required. For a short book, it would take him a hell of a long time to write. 'Each word,' he said later, was 'chipped from the breastbone.'

Tarka the Otter is an allegory of war, and the imagery of conflict is present throughout the book: the battles for survival; the otter hunt and the uniforms of the huntsmen, 'coloured as the dragonflies over the river', and the soldiers with their shiny brass buttons and regimental badges; the killing equipment – staves as opposed to rifles – and the bloodthirsty showmanship of deaths proudly notched into the huntsmen's poles; the crippling cold 'which poured like liquid glass'. War is also there in the noises, the commotions, the baying of hounds, the tooting of horns, the stampede of running feet. Williamson had been a soldier; he knew what it felt like to be hunted. By writing *Tarka* he hunted himself out of his darkest hollows.

Like Hirst, Williamson was looking death in the eye, but this time through the prism of war. Comparing these two residents, which must be done in the context of their times, is a clash between war and peacetime, light and dark, death and life, entry and exit. For Hirst, death can be made glamorous; for Williamson, it is not silver at all, but red in tooth and claw.

The path snakes along the Damagehue Cliffs and drops to Bennett's Mouth, the outflow of the Kinever Valley which collapses on the beach in flashes like a broken necklace.

A walk off-track, over the slabs and the humps, and into the cove's full embrace.

On the middle shore is a rock pool protected by a stole of bladder wrack and sea lettuce. The water is clean glass and there is much to see in it: limpets and beadlet anemone, periwinkles and the gesticulating waves of carrageen, and, most beautiful of all, the stiff finely branched pink seaweed *Corallina officinalis* with its tips of calcium carbonate. On the whole, you know civilisation has arrived when there is a beautiful garden into which a river runs: a *locus amoenus*. Indeed, it could be a model for God's own underwater Eden. Certainly, a location for love and sexuality; from *Corallina*'s generous urn-shaped sex organs to bladder wrack's flagellating sperm moving through the water to fertilise the egg, having been attracted by the female's pheromones, to the limpet's dramatic sex change.

And then in comes the wave; the clean rinse, the back swirl, and all the sick and dying are suddenly clinging on for dear life. Nothing will stop the tide or the expulsion from Paradise for those that are weak or unlucky, or the heinous murdering and the leftover body parts. Nature's engineering can also be crass, like many political and religious calculations. Our whole human history in just a simple rockpool, at the edge of the sea.

Bull Point Lighthouse gives guide to vessels navigating the North Devon coast, marking out the Rockham Shoal and the Morte Stone, sharp rocks that are like slow traps of steel for passing boats.

The lighthouse has been reincarnated three times. The original was constructed in 1879 after a group of local worthies appealed to Trinity House to counter the 'barbarous conduct of lawless wreckers'. The good folk of Mortehoe had become somewhat adept at luring ships onto their rocks, deliberately misplaced lights drawing them in like stars; the wreckers would then plunder the cargo, killing any survivors in the process.

The first lighthouse stayed in place for almost a century, until part of the headland on which it stood lost its footing, causing rivers of fissures to open up the structure. An old light tower was borrowed from elsewhere, until the present lighthouse was built further inland.

Not the most graceful of buildings by any means, it steadfastly refuses to lift 'its massive masonry' into the sky by standing at a mere thirty-six feet. It is fully automated and has no diaphone foghorn – barely a lighthouse at all, in fact – but its situation is unbeatable, a world's end location sheltered from all human habitation, down a long windy road where you almost tumble over the headland before you see it. It leans back, eyes closed, confident and smiling into the sun, like a small, barrel-shaped barn owl sleeping.

Later, I return from the pub, under a star-dirty sky, to the old lighthouse-keeper's cottage where I am staying. Out here, it feels as if I am suddenly no longer a member of a material world but of an ethereal region, and an insignificant part of it at that. This is the ancient light, one which has taken billions of years to meet me here, distances many times longer than the life I will live; stars studded into shapes like Hirst's diamonds into his skull cast, of crosses and centaurs, goldfish and toucans, crabs and rams. It is huge and beautiful, and almost incomprehensible. These are the ulterior edges, the ones that take us to the very extremes of a barely understood universe; a place where one answer goes on to create four more questions, pushing boundaries ever outwards, until they disappear into the distance. There must be an edge, surely, even if it is the outer surface of the atmosphere where meteorites, galaxies and gamma rays fly. Maybe it is where God himself resides.

If our perceptual powers can't take us there, and science is inconclusive, then thinking has to, metaphysically, theologically, poetically. W. G. Sebald, in *The Rings of Saturn*, tries to make sense of this immensity. He looks at our human insignificance through a series of rings around the planet. Each circle is history, and each history is made up of innumerable particles which he correlates to individual stories about people and places. Using books, historical events, pictures, maps, illustrations, he takes us on a labyrinthine journey, forever reminding us of our temporal condition as humans. He is telling us that stories once lost can never be found again, so we must create our own universes: capture every memory, every photograph. If we don't, the ravages of time will destroy everything we know and love, just as the universe has done to Saturn's rings, which were once large moons in orbit, but are now just particles of dust. He writes, 'On every new thing there lies already the shadow of annihilation.'

Similarly, the film *Nostalgia for the Light*, by the Chilean film director Patricio Guzmán, is a sensitively shot essay on the big questions of time, space, memory and how creatures so small and insignificant find meaning in a gigantic cosmos, sometimes as a distraction, sometimes in pursuit of redemption. Guzmán goes to a high plateau on the Atacama Desert, the driest place on earth, a landscape so hostile, made up of just salt, sand and lava, it is like a faraway planet. A place where the night is open and the stars shine so brightly they cast shadows. Here, he aims his telescope at some of the dimmest, least acknowledged reaches of the night sky, looking for remains from the cataclysmic distant edge of the Big Bang. He intertwines his discoveries with others also searching for the truth of the past in the desert: archaeologists studying ancient rock paintings and, more gruelling, the mothers of the 'disappeared', who we see digging manically through the desert for the bones of their loved ones, gone missing during the Pinochet era. Guzmán makes starwatching and archaeology similar quests, everything emerging and disappearing in their own period of history.

The owl awakens. He swivels his entire head in slow-motion eloquence so he can see in all directions. With an air of intelligence, and caution, he issues his warning gently, in light as soft, white and silent as a fringe of down on his feathers.

I lie on the grass, follow its silver paths and then look up at this huge sky, into the soft infinite darkness where diamonds are hanging on invisible threads and I recall a favourite quote which reconciles the science with the poetry and the magic:

> The amazing thing is that every atom in your body came from a star that exploded. And the atoms in your left hand probably came from a different star than your right hand. It really is the most poetic thing I know about physics: You are all stardust. You couldn't be here if stars hadn't exploded, because the elements – the carbon, nitrogen, oxygen, iron, all the things that matter for evolution – weren't created at the beginning

of time. They were created in the nuclear furnaces of stars, and the only way they could get into your body is if those stars were kind enough to explode. So, forget Jesus. The stars died so that you could be here today.

I turn my hands in front of me and think about the bones within, the ones that are most important to me, the ones that enable me to write. Calcium resides in them, a ductile silvery mineral that also came from stars exploding in supernovas that sprinkled and spread out across the universe before landing on rocky planets. The calcium spent the next five hundred million years in transit, through seawater and the skeletons of ancient sea creatures, then dinosaurs, then into the bones and teeth of all land-based animals. When my bones, my hands, are returned to the earth, we will transit together, in a geological fraction of a second, to somewhere new and, hopefully this time, eternal.

How can there be loneliness in this life when you have astronomy? It takes away absence, the insufficiencies of friendships, bereavement, pain. It tells us we are all part of a cycle that never begins with one person nor ends with them. It tells us that however fleeting our lives are, we are still part of a current, an energy, a narrative, that we are recyclable matter, so that when a massive star dies in your life it might blow off gas and shower you in dust, but eventually it will coalesce to form new stars, new planets, new life. Because you cannot hold onto stardust, it does not settle, it always has a job to do, another place to go. This is what I'm learning from the stars this quiet silver night: nothing comes to an end, but everything has a beginning.

Water

Croyde Bay to Westward Ho!

Over the sand dunes of Braunton Burrows to look for flowers, especially the orchids. Henry Williamson described this stretch in his book *The Pathway*. He writes, 'I'm told that every kind of English wildflower is to be found growing there somewhere.'

Indeed, the Burrows are one of the last really old and wild habitats left in Britain and extend southwards for about four miles from Saunton Down to the estuary of the Taw and Torridge. It is a landscape of miniature mountain ranges composed of millions of grains of sand. The winds blow the immense amassing of shifting calcareous shell-rich particles into hummocks, which in turn create refuges for botanical treasures.

In this mosaic of microclimates, over uneven ground, I find pyramid orchids, sand pansies, viper's bugloss – the most dominant – marsh orchids and bog pimpernel, and a bee orchid, which is quite beautiful, its velvety marked lip cunningly similar to the body of a hairy brown bee. Orchids just love dune-land; it's the liminess, the damp hollows, the opportunities for breeding. Their beauty and elaborate life cycle – seeds so minute that germination and growth of seedlings can take years – make them entirely exotic. To William Blake's question, 'A heaven in a wild flower?', the answer is yes, probably, but it would have to be an orchid. Orchids have forever drawn in the fanatics, just as they have the bees. 'You can get off alcohol, drugs, women, food and cars, but once you're hooked on orchids you're finished,' says Joe Kunisch, a commercial orchid grower from Rochester, New York. I suspect it's the vulva in them; legs akimbo, they just provoke desire. On its own a vulva is an ugly thing, but in love, in passion, the temptation and offer of it reveal the colour and joy of its complications. I think we might love this flower purely because it contains all the secrets of procreation.

What I so admire about the Burrows is that it is selective about the reality it accepts. The shoreline shoos away almost all plant visitors, bar the occasional kelp and plankton left languishing on a rock when the tide is out. It is formed from constituents, unlike its soil cousins, that discourage all forms of vegetation. But not here. Here the vegetation knows how to adapt to survive, because 'even on the stillest day the Burrows are changing ... every arc drawn by a bent tip of marram grass shifts grains of sand triturated by the elements. When the south-west is blowing the shape of a dune may be changed in a day, streamlining away in the vagaries of the wind ... the roots of the binding grasses hang loose when the air is still again,' Williamson writes. It's this wind that is vital in building the dune system and in distributing the seeds and other propagules; it supplies the dunes with nutrients, both inorganic from spray and organic from debris blown in from the beach. But it's the light as well, open and full, and the water, for luxuriant growth, falling on sand that has no water-holding capacity, bringing near-desert conditions.

Walking through it, discovering it, you admire the fight here. It feels subversive and revolutionary, each flower almost an act of resistance. It makes me think somehow of the old joining keep-fit classes, learning pottery, of my mother who already speaks many languages learning one more in her eighties. It's about reasserting themselves as relevant, adventurous, as primary again, as unreducible to the expectations of higher laws and an absolute refusal of settlement. Because nature will always try to make you into who it thinks you should be and when you should not be any more.

The Taw and the Torridge are the two rivers that drain off eight hundred square miles of this land, transforming it into estuary country. While the Taw rises on Dartmoor, the Torridge rises near Hartland, horseshoeing around in its large arc to reach the estuary only nine miles from its source. These rivers, though beautiful, are simply slaves to a sea that rises high in these parts. At low tide, only one and a half square miles of land lie under the water, while at high tide over five miles of it is drowned, and during floods or storms even more.

Today the tide is low. Mud everywhere. I look at the sheer bloody stubborn weight of it, the heavy haulage of it in its moving. It's a weight you can see; it escorts me along the estuary. Mud, I think, mud, the lump of clay you throw on the wheel, it's the bricks that enfold you, it's the glue that cements, it fills the trenches as war's companion. It's the weight you feel when your bones get old and you have to raise yourself from an armchair, looking out the window and seeing life flowing freely like a river.

It starts raining, long and hard and repetitive. Silver spears. And I am standing here on the edge, just as the ancients did, experiencing an exchange of water between two cosmic realms, from the water that flows on the earth in rivers and ocean currents and the water that falls from the sky as rain. It's that precious moment when the circle is joined and our ancient world is in movement again.

The word estuary is derived from the Latin *aestuarium*, meaning tidal inlet of the sea, which in itself is derived from *aestus*, a word which is applied to various things that are perceived to move in this manner: it could be heat or fire, it could be the swell of the sea or the tides or it could be used figuratively, referring to passion or uncertainty of mind. The Epicurean poet and philosopher Lucretius used *aestus* to refer to the flux of atoms that he believed was the cause of sense perception; of moving in a certain manner. You do get a feeling – walking beside these estuaries at high tide – of floating down with a body of water and being measurably diluted from all that is derived from the land, all the litter of your life, good and bad. Think of Sir John Everett Millais's *Ophelia*, singing while slowly being drawn downstream, through the dark water into another realm.

Is it possible that underneath all of us is a kind of water table? It might be a lake or just a pond, but it sits down deep, secretly, in the darkness, this element, our bodies holding on to it like a limestone landscape. If we leave it there too long, it tends to stagnate. If unswept by decontaminating currents, hydras, aliens, parasitic beings start to breed. The possibilities contained within might need to come to the surface. It might emerge as a dark brown shout of anger, sometimes as a whisper, a sigh even. If you vaguely understand this strange watery connectedness, you try to make your way here, or somewhere similar; you try to move towards the edge. You need to reach a place where the horizon is long and the air is open and where water is present. If you are lucky, you reach an estuary like this one, where the currents slow to a crawl and all those particles that you have carried with you on this journey, and are in suspension, finally begin to settle on the beds. The coastline, then, as a place of expulsion. The river's course is ended. Banks unfurl like fern fronds to become the seashore; the tidal influx of seawater begins to inflict itself on plant and animal life. At last you are mixing with the waves and the tides; at last you are flowing freely. In that sense, we are all of us rivers. This emotion is even dignified with a theory: it's called psychophysiological stress recovery theory, which was developed

by a Dr Roger S. Ulrich, and basically means finding an outlet
for stress recovery. The best public health resource for that – and
the cheapest – is to step out of ourselves and into nature. I know it
might be a rational type of abstract thinking about an emotional
phenomenon, but who cares? It works, this water cure.

My grandparents moved to Westward Ho! like many elderly
people have and will. They sold their house in Kent and moved
into a seaside villa my grandmother, Phyllis Nott, inherited from
her father, John Edmund Francis, the local GP for Northam,
Appledore and Westward Ho! My grandmother clearly wanted
to return to her roots. The sea had cast its spell on her early, and
anyone who has grown up beside it, as I have, will tell you the
same: it never stops holding you in its net. Her husband agreed
to the move on account of his love of golf, which led him to disappear daily to the Royal North Devon Golf Club, the oldest
golf course in England and Wales and over which the coast path
skirts. It is still played and manned by men from an England
that has passed.

Relations aside, I have often wondered why so many older
people swarm to the sea edge. Is it the biophilia hypothesis,
which says humans have an innate and genetically determined
affinity with the natural world? Or the sea bathing, maybe? Or
does sea air improve lung function? Or is it just joining the blue
zones, where it's proven that people live longer? Is it the search
for immortality?

But it might be something else as well. I think of rivers again,
and how we are like them. Rivers are not like mountains, or
hills or fields, they are not landbound things that subsist through
changing seasons and weathers, they move and flow. They squirm
like a snake over the face of the land, picking up content, moving
it, changing direction; they come up against edges in the form of
soft banks and destroy them, forming new landscapes. Nothing

can stop a river's determined one-way direction, although some try to swim against it, like salmon do. It is like life itself. As with the river, we also have a role, a task, and we are absorbed by it until that moment when we are released in our entirety into some other large heavenly body with undefined boundaries of which we know little.

My grandmother died slowly in Westward Ho! She had a terrible stroke and for seven years she would sit all day long, lopsided and disparate, by the bay window, her melancholy eyes overlooking not the sea but the tarmac road where cars entered and left the town. Death is a boundary like any other, and those heading towards it can enter it in different ways, from calm to violent, or, like my grandmother, something in between. Childhood memories are often made up of the exceptional, and the experience of watching her come to terms with the loss of her brain function felt overwhelmingly uncomfortable to me as a child. I hated entering that house, which had been divided into flats to provide an income. I hated the atmosphere, which was so weighted with my father's and grandfather's anxiety about her. And mostly I hated the ugliness of Westward Ho! It was a despoiled village which had been developed in order to satisfy the Victorians' passion for the seaside. Charles Kingsley, after whose 1855 novel the new resort had been named, had seen it coming: 'How goes on the Northam Burrows scheme for spoiling that beautiful place with hotels and villas? I suppose it must be, but you will frighten away all the sea-pies [oystercatchers] and defile the Pebble Ridge with chicken bones and sandwich scraps.' He was not wrong. By the early twentieth century it had been bought up by a local investor and in 1907 sold off in cake slices. It's been going downhill ever since, full of tawdry holiday camps, arcades and go-kart tracks, its only poetry coming from the sea and its famous shingle ridge, a massive accumulation of ovoid pebbles and boulders arriving from the south-west by the longshore drift.

At the end of her life, my grandmother was taken to Northam

to be buried. Looking out from the graveyard there, across Bideford Bay and the Taw-Torridge Estuary with the ships coming in and out across the bar, I feel content at last that she was given one of the most beautiful views this country has to offer. Over estuary country; over her country.

I like to collect talismans of places I have passed through, and as I cross Westward Ho! Beach I pick up three pebbles, roughly the same size, all of sandstone, although you would not know it to look at them. They are in different stages of undress. The first must come from the cliffs to the west, where there are many outcrops of similar rock. A chip off the ancient sandstone beds, falling along iron-stained joints to gain its colour, then clearly separating itself from its angular orange-brown block. It is still defiant: it will not be beaten, or rolled, or scraped to its end, which will be as gravel or sand; it is the colour of the Sahara, of Uluru glowing red at dawn and sunset, raw, untamed, with full pigment. It is the colour of my house in Devon, built out of the Redlands. The second pebble is not so insubordinate; it still has some stain in it but more like a sky glow, an orange aura, the one you find above an urban area at night. The third is entirely grey, rounded and polished: a Barbara Hepworth, if you like, all fine-grained and tamed, no longer a weapon. Three pebbles which are like photographs, snapshots of a life lived. But they also interrupt, arrest the slow flow of time which, anyway, is invisible to the human eye. They make it all seem tangible, possible even, the tick-tock, click-clock of it all. They show me the past but also the future.

I wonder what time will bring for these parts. A worrying map shows huge areas of Devon under water by 2050. The climate crisis is the most inclusive historical moment of our age. It has instilled in us a feeling of helplessness and a new kind of miserable melancholy. It's pretty much understood that it is coming soon and the new edge of our lives is an environmental doomsday, one filled with uncontrollable natural events such as hurricanes and tsunamis and flooding that will overtake whole countries. It's as if we are all perched on the edge of a cliff, like my first pebble, waiting for disaster to strike. Will we end up grains of sand as well? No, we must not be like the pebbles; we are cleverer than that, we must fight, forge a new vision for a viable future, create more irrepressible edge worlds. After all, we are living in the Anthropocene, the age of man; humans are now the force of nature that is reshaping our planet on a geological scale. That can work both ways, surely. Water may be our consoler, but we mustn't be tricked into letting it become our master. A rebellion is required against its authority. A mutiny. We must swim against the current like the salmon.

Barriers and Breaks

Westward Ho! to Hartland Quay

There is a row of candy-coloured beach huts as you leave Westward Ho! Small but sturdy wooden affairs summing up our island nation's stoicism and modest optimism, their unsegmented bodies clamped to the water's damp edge like molluscs. Some of their names: *Albatross, Chez Sooty Sweep, Shepherd's, Per Mare, Daybreak Hiscott, Water's Edge, Haggy's Hut, Attila the Hut, It'll Do, Peace Haven*.

What I like about beach huts is that they signal characteristic British eccentricity as emphatically as any other of their time-hallowed rituals; from talking about the weather to coping with class codes and envies, to squaddie talk and dog loving. They festoon the fringes in multicolour ribbons, provide shelter from harsh winds, open up the ocean in small, neat dreams.

Beach huts were spawned from the Georgian bathing machine, in which body-shy bathers could change out of their clothes before being wheeled into the surf. As our flesh became more exposed, so bathers started to hire or purchase sheds which could house home comforts, including electricity and even cooking facilities. During the last quarter of the twentieth century they suffered severe image problems; they were seen as being for the poor, rather like caravans, but by the 1990s this had changed again. No longer considered ugly and utilitarian, huts were back in fashion, with prices rising dramatically in more genteel locations such as Southwold and Mudeford. The humble beach hut is now something of a status symbol, and today there are close to twenty-five thousand of them across the country; most are found on public beaches, owned and managed by local authorities, but private beaches have huts as well, and very rarely does supply meet demand.

I get talking to a lady in a deckchair. The conversation starts, as it invariably does, with the weather, that unwritten code which has evolved to assist us in overcoming our social inhibitions. When the wheels of conversation are suitably greased, we move on to the huts and I ask her how much they go for.

'Anything from eight to fifteen thousand pounds,' she tells me.

I gasp. 'Really! That much!'

'That one over there is for sale. It's freehold, but you have to be on the waiting list to go for it and the seller picks who they want from that list. The sale of the structure is a private agreement, but the council charges a site rental. There is fierce competition when they come up.'

I ask her why they are so appealing.

'It's the simple life, isn't it? The one we all crave, away from the hurly-burly, no phone signal and all that. And I like the fact that nothing blocks my view. Everything is always blocking your view these days.'

I ask if she comes by herself.

'Oh yes, I come here alone, I make myself a nice cup of tea and sit and watch the world go by.'

And in the winter?

'Not so much, but beach huts attract vandals – that's why many don't have windows – and the sea and wind can be punishing so we come down to check it out every now and then.'

I say my goodbyes and walk on, but I'm left wondering if there is something deeper going on here than just primitive virtue and a view. This line of huts could also be regarded as an old-fashioned boundary marker. This, after all, is an artificial edge, one that has been built by human hands with human aims and mostly by a post-war generation which would slowly be forced to come to terms with the idea that Britain was no longer an island unto itself.

So is this some sort of contest, where the artificial is placed in resistance and conflict with the natural? Instead of thinking we are here because the sea is in our soul, because we are devoted to that which surrounds us, an obsession that has shaped our national psyche, maybe we are actually just fencing ourselves in and keeping others out. Maybe these huts are here to jealously guard the ghost of our island self. After all, this is no port, no opening. No, this is the end of something. It's about loving oneself and others within. It's about winners and warriors and those on sentry duty, sitting in their rocking chairs, going nowhere like the sea itself. It's about the loss of naval and merchant fleets, of a fishing industry, of people now preferring the beaches of Spain and Greece, about tunnels being dug under the Channel, joining us to continental Europe. It is more earth-praise than sea-praise, if you like. This line of huts, just as much a barrier as an opening.

The path continues south-west through wild, rolling mounds above curious folding formations on the beach below. When the tide is out it looks as if the whole beach has been ploughed. Farmers will tell you that there is something sensual and physical about ploughing, that it is fundamental to life. That all that undressing to reveal the fleshy innocence of the earth below is a God-like act. Some Creator has been rearranging the landscape.

I like Peppercombe Beach, I like it very much, and the secret cottage I stay in, in the woods just up from it, which sits beside a small stream that will end its journey to the sea in a waterfall. The cottage once housed another barrier force: officers of the

Preventive Waterguard, a group tasked with the prevention of smuggling that later evolved into the coastguard service.

The beach is large and wide and unpopulated and a rock-pooler's dream. Its boulders are smooth in chocolate browns, greys and reds, some struck by lightning streaks of quartz. The varied colours and their vividness, sometimes in contrast to the cliffs hovering over it, are what makes the beach so appealing; that and its splendid isolation.

In this red arena I notice kidney vetch growing up against the sandstone cliffs and their slow erosion onto the beach. The kidney vetch has a silky, pinnate foliage and crowded heads of many small flowers, each protected by a wodge of woolly down. They are usually yellow but here, sharing the same head, are red flowers as well, and what is so striking about them is how they are exactly the same shade as the sandstone. Is this a statement of kinship or have they been sent to colonise this bald ground, and by doing so thwart the haemorrhaging of these cliffs? I pick one and leave the rest to crowd around the rocks, earnest and sweet as nurses. It is a wound flower, they say, effective as gauze when staunching bleeding, and well chosen for the site because these cliffs are really an open wound of Triassic rocks. Long ago, 251,902 million years ago to be precise, these rocks covered everything, including the hard carboniferous rocks on the beach below; a burst even emerges west of here, sitting under my house near Crediton and travelling as far as Hatherleigh, but at Peppercombe that leg has been amputated from the rest of the Triassic, eroded. Here the cliffs are low and stumpy, and on a clear day it's difficult to imagine that soft, old, red, drought-ridden desert land before the sea got at it, leaving only the undaunted granite behind, a land that stretched from this beach to beyond the island of Lundy like long, tanned legs on a sun lounger under a Saharan sun.

*

On into woods, first Sloo then Worthygate. Thickets of willow, hawthorn and hazel and elderberries, wild mint, bramble and twisted oaks, zigzagging down to Buck's Mills, a hamlet hugging a steep incline into the sea where lime was brought across from the Welsh coast.

On its seaward slope, right at the edge, is a small cabin which was owned by the artist Judith Ackland and the poet Mary Stella Edwards. A former fisherman's store, they bought it at auction in 1948 for £625, having previously rented it. Mary Stella's diary for the day of the auction records the tension: 'The glorious moment of relief and happiness after agonising strain ... such looks exchanged between smiles and tears, such a clasping and grip of hands.' The couple stayed and worked here during the summer months between the 1920s and Judith's death in 1971. At that moment, the clock stopped; everything was left as it was, with Mary Stella never returning.

Judith would spend her time here painting watercolours of the coast and countryside around Bideford, where she had studied art before moving to Regent Street Polytechnic in London, the college at which she met Mary Stella. Their days were spent walking the shore where they explored rocks, 'looking so paintable – decorative and such lovely colours . . . watching waves as we walked along stretches of the beach, visiting rock pools . . . and indeed working till the rising tide lapped over our feet'. Their works followed no fashionable movements of the day, more what they saw in the romantic-topographical tradition, which meant detail, beauty and affection for what was laid out before them in the natural world.

As painters working within boundaries both would have known what it meant to be between edges, to be in between them, not as a border but as a limit, one that acts to frame, to shelter, to support their efforts. In many ways, the cabin offered the same provisional structure: it made Judith's life with Mary Stella possible. Coming here to Buck's Mills would not only open up possibilities to their emerging status as a couple and give them an energy that they would lack in everyday society but would establish a place of creation whose walls could be extended to the extremity of the landscape itself. From this epicentre love, art and poetry came like a spill.

Those walls extended in other ways as well. The women's artistic collaboration included a method of making miniature theatres or dioramas. The couple called the process 'Jackanda'; Judith would create tiny figurines from wire and cotton wool, and the backdrops were painted by Mary Stella. The subjects were often historical and in the 1950s brought them commissions, including five dioramas which are now on permanent display at the Windsor Guildhall. One particular scene, which would mark 350 years since John Norden's 1607 map of Windsor, reveals the recently built market hall with the old parish church behind. The scene, which could easily be seen as making a point about the social acceptance of their relationship, reveals a pillory where wrong-doers were punished by being forced to stand pinioned by their necks and wrists, tolerating catcalls, and probably well-aimed fruit and vegetables. 'Sapphist!' 'Pervert!' 'Slime!' 'Wife stealer!' There is a pig which has made a bid for freedom and is creating a ruckus; you can almost hear the bench overturn, the thud of apples, the shouts and shrieks with a well-to-do lady holding on to her hat as the commotion carries on around her.

In many ways, what the women were doing with their dioramas was what they were doing with their lives: bringing meaning in ever-smaller entities, reducing it to basic terms seen through a pane of glass. Indeed, both Judith and Mary Stella exhibited a formidable attention to detail in everything they did, and the smallest items were what intrigued them the most. They were fanatic collectors of every kind of small curiosity, natural and man-made – shells, unusual stones, fragments of china and pottery, old keys, all were brought in, marked and kept in miniature chests of drawers.

You are transported in time by entering the Buck's Mills Cabin, which is now owned by the National Trust and can be viewed by appointment. It is like entering another world, of a small artists' colony all of its own, full of quaintness, frugality and old-worldliness, to a time when free digital access to information and graphical media were absent and communication was distant. Once inside, one can see the economical furnishings, the doll's house-sized wood-burning stove, the tables and kitchenware; there are waterproofs and a kit for plein-air painting hanging on their hooks waiting for another excursion. In the upper room a plain and narrow iron bedstead and a wash jug and bowl, and a simple rail for hanging clothes with a tall dried teasel standing guard by the window. Everything simple, functional and pleasing. It is uniquely preserved, two tiny rooms enshrining all the goods and chattels of their life together while offering a faithful record of their artistic collaboration. The joy of it is similar to peering inside a diorama or a bell jar. It is about seeing something reduced, all the components of a life together, the essence of it, boiled down into some microcosmic idyllic scene.

Everything about Mary Stella and Judith's life at Buck's Mills is about skewering time and space, different realms with different edges existing almost like Russian dolls placed one inside the other; making ordered worlds away from external chaos. And what of those many summers, from the 1920s to the 1960s? What was happening outside their isolation and simplicity? What of the events of which they had no control? A new chancellor in Germany climbs onto the scales and his nation perches itself at the opposite end until the balance is equal. A war hero and leader becomes redundant with the peace. When clever states let off an explosion it forms a mini supernova, and the radiance from those thousands of suns turns everything to ash. In faraway countries people are pushed into cooperatives and told to give up ownership of possessions for the greater good; the complete antithesis of the space and atmosphere accorded here. A man comes out of the darkness telling us he has a dream of building the light. In the hatcheries of state, a distant war is inscribed into its cold war campaign and its youthful population rise up against the draft, morality, legality, pragmatism, values. In biblical lands a spirit of intolerance will draw up new boundaries of 'us' and 'them'. And a quarter of a million miles away, one small blue planet watches in awe as a spidery spaceship lands in a magnificent desolation, making hope infinite.

Gaston Bachelard, in *The Poetics of Space*, wrote, 'But we haven't time, in this world of ours, to love things and see them at close range, in the plenitude of their smallness.'

This is a place where you can. Where they did.

It is a good walk, this one, quiet and wild; it twists through woodland and out again, down inclines and up again, mostly staying parallel to the sea. Here the coast faces north-east, so it is sheltered from Atlantic winds and the bent waves around Hartland Point, which are coming soon.

Eventually I am on Hobby Drive. Built in the early nineteenth century under the watchful eye of its owner Sir James Hamlyn Williams, it was a project that had been started to occupy restless Napoleonic prisoners of war to cut a swathe through dense woodland. I can see nothing below. Not even the cave which is said to have housed the bloodthirsty Greggs, a family of cannibals who, in the eighteenth century, were said to have robbed, killed and eaten some thousand victims.

Eventually I am above Clovelly.

Tired and in need of rest – Hobby Drive had felt interminable – I order clotted cream with jam and scones in one of its quaint cafés.

Collapse. Mouth open and poised:

Adieu, bluish, watery, tasteless skimmed milks, polystyrene cheeses, soya milk that does not even come from a mammal but a bean. Here is my riposte to the nutrition police, those who exercise their rigid and repressive controls upon me in this our homogenised dairy world.

I say this now: nowhere is the erosion of our identity clearer than in our food landscapes.

Imagine me now diving into the fat; wading through the nutty, canary-yellow, grainy seductive sweetness of it. Clotted cream, the tonnage of it, barely moving, it's a weight you can see and feel like mud is, it's of the earth. Really of the earth . . .

A Friesian sways her head and loops a dark tongue around Devon's grass, pulling it from the ground into her mouth. The earth is rich and red and crumbly, a legacy of the iron in the underlying desert rocks which have slowly broken down over the millennia to form this sweet soil. From pastures, down sunken lanes, she has travelled to milking parlours twice a day for centuries to give me this.

Legend tells us of Jenny in her kitchen: she will heat the full-cream milk with steam before leaving it in a shallow pan to cool slowly. When the cream rises to the surface and forms its clots she will serve it to the giant Blunderbore (sometimes called Moran). He will fall in love with her and make her his fourth wife.

Bideford's popular postman poet Edward Capern, who wrote about the nature and people he met on North Devon's country lanes, wrote of it:

> Sweeter than the odours borne on southern gales,
> Comes the clotted nectar of my native vales –
> Crimped and golden crusted, rich beyond compare,
> Food on which a goddess evermore would fare.
> Burns may praise his haggis, Horace sing of wine,
> Hunt his Hybla-honey, which he deem'd divine,
> But in the Elysium of the poet's dream
> Where is the delicious without Devon-cream?

As for Clovelly itself, Charles Kingsley, whose father was rector here, said of this place: 'A straggling village of irregularly shaped lichen-covered cottages on so steep an incline that the base of the one is on a level with the roof of its neighbour.'

For H. V. Morton, whose *In Search of England* came out of a series he wrote for the *Daily Express* in 1926, Clovelly failed to live up to expectations. It was altogether too quaint, 'the old established beauty queen of England . . . an English Amalfi rising sheer from the bay'. It is, he adds, 'a beauty spot that has been sternly told to keep beautiful. Its washing is displayed discreetly on a certain day. No signs disfigure its bowers, no motor cars may approach within half a mile of its sacrosanct charm.' This is all, of course, true. But then there is no other village in the British Isles that bears any resemblance to it.

Only three families since the middle of the thirteenth century have owned Clovelly. It was George Cary, in the sixteenth century, who built the only safe harbour between Appledore and Boscastle. He erected a pier and quay, divers' houses built on either side, cellars and warehouses at the cliff base. He diverted waters to a pathway through the woods and down the cliffside to the beach, making a new waterfall of brick. When tourism replaced herrings, Christine Hamlyn, who inherited the estate in 1884, would tend it lovingly as if it was her own garden. Over a fifty-two-year period she started renovating the existing houses at the quay and built up from there, turning simple fishermen's dwellings into Arts and Crafts cottages with spacious bedrooms on two or three floors. She married a rich banker called Frederick Gosling in 1889 and persuaded him to change his surname to hers, and together they poured money into Clovelly's restoration and upkeep. Clovelly passed to Christine's niece, the Honourable Betty Asquith, before it was dispatched to a company in 1929. The estate is currently owned and administered by the Honourable John Rous. I see him floating around the village in salmon-pink trousers, an air of inspection about an intelligent face, stopping every now and again, in a friendly manner, to talk to some of his tenants.

Some years later I meet Rous, and he tells me that he was in his thirties, working in London, when the estate's trustees told him they wanted to install a keen amateur, a retired naval captain type, to run it. 'But I felt Clovelly at that time needed a bit of a kick up the backside. There was a huge backlog of work to be done with no obvious funding streams and I didn't want to sell off land to pay for everything so I came down here to live to sort it all out.' He said it's mostly been a story about adaptation: 'A hundred years ago Clovelly was principally a fishing village with a bit of tourism thrown in, now it is a lot of tourism with a bit of fishing thrown in.'

You can't help sympathise with Rous as regards the challenges of keeping this village going. Protecting hundreds of homes, some of them centuries old, from the forces of sea, wind and salt might sound like an easy task which provides an easy income, but it must also be a terrible headache: contending with supporting tenants, subsiding properties, living life in a vertical time warp, dragging anything from groceries to chest freezers on sledges over cobbles as there is no vehicle access in or out. As for the properties themselves, they look quaint enough, but they must be hell to live in: perched high on a precipice with low ceilings, tourists pressing their noses up against your windows, and not being able to park your car by your front door. No thank you. I ask Rous what type of people take up the challenge, and he replies that it is mostly people who can work from home. He has potters and silk printers, but tells me on the whole they are quite an eclectic bunch. He doesn't necessarily look favourably on relations of people who have lived there or provide tied cottages for estate workers. Still, he has had tenants who have lived in Clovelly for thirty or forty years and says if they get too old to walk over the slippery cobbles or climb the steep gradient, he moves them to houses higher up in the village, where access is easier.

'Some of them have funny backstories. I have an Australian tenant, probably of Chinese extraction, who married an American of Russian origin who fell in love in Clovelly in Australia and decided they wanted to start a life here together.'

Rous was determined, when he took on Clovelly, that it would be a living parish. He doesn't like the terms 'heritage village' or 'preserved in aspic'. He told me, 'I want to get across that this is a lived-in environment. And I do make it an absolute criteria that if you take up a tenancy in Clovelly you become part of the community, that it can't be a second home.' As a result, he has kept rents relatively low. The temptation to sell the odd cottage here and there has also been resisted, so it hasn't turned into another ghost village of second homeowners like Port Isaac has further down the coast. The deal is simple: those who want an all-year-round, old-fashioned, steep-cobbled village experience on the edge get it subsidised by people who enjoy it for a day but are more than happy to go home. Rous admits that for many of his tenants it is a bit like living in a museum, 'but by evening when all the tourists leave, it does return back to its sleepy old self'.

When I ask him if it's been an encumbrance, he says not; 'To me it's been a fun challenge but I am probably too much of a hands-on person, I probably should have a manager to do this, that and the other.'

I stay at the Red Lion Hotel, which sits beside the harbour. From my bedroom window I can see the semi-circle of the quay bending eastward. The blocks used to build it date back to the fourteenth century. In the downstairs bar, I get talking to some of the locals and I say how much I admire Rous for his commitment to this place. If he is seigneurial in his decisions about who gets a property, it is probably tied up with bigger questions such as will this family help keep our community going? Besides, this is a kingdom, it has its own sovereignty, even monarchy, in the shape of John Rous, and great kingdoms are usually shaped by the ideas of those who sit on its throne. And the locals nod in agreement when I say this, saying they wouldn't want to carry the burden of the village's upkeep.

That night I think about Clovelly again, about its strangeness, how it is rather similar to the dense forest that surrounds it. To me it has a kind of metaphysical timelessness. I don't mean unexamined assumptions that have not been logically explained; it is, after all, still subject to movements, struggles, seasons like any small village, but what it isn't is a world that keeps alive any sense of continuing creation. The truth is, heritage busybodies probably wouldn't permit that anyway.

For me, it's another important artificial edge story. Like the beach huts, it's about a building battle in a place so mutable only the most hardy and adaptable can survive. The families that have owned this place have lived a difficult life of rock and shore, displayed their toughness by moving into fissures and crevices, they are part of a fraternity of creatures that live in the sand, hide in caves and under boulders, they are from the group that tunnels into solid rock and bores into bare soil. They have tried to hold the sea back. Tried to defy the ebb and flow of tourism and society. But Clovelly, Clovelly is a spectacle that just refuses to die. As Rachel Carson, in her book *The Edge of the Sea*, says:

Underlying the beauty of the spectacle there is meaning and significance. It is the elusiveness of that meaning that haunts us, that sends us again and again into the natural world where the key to the riddle is hidden. It sends us back to the edge of the sea, where the drama of life played its first scene on earth and perhaps its prelude; where the forces of evolution are at work today, as they have been since the appearance of what we know as life; and where the spectacle of living creatures faced by the cosmic realities of their world is crystal clear.

Clovelly has an edge over its rivals. A superiority. And that always puts people on edge. It puts them on edge because most people's hearts carry cowardice and procrastination when it comes to the forces stacked up against them.

*

It is lonely between here and Hartland Quay but beautiful, still green and rolling and occasionally wooded over high cliffs and deep valleys. I tramp over ancient hillforts and pass uninterested Friesians who barely lift their heads. The meadowsweet is out in abundance. I am drawn forwards by a radar station rather like a huge mushroom that comes into view some ten miles ahead. Installed by the Ministry of Defence at West Titchberry Cliff, near Hartland Point, it is used for air traffic control of both military and civilian aircraft. Or so they say. When you get up close you can hear it hum, challenging the natural symphony of the surroundings. It is mildly depressing that even in this wild and windswept place we are being bombarded by wireless trans-missions, but of course that is why it is here, at the edge, free to transmit and away from human habitation and controversy. I shut my eyes and eavesdrop, as if listening to a piece of orchestral music that is in a single continuous movement; a tone poem that evokes a tale of a hero not dissimilar to St Sebastian who is being pierced by the arrows of technology. Somewhere in it – I'd like to believe – lies the message about the torment we should all feel for our own foolish martyrdom to modernity and communications.

In the Beginning

Hartland Quay to Marsland Mouth

The edge never looked so dangerous as it does here, around Hartland. It is intimidating, tyrannising, a repository for features that reject all the primacy of human life. Everything is shaped by movements we would find unmovable, in seas that gather, wash, remove, in an unhurried, vague metonymy of motion and time. This area is jam-packed with *'in the beginning'* junk. Here, you can bear witness to the groundwork that was laid, the surfaces; a rare invitation to see a primeval cataclysm in action from a time when 'heaven and hell mixed as they spun'. Because this is God's own country. Truly. All the clever stuff will come later: people, religion, compassion, intellect, that sort of thing.

The prologue starts a mere 320 million years ago, in a raw and youthful earth, when this region was the floor of an independent arm of a formidable ocean straddling the equator. On this flat base it deposited a cake, not sandwiched by cream and jam but by sand and mud, fruited with ammonites and fish, baked by a nascent sun. And as this juvenile earth was buried beneath soft layers so it was compressed, until the top of the cake is what we see today, pale sandstone and darker mudstones which make up the rocks around Hartland Quay.

The drama in this narrative is not the layers but the upheaval of them. The reason why they are no longer horizontal is that way back in the 'carboniferous' – that's 320 million years ago – the peace of this ocean floor was disrupted by the approach of two super-continents from south of the equator. They went by the glorious, almost gorgonesque names of Eurussia and Gondwana. Eurussia (North Europe, Northern Asia and North America) was taking it slow travelling north, but Gondwana (Southern Europe, Africa, South America, Australia and Antarctica) had more of a pace as it travelled in the same direction. A collision was all but inevitable. And what a collision it must have been, two huge land masses crumpling and compressing all that was between them, creating an extensive mountain system. In effect, a rough sea of stony waves.

And so those calm, flat beds of the former ocean were squeezed into upfolds and downfolds, as the ones seen at Warren Cliff, with all the action occurring deep within the mountain chain, more than three miles below the surface. So strong was this compression, from both directions, that all the water from the ocean was wrung out and its thickness reduced. If you look at this old ocean now, from Hartland Quay, you can see it swing up and down like a heart monitor screen as it was squeezed and pushed.

Devon and Cornwall folded, fractured and was crushed into a huge and high Alp-like mountain range; it hardly seems possible, and where have they all gone? You can only really get your head around it if you wrestle with the true concept of time and its span, in this case 290 million years. Considering the Alps and Himalayas are a mere fifty million years old, you quickly realise that is a hell of a long time for erosion to take place. It reduced the mountains down to their bare roots, creating a rock plane, an erosional surface so soft and calm, gentle and sweet that there was no energy provided by the incline, meaning erosional processes were unable, at the time it was formed, to continue any more down-cutting below this base level. These plateaux now dominate the surfaces of the two counties. Travelling by car across them, you are completely unaware of the intense drama of rocks that have been folding for millions of years beneath you.

What is so utterly absorbing is that you can see this story in the stone right here in the Hartland Quay area. It must be why there is a group of geography students from Exeter University sitting like time travellers on the grass above with their clipboards, surveying all that is around them. I see one of them lifting a small rock beside him, trying to peer inside the interior of this natural thing as if looking for a window but the rock's strength and memory is all bundled up like a closed fist: it wants to retain its essential edgefulness in its patterns, and the student knows he will need the strength of gods to open it up to see them; just like the rocks around him, with their own profound interiority, they can only be disturbed by something more massive than themselves, by earthquakes and volcanic upheavals or other colossal events out of their control. What he is learning about is the resilient inner core, about the intact and unseen, about the integrity of composition. That there is stuff in this life we can't always alter, stuff that remains independent in existence and in concept: that are 'conceived through themselves alone'.

And there is just so much to see here. At the left end of Warren Beach, a thick bed of sandstone forming the roof to a wide sea cave. Black cliffs which jut out into the deep sea in castles and spires and obdurate wings of ironstone. Or the spectacular contorted folding at Embury Beach, moving like a bucket of worms waiting to be used as fishermen's bait. The ribbed beds of raw rock caused not only by the constant wetting and drying of waves but boring animals and the growth of salt crystals in the rock cracks as they dry out. The isolated stacks and reefs making their last stands while the rocks around them are left slumped and scattered like the hopes and dreams of warriors on the losing side. Dominating everything is a sea, the victor, always the victor, which rampages as a young, untrained colt might do, unafraid to trample over any ground or enter any inlet in search of its freedom.

Further on, at the side of a sea-dissected valley, another rare feature much vested by geologists and geographers is St Catherine's Tor. It was named after a mariner's chapel that once crowned its summit, but which came crashing down to the sea along with one of its flanks. It is remarkable because of its isolation, separated from the rest of the coast by the flat plain I pass through. Dark shadows on the landward side emphasise its steepness. Something angry out there, clearly, did not want it to live. From its summit, if you could ever get up there, you would be able to see how wide the wave-cut platform is along this coast, 250 yards from this point, a rocky illustration of the coastal erosion that has occurred.

Speke's River once ran along the foot of the tor, along the valley past Hartland Quay and on further north. But the water now drops to the sea at Speke's Mouth, in a series of dances. It falls and cascades, plunging first fifty feet, before taking a new route that follows the structure of the rocks which, like all good dances, ends in a perfect 'dip', down to the beach below. This is what is termed a coastal hanging valley where a water's profile has, up until this point, been long and smooth, and is then ended abruptly by a sea advancing onto land. Here, the valley must have extended a considerable way and flowed gently down to the sea edge as the drop is some 160 feet above the beach.

The area through Hartland and beyond is wildness personified. There is no culture here, it is just a big open stage of the elemental. Nothing is in a display case. Nothing is neat or small. Or inside. From the Point and its massive crags – this is the most extreme north-westerly point in Devon – the land is all victim. Erosion is everywhere. The top of the reefs are sharp as upturned knives. The water, already an elemental mystery, allows for massive ground swells; it casts the tides in deadly opposition, it sends up great walls of water that rear, crest, fall and recede before repeating again. There was a quay that threw out a protecting arm, but it was gobbled up in 1887, and again in 1896 when storms tore the limb out of the water, leaving just a stump behind. The forces are like monsters here; all mouth, they open their jaws in a growl, display their teeth, lunge at ships, grind their timbers, steal sailors' souls. Edges don't get more treacherous than this one, particularly for shipping and particularly for the ketches and schooners that plied this coast in the days of sail. At the quay the roll call of lost ships is long: SS *Rosalia* and SS *Ginetorix*, *Edward & Ann*, *Test*, *Eclipse*, *Jenny Jones*, *Zuma*, *Deux Freres*, *Royal Saxon*, *Londos* and *Clipper*. Many more could be added to the list from around Hartland Point.

But there is also a discernible independence about the place. A strength of character. And individualism. An impressive church, known as the Cathedral of North Devon, rises high above the landscape at Stoke; farmhouses stand firm, there is a lighthouse, a dialect, the ghost of an abbot that walks by Abbot's Oak in Hartland Abbey Park, sea pinks grow at the edge, oystercatchers dive and shrill, seals bask. Everything is soldiering on, everything is determined, both the good and the bad. Dodder, for example. Its alien-looking red threads cover the gorse in small explosions just up from Hartland Quay, as if hanging on to a wreckage itself. Dodder is a totally parasitic plant that lacks chlorophyll. Its propagating methods are pretty twisted too; after its seeds germinate in the soil it sends up small shoots, but unlike other plants the stem grows up in a circular motion rather like a tornado, spiralling until it picks up a nearby plant which will act as its host. The dodder's stem then begins to twine around the neighbouring plant, inserting suckers to draw out nutrients. Once this contact is made, the dodder's original stem wilts and breaks from the ground, and it starts to leech off its host for nourishment.

There are shelters as well. Places that pull you back from the edge. The steep-sided coombe of Milford Water, for example, dug into the edge of this high plateau. It would have provided some comfort for weary travellers, backs bent from the weather. There are glens like this all along the path which slice the high table-land, that travel through hunched small woodlands of rich oak and hart's tongue fern, coming away from the ocean, where the footsteps of farmers collecting sand to apply to their heavy acid soils, and smugglers and the wheel rolls of their carts have worn down paths to make walls of species-rich hedgerows. Places that show compassion in the wildness, rather than beating against the ground you stand on.

A. L. Rowse, the Cornish historian, wrote that the Reverend Robert Stephen Hawker was 'one of those men of strange and original personality who impress themselves upon a place in such a way that one cannot think of it without thinking of the man'.

I am now entering Hawker country, and I have even booked to stay at his sprawling rectory, which he built on the site of the old vicarage, using stone quarried from local cliffs and completed in 1837. The house sits lonely in its own tree-lined valley, and Hawker chose the site because he had seen sheep shelter there in a storm. He wrote in a letter, 'I find that by a sweeping abolition of fences and the old Vicarage Buildings I can contrive that my Church and Churchyard shall stand just in the centre of my future lawn. The only objects then perceptible from my two fronts will be the Church and the Sea, the suggestions of both of which are boundless.' He would add a few eccentric and ecclesiastical spins to the building, including a set of chimneys copied from favourite church towers and a 'Gable on one front surmounted with a cross', as well as a set of arched stained-glass windows. The result is a sort of architectural purgatory, neither one thing nor the other.

In the light-filled drawing room I imagine Tennyson, an admirer, sitting with Hawker discussing Arthurian myths and poetry, or Charles Kingsley in the library, another fellow priest and social reformer seeking inspiration from Hawker's compassion for his fellow man. A towering figure of nineteenth-century Cornish cultural history, Hawker was very much a celebrity in life as much as he was in death. He composed the lyrics for 'The Song of the Western Men', Cornwall's national anthem, kept a pet pig, requested mourners wear purple rather than black, matching his own long purple cloak and, according to local legend, in his youth once dressed up as a mermaid and was seen wailing on a rock in Bude, frightening the people out of their minds. He also believed birds were 'filled with the thoughts of God's own mind'.

After the death of his first wife, Hawker 'fell into a condition of piteous depression, and began to eat opium', according to Sabine Baring-Gould, Hawker's biographer. And it was during those distressing months that he penned his rendition of the Arthurian grail legend, 'The Quest of the Sangraal'. Happiness returned a year later, when he married a governess of Polish extraction, Pauline Kuczynski. He was sixty years old; she was twenty. She managed to squeeze out three children, the youngest of whom died in 1950, having been a nun for sixty years.

Hawker's incumbency at Morwenstow, where he stayed until he died, must be put in the context of his times. Morwenstow was no romantic idyll as it is seen today; it was a wild parish, consisting of a group of hamlets without a centre; its main occupations were smuggling, violence and, above all, religious non-conformism. There were few manor houses and no 'gentlemen' in the vicinity; Hawker's parishioners, mostly farmers and labourers, lived in desperate poverty. 'My people were a mixed multitude of smugglers, wreckers, and dissenters of various hue,' he wrote in his 'Remembrances of a Cornish Vicar'. 'Mine was a perilous warfare … I had to soothe the wrecker, to persuade the smuggler, and to "handle serpents", in my intercourse with adversaries of many a kind.'

He is credited with introducing the harvest festival into his church, a period in the farming calendar he delighted in. In 1843 Hawker wrote to all his parishioners (even though most of them could not read), a letter which included the words 'let us gather together in the chancel of our church on the first Sunday of next month and there receive in the new corn, that blessed sacrament which was ordained to strengthen and refresh our souls'. Hawker particularly admired the old tradition of 'crying the neck', a ceremony at the end of harvest when the last sheaf, in which the corn-spirit was believed to dwell, was cut amid great rejoicing. He would remind his parishioners that the final sheaf was waved in the air three times as the Hebrews did on God's command, and he believed the treble 'cry' symbolised the holy trinity. In his sermons, he would tell his flock never to use a rake to glean ears of corn remaining on the ground because, he declared, they were for the poor of the parish and also for God's birds.

In his house he hung the neck, decorated with ribbons. It was to be used as a fertility and good luck symbol until the next harvest came, when the corn spirit would miraculously transfer to the growing corn and a fresh neck could be made.

'The earth is an orb of emblems,' Hawker wrote. 'God made this world for a man to see him by.'

One of Hawker's saddest and most harrowing duties was to give a decent burial to sailors after shipwrecks, which were a frequent occurrence around these cliffs. Previously the bodies were buried where they washed up on the beach, or left in salty waters. After a wreck under Welcombe Cliffs in December 1874, Hawker wrote, 'We expect bodies every hour.' Sometimes decomposition was so severe Hawker would have to dose up members of his burial party with gin so that they could get through the agony of bringing the bodies before God in a Christian burial.

The most famous incident of this kind was the sinking of the *Caledonia*, a ship bound for Gloucester from Falmouth, which in September 1842 hit a fierce north-westerly gale, ironing the ship against the shore; when the mast snapped the crew was forced into the sea. No one knows whether the *Caledonia* was enticed onto the rocks by wreckers with false lights, not least because the practice is more one of legend than truth.

Hawker was asleep in his bedroom when a loud knocking pulsed at his door at daybreak. It must have split his dream, placed something at the side of it. There are gentle ways to wake people up; this was not one of them. It must have come at him like something waiting at the end of a tunnel. The panicked voice and knocking came from a young boy who worked in his household, it was telling him to get up, that there had been a shipwreck, down on the rocks. Hawker hurriedly dressed, went outside and started a monkey crawl down the cliffs, the last three hundred feet treacherous. As he went, he was full of foreboding, and he was right to feel that way: what he found were dead bodies scattered like seals on Vicarage Rock; it was utter carnage. He described the scene as one to be looked on 'only once in a human life'. Far too late for a hero's welcome.

The rocks and the water bristled with fragments of mast and spar and rent timbers; the cordage lay about in tangled masses. The rollers tumbled in volumes of corn, the wheaten cargo; and amidst it all the bodies of the helpless dead – that a few brief hours before had walked the deck, the stalwart masters of their ship – turned their poor disfigured faces towards the sky, pleading for sepulture.

Hawker led the funeral procession as local men carried the bodies up the cliffs, and the dead sailors were placed in the vicarage overnight. When the coroner arrived the next morning, an inquest was heard and the usual verdict of 'wrecked and cast ashore' was given. Hawker was then able to inter the dead sailors. He tells us that eyes gathered there that day were moist: 'For who could hear unsoftened the greeting of the Church to these strangers from the sea, and the "touch that makes the whole earth kin", in the hope we breathed, that we too might one day "rest as these our brethren did"?'

The churchyard was to be their final resting place. Over

the body of the *Caledonia*'s twenty-eight-year-old captain Peter Stevenson, Hawker would place the ship's figurehead. Later it would be joined by three upturned keels with oars forming a rough cross.

Figure-Head of the 'Caledonia' at her Captain's Grave
By R. S. Hawker

We laid them in their lowly rest,
The strangers of a distant shore;
We smoothed the green turf on their breast,
'Mid baffled Ocean's angry roar;
And there, the relique of the storm,
We fixed fair Scotland's figured form.

She watches by her bold, her brave,
Her shield towards the fatal sea:
Their cherished lady of the wave
Is guardian of their memory.
Stern is her look, but calm, for there
No gale can rend or billow bear.

Stand, silent image! stately stand,
Where sighs shall breathe and tears be shed,
And many a heart of Cornish land,
Will soften for the stranger dead.
They came in paths of storm; they found
This quiet home in Christian ground.

I walk the grounds and enter the graveyard. It's difficult to quantify the atmosphere here, but there is something not quite right. I stop under whispering trees. Above there is a difference in the birds' cries, a warning perhaps. This ground, after all, is jammed with dead sailors who have left mothers and sons behind weeping; it is not like a typical graveyard where acceptance is the norm. Somehow here, you can't feel without conscience, without humanity.

For generations, the distinctive white figurehead was maintained and occasionally repaired by parishioners, but an inspection in 2004 revealed serious internal damage caused by rot and decay. The figurehead was moved into the sanctuary of the church itself, and a replica placed over the sailors' graves.

I walk into the church to take a look at the original. With its sword and shield, poised as if over the cutwater, it looms like a flying ghost. I stare up at this famous figurehead and get the sensation, almost at once, that all the sailors' hearts and those of their loved ones are trapped inside its carved pitch-pine white chest. The image then moves to one of a caged dove, flapping desperately to get out of this church and its surrounds, away from the bundles of broken hollow bones under the trees, away from its veneration and its association, so that which is within can be of reminiscence and memory, as if all it really wanted to do was take those imperishable souls out over the water once more, to dream and renew.

You pass Hawker's hut as you walk back to the coastal path. It is hidden down a few steps, scooped out of a bank and camouflaged with a turf roof. It is built out of driftwood from a ship's timbers. Sit here for a moment, as there is no better place to feel the man's spirit. Shut your eyes and imagine he is next to you: this tall and powerfully built man, with fair hair and blue eyes and ruddy complexion, smoking opium in this hut looking out to sea. His garb will be unconventional, a long coat of purple, and under it instead of a waistcoat a blue jersey in a nod to what he believed he was, a fisher of men. A small red cross, symbolising where the spear entered Christ's side, has been stitched into it, and against the wall leans his 'pastoral staff', a cross-handled wooden walking stick resembling a sword. Here, from this very sheltered spot, you can share the delight in all he surveys; the isolation, the wildness, the traditional way of life, all that gives succour to his imaginative temperament. A place of steady quiet in roaring music.

Albert Einstein perhaps got it right when he said, 'A human being is a part of the whole, called by us "Universe", a part limited in time and space. He experiences himself, his thoughts and feelings, as something separated from the rest – a kind of optical delusion of his consciousness.' But he says that this delusion is a kind of prison, restricting us to our personal desires and affection for a few persons nearest to us. And that 'our task must be to free ourselves from this prison by widening our circle of compassion to embrace all living creatures and the whole of nature in its beauty'. Sitting in this hut, and thinking of Robert Stephen Hawker, no words feel better applied to his character than these.

There is another hut on this route, another place designed for thinking, where philosophy was moulded in the three-sided collaboration between place, the environment and a questioning mind. It was occupied by an alternative poet who for twenty years of his life also needed to withdraw, someone who viewed his thoughts and feelings as 'something separated from the rest'. He was the little-known but talented writer Ronald Duncan; his hut, formerly used by the Admiralty during wartime, also looks out on all the immensity of cliff and surf that the Atlantic calls its own. The hut has been lovingly restored by his daughter Bryony in his memory and now walkers can enter the poet's biosphere and be left slightly intrigued as to who he was and the work he left behind.

Trying to get to know this giant intellect is no easy task. I have one book of his poems and two volumes of his autobiography, but that's about it: his books are now quite hard to track down; you mostly need to direct yourself to dusty library shelves. Back home I am more than intrigued, as with Edward Thomas's lines: 'To-day I think / Only with scents, – scents dead leaves yield'. I discover that Duncan was a man of huge range and that he also lived in a swamp of ideas and emotions, from the simple to the complex, from the dramatic to the pastoral. Digging around in the dark I find his influences included Gandhi, with whom he lived and worked in 1937 and whose prose he selected and edited for publication. He also was a friend of T. S. Eliot and Ezra Pound. That he worked in a coal mine, was arrested for vagrancy, founded an agricultural commune, served time in prison for being a pacifist and claimed that his father had been the great-grandson of the last crown prince of Bavaria. He wrote the libretto for Benjamin Britten's opera *The Rape of Lucretia* and, finally, I learn that he produced a five-part poem of epic proportions entitled *Man*.

I have the first few pages of *Man*, but the rest I cannot find without spending considerable money in an online bookshop. And those words and lines I have are dense with heavy scientific references. Duncan tells us in his introduction to this great poem that he had started out writing his autobiography 'in the conventional fashion' in a small luxury flat in London. It was there that that he started to think that the date of his birth was inaccurate: 'I was not forty-seven: some parts of me were possibly twenty thousand years old.' And so his journey back in time began:

A year of years lie behind my name,
    A century of centuries has waited for this hand.
It took all time's tide to reach me;
    The expanding darkness has groped for me;
Through the leafless wood, the blind wind's blown to me;
    Beneath the heavy ocean, the patient coral's
    reached for me;
I am the miracle: man.

In North Devon, he locked himself away in this hut and began to write a full-scale biography of the species to which he belonged, within the four great eons of earth's history. *Man* explores the knowledge of the universe, from its origins to the formation of the planets, the development of life on earth, the development of humans, the development of cultures and societies and even projects itself into the future. Central to all of it is the isolated figure of the epic hero, and that hero is of course Duncan himself, fixed in time to the moment of writing but wandering backwards and forwards in history through learning and cognition. What he found was that there was much poetry to be found in science, and that both should be intimately linked. 'Without an awareness of science, the contemporary sensibility is fractured and its literature will become a cul-de-sac, a diatribe of "subjective hosannas".' He cites Donne and the metaphysical poets as those who had managed this 'integrated sensibility'.

The poem must have been a massive undertaking for Duncan because it required a huge bout of self-education in immense areas such as physics, geology, biology and anthropology. Duncan's journey, alone in his hut, had been so cerebral, so immersive, yet when the poem was finally published in the 1970s it was barely acknowledged, and if it was, it was wilfully misunderstood. Literature is of course littered with similar cases, where weighty artistic endeavour often lies disregarded until someone has the patience to dust it down and take it on. More often than not that fails to happen. One can't help but feel melancholic for Duncan and his unrewarded efforts and equally melancholic for all that is lost through a lack of attention in our world.

Duncan chose to live on this coastline for forty years of his life because it was untouched. Every which way you look there is no evidence of Man ever having been here, only God. And that was perhaps his fault line; Duncan sought to use his self-consciousness to conjure truth about the world, but paradoxically it drove him into isolation from it. Unable or disinclined to break with the incompatible contradictions between himself and creation, he became increasingly occupied with the mirror of his own deeply critical self. It is no coincidence that he produced not one but four autobiographies.

And that is the fundamental difference between the two huts on this coast and the two men who took ownership of them.

Winds, Waves and Windows

Marsland Mouth to the Dizzard

The fog comes with me on 'little cat feet' as I walk across a simple bridge over a small, uninspiring stream that separates Devon from Cornwall at Marsland Mouth. Its modesty feels somehow appropriate. After all, the Cornish people were for centuries largely cut off from the rest of England. They were detached, hidden, making a living from fishing on the coast or tinning in the moors and valleys around the granite hills. Only a few hundred years ago you could find a Cornishman who would tell you he had never even been to England. And this is where his psyche lies, for Cornwall is *not* England, a Cornishman is *not* an Englishman; he is closer to a Welshman; he is essentially British. And he was inhabiting this island called Britain long before the English came. A brew of two races: the first nomads from the Mediterranean shores, the other Brythonic Celts from south of the Alps.

When I, so quietly, walk into this land over this small bridge, I enter a non-urban and ceremonial county, a duchy and a Celtic nation, where in the water and in the air and in the sodden boggy ground of moorland a different culture has been drawn, one that is physical and unafraid, where imagination has been born under every stone, one which was started by men who first give their labour to dragging and pushing great slabs of rock and continued by traders of tin over stormy seas. When the barbarians shouted at the gate to let them in, they refused to acquiesce, knowing that once they let them through, they would own the land and the customs, dilute or take away their language, laugh at their beliefs, and soon those outsiders gave up trying. Only men of spirit like John Wesley made any headway. Besides, who wanted to be cursed among the Devil's quoits and frying pans? Or to cross the legend-tough spriggans, those minute and hirsute fairies found under cairns and detached stones who, when angered, can grow to eight feet tall, who steal all you hold dear? Who wants to live a life in an inferno underground? Smell of fish or be dusted in clay? Who is brave enough to walk among the spirits that swarm over the holy wells and ancient burial grounds?

For all those who enter here come to a land set behind an imaginary barrier; you enter a spell. Cornwall is where you leave materialism behind, a place where you make room for the spirit, for that which observation cannot detect. There is so much here that is invisible, inaudible, untouchable, you enter a living environment of poetry and reverence and presumptions of immortality as if there is some supernatural force that helps all its objects and people fulfil their purpose.

Cornwall is a land of edges. Of borders. Of portals. On its eastern edge it is separated from Devon by the River Tamar. This rises where I walk now, in its extreme north-eastern corner, four miles from the cliffs of Hawker's Morwenstow. It is bordered to the north and west by the Atlantic Ocean, to the south by the English Channel. It is the westernmost part of the South West Peninsula of Great Britain. Land's End, where this journey will end, is the south-westernmost point, and the southernmost part of England – discounting the Isles of Scilly – is at Lizard Point.

It is virtually an island to itself. It is foreign. In fact, until not so long ago it even had its own language, a Celtic one, in origin not as early as Irish, but probably older than Welsh. In the parish of Paul, where I grew up, and the whole of the Land's End district, it was almost universally spoken as late as 1650. The last woman to speak it, Dorothy Pentreath, an old fisherwoman of Mousehole, is buried in Paul church.

Of course, there have been tussles, border disputes, like everywhere else. The Battle of Deorham in 577, when Wessex forces led by Ceawlin and his son Cuthwine led to the separation of Dumnonia (and therefore Cornwall) from Wales. Some rebellions in the Middle Ages as well: in 1497, Perkin Warbeck landed near Sennen Cove, claiming to be one of the princes murdered in the tower; he was defeated in a battle at Exeter. The Prayer Book Rebellion of 1549 saw many Cornishmen decapitated. There was the Spanish invasion at Mounts Bay in 1595. And there were a number of battles and sieges during the Civil War. Not forgetting the Monmouth Rebellion of 1685 and its bloody aftermath. But on the whole, Cornwall was always considered to be a land separated from the rest. Not even the Romans had much influence: their last major settlement is to the east, at Exeter. For them there were too many desolate moors blocking their path: Dartmoor, Exmoor, Bodmin. The dark rocks and jagged reefs meant there was also a shortage of safe ports. Yes, they came – ornaments and pottery have been found, a villa at Magor between Camborne and the coast, a marker stone in Breage churchyard, coins found in Zennor Quoit – but there is little evidence of Roman civilians migrating here in large numbers. This was always uncouth country to their sophisticated eastern eyes. A land of barbarians.

I first came to Cornwall as a three-year-old, when my father was elected as the Member of Parliament for St Ives on 1 April

1966. We lived in a small house above Newlyn Harbour, overlooking the fishing fleet there, before moving to a cottage at the
edge of Chyenhal Moor, a boggy shallow valley on the southern
side of the Land's End peninsula. My earliest memories are of
that small moor, of its colours, textures and sounds. Although
swampy, it was always a vital and rich habitat, full of willow
carr – cut regularly for making lobster pots – flag irises, wavy-
leaved St John's wort and pillwort, a rare fern of wet heathland
and acid pools. The rainfall, poor drainage and acid surroundings constraining the bacteria which would usually break down
the plant material meant it was also a place where peat could
thrive. Until the nineteenth century, livestock was grazed here
and furze (gorse) cut for fuel.

But what I quickly picked up, even as a young child, was how
this was a land of thresholds. From our cottage there was a discernible demarcation between the outside open world and an
inside, guarded, mysterious, covered one, and if you crossed over
the land under the portal you could be led into fear-provoking
and cruel places. Not so far-fetched, considering this particular
ground was known for yielding tin from the alluvial deposits;
adits ran under the fields and there were rumours that one
could walk to Newlyn inside them. The moor was surrounded
by smallholdings and the horses that ploughed the fields, and
later the tractors, often sunk through the ground. At Rose Farm,
part of a barn collapsed down a mine shaft. Very early on I was
made aware that a wrong foot here or a slip there and the earth
might just gobble me up, damned and screaming down some
kind of pagan hole.

There were other doors, other portals, as well, between the
living and the dead, a whole underworld that promised immortality, marked by heavy stones, pulled and raised in solemn rites.
Man's old dance with the trials of death. The standing stones in
and around Chyenhal Moor are part of a significant alignment
linking sites of importance from the Neolithic period. In a field

to the south-west of Tresvennack stands a magnificent menhir, the tallest, most elegant stone of them all, standing a superior eleven feet high, with another four feet of it in the ground, pressing down its memory into the earth. Its silicate flecks of mica shining out of the granite give it added allure. In 1840, a farmer found a large stone slab two feet south of the stone and discovered that it covered a pit, cut into the subsoil, which contained two Bronze Age urns. One was extremely large and held cremated human bones, the other a powdery substance. They were removed to the museum at Penlee House, where they can now be seen behind glass.

Unsurprisingly, I had no knowledge of these facts back then. I was much more interested in listening to the embellished tales of our farming neighbour, Mr Barnes, who told me that the menhir had been there since the beginning of time, erected by ancient people, that it was a grave marker for a great warrior who now swirled around this moor in his haunting. It might have just been another of Cornwall's many mythical projections, but it was enough to unnerve me. When my brother Julian took Mr Barnes's carthorse, Gypsy, onto the moor, she would refuse to proceed across it, and he would often grumpily return home without her on foot. It made me immediately suspicious.

From a fear of that moor, I moved on to stories of mermaids and sea monsters, of the pobel vean or little people, how King Arthur lived on as a chough and flew around his one-time home in Tintagel until he needed to return and serve his country again. Then there was the lost land of Lyonesse and the tragic romance of Tristan and Iseult. I learned that I was living in a land of mystery, of uneasy tensions. What Cornwall gave me very early on was the understanding of a sixth sense, an ability to know that some things cannot be learned by using just sight and hearing, that there were other things we can call on – perception, intuition, patience, legend – to understand the world, that there is often something extrasensory to be found in the winds and in the whispers. That not everything lives inside an orderly mansion of understanding.

But something else as well: this persistent feeling of how the authority of a place can be compressed inside us, always ready to be stirred, to be woken. It stays lodged inside our bodies long after we have left that place. In that sense we are deeply subject to place. Place is us, in us. Our surroundings when young become key to the creation of our identities.

There is a foam party on the edge of Bude; blustery winds and torrential rain have churned up the algae in the sea, ruffling the western end of the town into a thick off-white duvet of natural fluff. As the waves break on the shore, air is trapped with the organic matter forming bubbles; the resulting foam, which can be as light as a kiss, is blown onshore. They say this is a good sign of a productive ocean ecosystem.

I walk all day and intend to walk all week. The path out of Bude passes the Temple of the Winds at Compass Point, Thomas Acland's 1840 replica of the one in Athens, with the points of the compass carved into its octagonal sides. From there, the path hugs the clifftop, backs the beaches and follows the road, dull, all the way to Widemouth. The winds follow too, bullying, pushing. Occasionally you hear a high-pitched shriek; it could be a young girl being pinched and punched by a playground bully, but it is the wind. Or other high-pitched sounds: they are also the winds. There is a large sun, high and smiling. Then there is spitting. Rain.

It's Saturday. Surfers begin to assemble in a long necklace of black rubber baubles along the surf at Widemouth Bay. They take to the waves as if they are in conflict with them;

insubstantial boards head-first into the swell. If they are lucky, they will be lifted, perilously, in that small moment of flight, their bodies mastering the universe until the universe tosses them over into the foam, laughing. I watch the faces on the ones that come ashore, exhausted and defeated, always defeated.

Waves are the product of winds blowing over and goading the water surface. The brawnier and more shouty the winds are, the more commanding, superior and higher the waves become, and the greater the energy transfer from wind to sea. They are usually born far out in the Atlantic, perhaps in some distant storm, and as they spread out, characterised by regular wavelengths with crests which in deep water are smooth and unbroken, they lose little of their power as they arrive at the edge. But the edge is a great disruptor, it is where everything changes; it forces the waves to become unbalanced and collapse in lines of breakers so beloved by the surfers.

The edge of waves represents in outline the deeper patterns of underwater currents, ones I cannot see but I know are working there. In the same way, wrinkles on a face can signify a locked-in hardship. The face, after all, is an edge. Edges are endings of whatever lies around and under them.

I sit down and wave-watch for a while; the hush and the hiss of them, and the repetition and collapse. It brings a certain comfort. Maybe Heraclitus was doing the same thing when he said 'everything flows and nothing abides, everything gives way and nothing stays fixed'. The world is indeed filled with waves: quantum waves, sound waves, light waves, the child becomes a parent who becomes a grandparent, until there is nothing, the dissipation of energy at the end of a life equal to a wave. Our whole story, somehow, right here.

The force of an Atlantic wave can be something else. When it smashes up against a solid object such as a wall the power is insane. Although water cannot be compressed, breaking waves can trap air in cracks in the rock face and, as the wave recedes, the air will explosively expand. This can blow fragments from the rock face, adding to the litter on the beach; that rock litter in turn can be picked up by the waves to batter the solid rock again.

Waves of industry have moved into Cornwall and out again, leaving their own debris. For the hundred years since the Cornish tin industry was overtaken by better tin mines world-wide – and Cornish miners left to go and work them – the county has taken a similar beating. Farming, defence, fishing (pilchards disappeared in the 1920s) all foundered. Locals left, retirees and second-homers arrived. Over the decades Cornwall, by means of compensation, was awarded millions of pounds' worth of funds from the EU, whose aim was to help reduce differences in social and economic conditions within the European Union. It was uncoupled from neighbouring Devon and seeded useful infrastructure projects and new universities. Now that Brexit has arrived, the money has been withdrawn and we are waiting to see what wave comes next.

The sea is normally quiescent, on the seabed even in a storm, and vigorous changes limited to a narrow zone between high and low tides, but undercutting still goes on. Here that under-cutting is taken on by the nationalists who say, quite rightly, that Cornwall has a non-English culture, typified by its language, Kernewek, which was officially recognised by the government in November 2002. Yet, they complain, the government still refuses to give it official protection or to support the culture of the Cornish minority. The Cornish also still retain a legal system, but its legislative authority, the Cornish Stannary Parliament, is not officially recognised. The Cornish have their own folklore, traditions and customs that differ greatly from those of the English majority. They hoist their flag depicting the black and white cross of St Piran, they insist on a greater teaching of the Cornish language, they push their demands for regional self-government, protection of local interests and greater self-assertion. There are even home-grown terrorists working for the Cornish National Liberation Army, who are partial to issuing threats. They say this is because legitimate efforts to achieve recognition and official minority status have gone largely unheeded. Cornwall, after all this time, is searching for a new identity, one that matches the fiery independence and stubborn pride of its people, past and present. The Anglo–Celt debate rumbles on.

Blackthorn sloes and leaves on the road to Wanson Mouth, by Penhalt Farm. They are black and globular, swathed seemingly in an ultra-violet light. This grey bloom means they are ripe for plucking. The sloes are woven in on the loom of a hedge already filled with the interlaced threads of other species: gorse flowers, beech leaves, hawthorn berries and leaves, blackberries, honeysuckle, ivy, rose hips and leaves and hazel. Before the development of chemical dyes, these hedges were where you came for colour, particularly the earthy, fire shades; yellow and green from privet and bracken, sloe for the blues and the browns, blackberries for reds and blacks and browns. Even nettles were used by the ton to dye Second World War camouflage nets.

One could spend hours looking into a hedge, particularly ones along this route; they are probably the oldest thing you can see, older than buildings and churches even. And the hedges that have the most species are usually the oldest of them all, potentially hundreds or thousands of years old. They should be esteemed for their steadiness, their endurance; the uninterrupted actions of the soils that anchor them should be valued, as should their abundant pantries of seed.

When large-scale removal took place after the Second World War, spawned from a government directive to make the country self-sufficient, and in which financial incentives were offered to farmers, it is thought that half of the country's hedge network was lost. Farmers also had to negotiate the big fields with new machinery as their old equipment was designed for smaller plots. These large machines clunked and colluded with the removal of wildlife. Suddenly, farmers were no longer considered custodians of the land but destroyers of it. Worse, they came armed with terrible sprays and machines that prune in straight lines, making what remained straggling and thin in places.

But waves come in fashions, ideas, political imperatives as well. The rewilding movement, the one that wants us to return to an age of ecological innocence, now wishes to remove barriers and create swathes of wilderness. The rich among them, from politicians to guilt-ridden pop stars offsetting their plane travel, are clearing the land of hedges again – as well as tenants and cabbages, expelling sheep and cattle from the moors and disheartening and discouraging people like me from walking over them. Some even believe the way to stave off environmental disaster is to eat food grown in laboratories from enriched bacteria, protein pancakes. There are some, like the journalist George Monbiot, who see farming as 'the most destructive force ever to have been unleashed by humans'. All hail the new heroes and their urban followers. Rewilding Britain lists fifty-eight projects, covering a quarter of a million acres, on its website, illustrated with a pair of lynxes. They will soon, no doubt, be joined by polecats, wolves and boar. One can almost hear them laughing at the pastoral tradition.

Borders have histories, they contain memory, culture, and with them we have created mini Edens. They are not zones of exclusion as rewilding zones are. Hedges hold the soil together, prevent erosion and flooding, they link up woods and copses, they support wildlife such as dormice and butterflies, they support farmers, the men and women that we need to run sustainable, regenerative plots that are soil-rich and who use native breeds and capture carbon.

In fact, this edge has been farmed since the world as we know it began; you can tell by the geometry of the fields and the relics left behind. On the high ground at Forrabury, as you leave Boscastle, which is coming further down the path, there are forty-two stitches: long gently curving plots or strips of land scored into the earth, a form of Celtic land tenure known as stichmeal. It is one of only three surviving examples of stitches still being farmed in Britain today. Managed as hay meadows, they contain a wide variety of plants including orchids, hay-rattle, bird's-foot trefoil and sawwort. The ploughing of the strips allows the arable plants to exist. Most of the species are common, such as speedwell, bindweed, fathen, but some – lesser snapdragon and corn marigold – are nationally rare. In winter, the stubble on the stitches provides cover for overwintering birds such as finches and buntings, as well as those birds that have been driven off the land by the loss of farmland habitats. In these few strips, there is a rare place to view ancient farmland unpolluted. And there are messages here about the future if you care to look. Agriculture was humans' first great revolutionary intervention; it was a radical and surprising innovation and it will be again. Farmers are our greatest hope, not rewilders with their paying guests and wildlife sanctuaries. Farmers are the ones who will help our country to produce more of its food sustainably. The plough is not our enemy, in fact it might well save us, but we have to make it pay. Let's slay the agri-industrial dragon and return to something more old-style, methods that are nature-friendly, climate-aiding. Let's wear wool from sheep rather than synthetic fleeces when we are cold. Vegans could start taking their protein from gorse, which can be harvested from our moors. We should have high tariffs for meat and dairy imports, discourage unethical cheap imports. The power to heal is contained within our own hands.

I look out at the crests of breaking waves again, the moving ridges where the top of a wave breaks before it tumbles over and down, the last moment when everything is held together as one body before dissolving into an ill-defined form. We are also on the cusp of something, a new way of looking at the land. But look again at this confluence of currents. Just as farmers have built on the work of generations of their forebears, much as one cusped wave gives way to another, they also never bring the work to completion but to a new level of accomplishment, enabling the farm to move on to another stage. Because a cusp is not a straight edge, it is elastic, it is ever-changing, porous even; it comes and it goes. In that sense it is more like a boundary than a border, it does not exclude or inhibit, it does not form a partition but offers a design, an open design of incessant change, and the hedges with their tousled mass of threads studded with garlands and fruit are just part of that ancient contract.

Mystics and Mayhem

The Dizzard to Tintagel

We are in and around the autumnal equinox, that day when the sun rises exactly in the east and sets exactly in the west. The solar decrease is about to begin. The dark half of the year is almost upon us. On my walk I am seeing the plants already cowering, the leaves dropping. I am feeling a cold northerly wind, bringing with it migrating birds and a shiver. Day and night will soon be equal. We are at the start of that long, magic moment before we wake again. We have jumped another boundary.

On into the Dizzard, another stretch of ancient woodland at the edge, dominated by dwarf oak that stretches from the top of the cliff down hundreds of feet to the sea, where the salt-laden winds and weather have reduced these mighty creatures to a mere three feet tall, a Cornish version of a bonsai forest. This grove is thought to have been continuously wooded, back to the pre-Neolithic wildwood which once covered the whole land.

This really is the wood of all our dreams: ancient trees free-growing and wild, sculpted by savage but clean south-westerly winds. A place so far beyond the conventions and authority of our age it has the potential to fulfil all our imaginative cravings. I like to think there is the flicker of some pre-Christian civilisation here, of a time when humanity was undeveloped, and perhaps of the presence of the druids, those mysterious teacher-priests of an old Celtic religion that worshipped the oak. For them, it was the king of trees; their wands were made from its wood, oak galls, known as serpent eggs, were used as magical charms and acorns were gathered at night because they held the greatest fertility powers. Did they, long ago, sit under these rustling leaves seeking divinatory messages? Did they burn these oak leaves to purify the atmosphere? Certainly, there is evidence of coppicing, which is strange for such a remote, steep place; indeed, local history finds no evidence of people coming down here to cut wood. Julius Caesar wrote about druids in *The Gallic War*, telling us they were part of a priestly aristocracy: 'The cardinal doctrine which they seek to teach is that souls do not die, but after death pass from one to another; and this belief, as the fear of death is thereby cast aside, they hold to be the greatest incentive to valour. Besides this, they have many discussions as touching the stars and their movement, the size of the universe and of the earth, the order of nature, the strength and the powers of the immortal gods, and hand down their lore to young men.' Is that why many of their beliefs and traditions are immortal in Cornwall, such as crawling through stones to cure illnesses and the celebration of fire festivals?

But there is much else besides Celtic whispers in the wing-clipped canopy of sessile oak, in this temperate rainforest, where the drip-drop of rain from the treetops above is laying down time in this moss-green, damp, ancient plantation. Here, also, among the lushness and the growth you can find rowan and the rare wild service tree. The ground cover features ramsons and lords and ladies and meadowsweet. There are ling and bilberry and cow wheat and even hay-scented fern – a veritable larder of prehistoric treats. And such is the purity of the air that lies above it, and such is the lack of disturbance, the oak branches are completely hirsute with slow-growing lichens, the best indicators of ancient forests we have. There are meant to be more than

174 species contained here and many are extremely rare, each
the result of a symbiotic union between fungus and algae – the
fungus offers protection and essential nutrients to the algae in
exchange for photosynthesised food. Two creatures, one life, just
like a marriage built on love and dependency, when one goes so
will the other shortly afterwards. The lichens embody eternity
and endurance; their long silvery threads, small grainy patches
in sea green, lend character to the place, as a beard might to a
craggy old man.

Most attractive is the showy tree lungwort, *Lobaria pulmonaria*,
which looks like savoy cabbage leaves affixed to a tree. It got
its name from the doctrine of signatures, the ancient theory in
which plants resembling certain human physical attributes were
believed to be beneficial to the part of the body they resembled.
Lungwort – which resembles the tissue inside the lungs – was
thought to be an effective remedy for respiratory ailments. It is
still bought as a herbal remedy today, in capsules and tinctures,
and used for treating conditions including pneumonia or tuber-
culosis, although the positive effects lack scientific proof. Still, I
like the idea that places like the Dizzard can be seen as ancient
pharmacies. Shelves of plants and fungi that can mend.

It's important to come to places like the Dizzard, a place so
devoid of pollution, so clean of air, to remind us how far out into
the clearing we have come, and how much we have built and
torn down. So absorbed are we by our advances, every now and
then we should take our foot off the accelerator and return to the
silence and darkness of the wild woods, because only then can
we really differentiate between human time and deep time and
become environmentally aware, only then will we understand
our inferiority. Wendell Berry, in *The Art of the Commonplace*, says
that these visits are crucial to understanding what the land is:

Perhaps then, having heard that silence and seen that darkness, he will grow humble before the place and begin to take it in – to learn from it what it is. As its sounds come into his hearing, and its lights and colours come into his vision, and its odors come into his nostrils, then he may come into its presence as he never has before, and he will arrive in his place and will want to remain. His life will grow out of the ground like the other lives of the place, and take its place among them. He will be with them – neither ignorant of them, nor indifferent to them, nor against them – and so at last he will grow to be native-born. That is, he must re-enter the silence and the darkness, and be born again.

A magnificent and exhilarating walk from Crackington Haven to Boscastle in country that is remote, unpopulated and wild. It follows high clifftops offering commanding open views in all directions but it's strenuous as well, plunging into deep, sharp valleys and then up again. One of the summits is High Cliff, the highest point on the Cornish section of the path. At Rusey Point the wind is so fierce I have to crawl on my hands and knees to reach shelter, and at Pentargon – the finest coast fall in the county – the water drops down for about eighty feet, hits a shelving ledge and leaps all the way back up again in spray form.

Boscastle comes into view below; the sun is out. The sea concertinas like a snake with glazed skin into a rift in the rocks; it trails its aquamarine slackness in and out of the bends in sly fashion. The tongue flickers right up into Boscastle's heart. But then, water is predatory in these parts, and never more so than here.

Boscastle was built here for a reason. Misguidedly, it was considered a place of great safety, the only natural inlet where a harbour could be considered along forty miles of intimidating north coast. It grew busy on its maritime activity, particularly in the nineteenth and early twentieth centuries, when cargo vessels traded with South Wales, Bristol, Gloucester and Appledore.

But it always had one problem, which made it less safe: it had an uneasy and complicated relationship with water. This is because Boscastle Valley's catchment area exceeds nine miles; it spans inland to Bodmin Moor, where many small rivers start their lives. The 'flashy catchments' – the steep-sided valleys – act as huge funnels and can produce true flash floods after prolonged and heavy rainfall.

That heavy rainfall came one afternoon in the summer of 2004. Thundery showers had developed across the south-west, remnants of Hurricane Alex, which had recently crossed the Atlantic. Bands of showers aligned themselves with local winds and proceeded to gather menacingly on the high ground in and around Boscastle. This, along with the topography of the area, was the key to the catastrophe. During that afternoon five millimetres of rain was recorded in a one-minute time span, which is equivalent to 139,000 gallons. Two million tonnes of water would flow through Boscastle that day, creating a major incident.

The peak came at five o'clock. Cars were being washed out of the car park. Then there was a huge crash and the whole of the visitor centre started to shake; soon after, the end wall collapsed, along with the roof. The waters were by now eight feet deep and lapping the attic ladder. Nine people managed to climb out of the skylight onto what remained of the roof, but three were left inside. In the end, more than 150 people were either airlifted or assisted to safety by the emergency services. Modest, you might think, compared to global standards, but Boscastle would enter the history books as one of the worst floods in modern British history.

Water is the most intrusive of invaders, and it is indiscriminate; it favours nothing or no one, it takes off with things and leaves others behind. In the Museum of Witchcraft and Magic, it left more than six feet of sewage and water, it knocked down walls and filled up the entire ground floor, destroying archive material. There were whispers, of course: that the Devil had come to Boscastle. Why else would the town have a witchcraft museum? Water is, after all, the gift of God; through water he had led the children of Israel from slavery in Egypt to freedom in the Promised Land. In water his son Jesus received the baptism of John and was anointed by the Holy Spirit as the Messiah, the Christ. A flood carries with it all that mythic and biblical status, it raises questions about our place in the world, if a primal act of destruction takes place it is only because a vengeful God wishes it.

The Museum of Witchcraft and Magic, with its now redesigned layout, houses the largest collection of witchcraft and Wiccan-related artefacts in the world. Its main contents were collected by the neopagan witch Cecil Williamson. In the 1930s, Williamson was working as a film production assistant when he became interested in investigating the occult and started acquiring objects. But whenever he attempted to set up a museum, he found himself witch-hunted by Christians zealots, and was chased out of such places as Stratford-upon-Avon, Windsor and Bourton-on-the-Water. The fanatics considered him to be in league with the Devil. He tellingly settled his collection in Cornwall, the last serious stronghold of witchcraft left in the country, a place where the land was already littered with evidence of old religions and sacred places such as ancient woods where the sunlight dances through the limbs and clifftops with raging sea views, or streams where kingfishers fly. Williamson died in 1999 but the new owner, Graham King, had his own battles; the gift shop across the way was run by a born-again Christian, Trixie Webster, who sold a good collection of anti-witchcraft books in order to counter the dark spirituality emanating from her neighbour's premises.

The truth is modern witchcraft, or Wicca, has nothing really to do with Devil-worship and Satanism; it is a nature-based religion and lifestyle. Participants celebrate the changing cycles of nature in the eight major festivals of the year (sabbats), with a few spells – similar to prayers – thrown into the pot, and those are mostly for the greater good. It seems to me that both Graham and Trixie had a strong awareness of a god or deity being present in everything around them. Witchcraft simply uses different methods in expressing this.

I go into the museum alone after a hard day's walking, not looking for anything in particular. There is the corpse of a dead witch and mandrake roots, charms and dolls with pins stuck through them, many stories of rituals and regalia. But I am fascinated mostly by a large piece of slate with a carved unicursal maze or labyrinth. The slate was found at a farm not far away in Michaelstow. Cecil Williamson thought this piece might reveal a portal to the Other World. 'The Labyrinth has always been associated with Mother Earth and the entrance to her underworld. Notice the shape of the entrance to a labyrinth and its womb-like centre,' he said. (Incidentally, similar circles have been found carved into the rock at Rocky Valley, which lies between Boscastle and Bossiney Cove.)

We are told, in the information about the piece, that slowly walking a labyrinth can induce a trance-like state suitable for the journey into the Other World. With a unicursal labyrinth one can't get lost – you start at the bottom and slowly follow the raised path, you will as a result be moving deosil (sunwise) as often as you are moving widdershins (anti-sunwise). Eventually you will arrive, well balanced, at the sacred centre of the symbol and maybe in another world. Of course, it makes me think instantly of my own unicursal labyrinth, the South West Coast Path, one that is well labelled and trodden. One can't get lost on it either, and it lies mostly on a raised track at the edge of the world. It is a pilgrimage in itself, through an environment we have partly created and damaged, a journey through time and meaning and faith. Certainly, you feel an adventurer in your own land, but sometimes well balanced. This is mostly through a sense that you have come close to things sacred, by which I mean things so much bigger than yourself. Really, there is no riddle to the maze

stone. Its's about the journey of the human soul; the goal is clear
but the way to achieve it can be very confusing.

A cynicism prevails: I will not get caught up in those hazy
Arthurian connections when I reach Tintagel, I will untan-
gle myself from all the myths and legends and the medieval
romancers. I am, after all, reliably informed by twelfth-century
literature (derived from oral traditions) that this was the seat of
the rulers of Cornwall and a significant royal stronghold in the
sixth century. The dominant ruins found there today are the
work of Earl Richard, who built them in the thirteenth century, no doubt attracted by the potential symbolic authority it
offered. It might also have been the case that he just wanted a
seaside property.

Yet when you get to this edge you understand immediately
how history, legend and myth have merged so cohesively into
the landscape. This is the point of the place. It is a world that
has been resketched through a narrative thick with characters,
romance and metaphor and place, it provides a connection
between what is seen and felt and understood and desired.
Tintagel has been designed around a complicated network of
myths that have developed over aeons, through an evolutionary
process in which the myth itself has taken on a life of its own.
Myth might be a palace like this, but it can also be a prison; it
can transform itself into a truth when it is not one. Does it matter?
Not really: human beings have always used stories and beliefs to
give their life meaning. Do we want to be crushed by the awful
bleakness and discomfort of these surroundings? Or do we want
to see this land as a sacred place above a raging sea, a meeting
place between past and present, between heaven and earth? Do
we not want to keep it as a safe haven for old gods and old heroes?

The Arthurian cult is actually relatively new. The first stone
thrown in the pond here, creating later ripples, dates from the

early years of the nineteenth century, when J. M. W. Turner painted a view of the castle in 1819. He was followed by our own Reverend Hawker, who stayed here for a month with his much younger bride in 1823. It is not clear whether Tennyson was influenced by Hawker's work or that he had already become wrapped up in the whole concept of chivalry as promoted by the novels of Sir Walter Scott, but in 1859 Tennyson began his *Idylls of the King*. It was a reworking of the *Morte d'Arthur*, Sir Thomas Malory's version of the Arthurian legend first put down by a dubious historian from the twelfth century called Geoffrey of Monmouth, who was the first to name Tintagel as Arthur's birthplace.

The North Cornwall Railway would bring yet more visitors, forcing the erection of the hideous Arthur's Castle Hotel which was built in 1896 and opened three years later. Such a threat to the surroundings was it that a newly formed body called the National Trust bowed to local pressure and bought fourteen acres of Barras Nose to prevent the hotel being located on the headland. Super-saturation of the legend probably took place in the 1930s, when custard king Frederick Glasscock built King Arthur's Great Halls in the high street. He was also inspired enough to found a modern Order of Knights of the Round Table, which generously included women.

There is one problem with myths, and that is you cannot determine their direction. You can't choose the path they take or the people who carry them along. Sometimes you find them like stolen vehicles, joy-ridden, off-road, burnt out and abandoned. The straggling village of Tintagel feels a bit like that now. It has been in flux for a while, its character barely changing. Of course, the heritage industry likes it that way; it's far more convenient for them to freeze-frame what they already have. And yet, imagination is always stronger than data, myth more exotic than history, illusion more powerful than reality; in the way a weed breaks out from the confines of a formal garden and flourishes under new conditions, so will the myth's tendrils latch onto new victims.

I walk up to the hotel, now named the Camelot Castle, to snoop. There is an uninterested Polish receptionist sitting behind the desk reading a magazine; apart from that, it is empty. I ask if I can take a look and she gestures me through without moving. I scoop up a copy of 'London's International Newspaper', *The Westminster Independent – Camelot Castle Special*, as I go.

The run-down rooms are dominated by extraordinarily large and tasteless paintings by an artist called Ted Stourton. In fact, the whole atmosphere is deeply and unnervingly surreal. I think I might order a drink, so I sit down and wait for someone to appear and read the paper to discover more.

The front page is dominated by a picture of the hotel owner's flame-haired wife Irina Kudrenok-Ablakova-Mappin – Camelot Castle's very own Lady Guinevere. We are told that Irina has 'indeed been the mind behind much of Ted Stourton's success in the international art world': she is Mr Stourton's creative muse, and that of several other powerful international artists besides. Indeed, the local airport at Newquay is apparently getting quite used to the roar of Gulfstream jet engines as Stourton's collectors detour from 'Nice airport and the beaches of Monaco and St Tropez and the ski slopes of St Moritz, Gstaad and Courchevel' to come and purchase this great 'art'.

The paper tells me that while Kazakhstan-born Irina remains almost completely in the background and has little interest in personal publicity, 'her formidable mind is primary in the exceptional expansion that is occurring from Camelot Castle'. There is not much evidence of this, however, Lady Guinevere being publicity shy: page 4, Irina in black and diamanté ballgown; page 5, Irina during the celebration of President Nazarbayev's birthday at the castle. For the record, he happens to be the dictator of Kazakhstan. There are pictures of Irina with E-list Hollywood celebs. Pictures of Irina on the ski slopes. Then it gets a little bit odd, with a page on the pyramids of existence, which is essentially again about the power of myth:

The Arthurian myth, more than any other, acts and serves
to control, strengthen and weaken, increase or decrease
the 'HOPE NEXUS' in the environment and perhaps most
importantly in the mind of mankind. And as this story perpet-
uates and is transferred from mind to mind whatever medium,
it maintains and represents the very simple but valuable idea:
'The idea that "Truth" might exist.'

It's like deciphering a whole new language, but the gist of it
is that the good folk at Camelot Castle are focused on helping
new 'ICONS' come into being, for it is they who will, like King
Arthur, shape our culture.

The rest of the paper is filled with appalling poetry, articles
about unlocking the door to artistic viability and a page in
screaming red ink about the dangers of psychotropic drugs for
children. What this has to do with anything I am not entirely sure.

In the end I do not order a drink; I find the whole experience
slightly unnerving and leave. Further investigations reveal that
Camelot Castle Hotel is partly owned by the conspiracy theorist
John Mappin, who at the time of my visit was a prominent figure
in the Church of Scientology and was said to be involved in dis-
seminating Scientology across the UK with a recruitment drive
that favoured drug addicts, criminals in jail and struggling artists. Today, Tom Cruise and David Miscavige have been replaced
in Mappin's affections by one Donald J. Trump, whose picture
now looks over the reception. Back in 2020 he even hoisted the
QAnon flag over the castle.

The Arthurian myth might well be a stolen vehicle, but it is not
yet abandoned. Just as used cars often become dens for children
in the rough edgelands of our towns and cities, the same could
be said of Camelot Castle; it has transformed itself into a secret
space where imagination has been allowed to turn an immobile
myth into a truth. Is it tacky? Yes, but it does also represent a
human need, which is to grasp the tangible aspects of landscape,

to find personality in its form, to lift spirit, emotion and light from it. And why do we need to do that? Because the world is too sure of itself, too dense, we need to take a step down, into a place where nothing is certain, where beauty lies in something that is unhuman, intangible, where we can give meaning to things that touch us and in doing so free them and ourselves from the brutal hostilities of this world. It is about escape.

Walking away, with the castle at my back, I stumble across a touchstone in slate almost hidden by the grass. It reads, '*Courting down't Gilla adders meet, amidst the tab mawn lover's end.*' Here is a place where lovers came to court, where adders squirm among the sea daisy.

Exploitation

Tintagel to Port Quinn

From Tintagel, the edge is a harvest field.

I pick up a fragment of slate at Lambshouse Quarry. It is such a hard, dark rock, full of internal contradictions, and yet it offers up such a smooth, quiet surface. This particular piece is from a disordered heap of slate waste associated with the cliff quarrying which has been going on since the fourteenth century. All along this stretch between Tintagel and Trebarwith there are places where a stone massacre has taken place, where the cliff face drops suddenly as a jaw might in shock. Fragment upon fragment of blasted rock that has failed to make the donkey's pannier lies abandoned, its muscovite mica shimmering under the sun, as if some kind of old glass mirror has shattered into smithereens.

As a stone, it has been on quite a journey since it first lay down as mud some 410 million years ago on a tropical ocean's bed: all that pressure that came to bear upon it from other sediment; the heat that baked it into sheets; the civilisations that used chisels and bettles to hack into its cleavage for cleanly split pieces to use for their buildings and blackboards. If there is stamina in rocks, slate has it by the bucketloads: it is almost waterproof, it does not burn, it is never dull or moody in colour, and it takes to the mason's knife like no other.

Do we choose things for a reason? I am thinking of Sir John Betjeman's slate gravestone further up the coast at Trebetherick. I wonder whether such smoothness, consistency, calmness in this rock is the reason it is used for headstones, certainly the more beautiful ones; a pre-condition for making the onlooker believe, by a kind of deceptive showmanship, that one's wretched life was able to take the knocks, that it was in itself quite ordinary yet well ordered, that beautiful things could and were written upon it.

Or is it to compare and contrast? Is it there to remind us that physical matter is indestructible and completely transmutable; that it can change from one form to another, from mud to headstone, from liquid to solid? Is this slate tombstone telling us we are not so lucky, that we are unconvertible matter? Or are we? Do our beliefs not perpetuate us in another form? Maybe it's to do with respect: what we take from the earth around us we must and will put back as redemption for our sins.

Or it could be all a deceit? Certainly, in the graveyards around here it might just be having the last laugh.

Port Gaverne might be located within the dominion of Port Isaac but somehow it escapes the village's control. It is its own hamlet with its own history. I approach it along the Great Slate Road, which was cut from the rock in 1807 to facilitate horse-drawn wagons carrying rock from this coast to ships waiting in the harbour. The slates were loaded by women who then packed them in straw to protect them on the voyage.

It is high tide when I go down to the beach. I notice the shingle is not that golden sand composed of slate and fragments of shells as on most north Cornwall beaches, but of flint. Later, I consult a guidebook, which informs me that the flint was used as ballast for incoming ships when collecting the rock. The bigger boats had to be pulled in and out of the busy and somewhat cramped harbour using ropes and chains. The harbour stayed active with its export of slate, sand and pilchards until the North Cornwall Railway Company linked the Delabole mines to Launceston and Plymouth and the fish changed their migrations.

Port Isaac, which looms overhead, is very much the starting point for a stretch of coast that caters for a certain class of English tourist – middle class, that is. It is unquestionably quaint, but it feels somehow as if it has gone under the taxidermist's scalpel and in that act of preparing, stuffing and mounting it for artistic display, all its blood has been drained, all its spirit lost. Most of the houses are now second homes and the 'real' people live on the outer edges.

The storm brewing here, although considerably smaller in scale, is not dissimilar to storms occurring elsewhere, such as in Venice, Barcelona, Dubrovnik, New York City, the Isle of Skye. All over the world, summers of discontent are happening where water rubs up against land. Tourism is growing at such a phenomenal rate that the number of international journeys worldwide is now projected to double to 1.8 billion trips a year by 2030. The worst culprits are the cruise ships, which disgorge bulk numbers on shore, blocking up the arteries of the places they visit on streets too narrow to walk, bridges not designed to take such weight. In Orkney, a hundred thousand tourists visit each year – double the resident population – the larger ships dropping off three thousand passengers in one go; that's three thousand people visiting ancient heritage sites such as Skara Brae in one four-hour window.

The industry retaliates by labelling critics 'hypocrites' or 'snobs'; they say these people were perfectly happy when these places were playgrounds for the rich, but less so when the masses came in behind. It's a fair criticism. And tourism has been proven to help a developing region's economy; it has certainly transformed Cornwall's fortunes for the better.

So how do we judge saturation point in a place like Port Isaac? I reckon the test is a simple one: when a gift shop is replacing the hardware store or there are more cafés than grocery shops, alarm bells should start ringing. So should they when a community is gone and a place exists merely as a tourist destination. Or when a village has lost its soul. It's then that management and timing is required. In somewhere like Clovelly that's a lot easier, because there is a single ruler in the form of John Rous; in places like Port Isaac it's left to the local authority to take a view on what is needed and what isn't. This is not helped by a rotating cast of councillors, nor the shadier side of town and country planning, which sometimes involves secretive lobbying, conflicts of interest and the offer of excessive gifts and hospitality. Although full-blown bribery is still fairly rare, if you read *Private Eye*'s 'Rotten Boroughs' you can see how councils lack essential safeguards to prevent exploitation. I don't have the answers and I don't think many others have either, but it's an environmental crisis of our modern age and one that I'm convinced has to be delicately negotiated on an individual rather than universal level. What I will add, however, is that everything is expendable, that it has a life, then it has another life, therefore we must not mourn its loss because everything comes around again, just in another form; it is a reincarnation. In the end nothing belongs to us, or to a place; we are bound to what preceded us and what comes ahead of us, and by each right and each wrong we will learn to create a future.

From the south side of the harbour I turn right up Roscarrock Hill and follow the narrow lane past the Wesleyan chapel to the end of the road. Cornwall is littered with these chapels, somehow left unfulfilled if not converted into dwellings, standing humbly in a crowd of buildings or lonely outside them, a thoughtful building, stone layered upon stone with no embellishment, inside its soul empty, its master and movement gone.

That movement owes its origins to John Wesley and his brother Charles. While at Oxford they had formed a club, which pledged to meet regularly for prayer and Bible study. It was a kind of forerunner of today's book clubs, where they would 'read over' the classics and then meet to discuss their responses to the texts. The members of the club were also dedicated to pursuing a pious life: in Wesley's words, 'they resolved to live by rule and method'. This saying gained them the name of Methodists. From Oxford, Methodism would stretch wide, and nowhere more so than in Cornwall.

The true Cornish have always been at the mercy of their emotions; their feelings are easily excited and often openly displayed. They are prone to the mysterious which ultimately accepts true art and true science, but they need an outlet for their passions, they need a sense of being in the world through a common union. For many years there was a vacuum in this respect; the established church had become complacent, an easy ride for the younger sons of the landowning squires, men who had little propensity to preach and even less to minister to the poor. Churches were empty, sermons uninspiring, respect minimal. So when John Wesley came west in 1743 he hit the ground like a tornado, threatening established codes, upsetting the faithful, horrifying parsons, who tried to pull up the drawbridge to protect their livings. The easiest way of doing this was to ensure that Wesleyan lay ministers, who came under the banner of being able-bodied but without occupation, be press-ganged into the navy. The most notorious of these clergymen and persecutors was a Dr William Borlase, who also happened to be a magistrate. Others spread the rumour that Wesley was a supporter of Charles Edward Stuart, the Young Pretender, even that the claimant to the Hanoverian throne had disguised himself to follow in Wesley's footsteps and was lurking among the congregation under an assumed name.

Wesley saw them all off. He continued to visit Cornwall for the next forty years and despite the occasional public protest,

obstructions and expressions of loathing issuing from his ene-
mies, he most definitely created something of a revolution in this
leg of land. What his detractors couldn't control was his mag-
netism or his message to the ordinary working man, which was
to abandon apathy, despair and general anarchy and replace it
with a greater good.

How did Wesley entrench himself so deeply here? At the edge?
Probably because Cornish innocence offered perfect possibilities
for exploitation, but then that is how religion thrives, does it not,
the strong versus the weak. What also helped was that he didn't
consider these people as barbarians, he held no division of persons: he reached out for the souls of fishermen and miners alike;
he blessed their children and visited their homes; he rattled the
cages of a bewildered people with hellfire and told them of their
failings, but he also showed them a route back. Of course, at first,
they hated it – who was this intruder? – but slowly, curiously,
they emerged blinking into the light, then they flocked, then they
followed, then they built chapels in every village and every town
in his name. At last the Cornish people came to have their own
form of worship in their own form of meeting house, at last they
did not need to submit to a governing class. And Wesley, like the
rest of them, did it through chemistry, because chemistry is the
science of change. It looks at all the elements and how they inter-
act with each other, and blends them together. Here it was sea,
rock, the underworld, belief, song, prayer. The change that came
was a new pride in work, a dignity in living, a sense of family
and morality. Drunkenness declined, smuggling was abandoned,
Cornwall's psyche was restored by the efforts of someone whom
we might today call a cult leader.

Wesley visited Port Isaac around a dozen times, preaching
in the town and noting that, over the years, it had become 'the
liveliest place in the circuit'. He was clearly pleased by the work
he had done there, writing in his journal on 21 September 1762
that he 'rode on to Port Isaac. Here the stewards of the eastern

circuit met. What a change is wrought in one year's time! That detestable practice of cheating the King [smuggling] is no more found in our societies. And since that accursed thing has been put away, the work of God has everywhere increased. This society, in particular, is more than doubled: and they are all alive to God.'

I continue on my walk, heading towards the cliffs again, through a kissing gate and up the steps beyond. The coast path will take me around Lobber Point, and with it I drop down into Pine Haven. Beside me, a Cornish hedge: a drystone wall built in a herringbone pattern. This style is known locally as 'Curzy Way' or 'Jack and Jill', and is unique to north Cornwall, possibly introduced as far back as Roman times. Since the fishing of pilchards and mining of slate were such huge industries here it seems right that the walls that contain these livelihoods resemble the skeleton of a fish.

The herring has long been a symbol of nature's indestructibility thanks to their abundance for long periods, no more so than in these parts, and these walls remain constant in the face of harsh and debilitating weather conditions, as do the people who have lived and worked this coast. There is another link, that of colour. Slate is composed of many parts: of quartz and mica, often accompanied by biocite, chlorite and haematite. These minerals lend distinctive colouring, from dark grey to green to purple to silver. When the slate is packed together – interestingly, when spawning, herring also lie one on top of another in layers – its tonal range is similar to the fish, from its scales on the surface of the water to the beautiful dark green of its rear parts, not forgetting that wonderful illumination it retains for a few days after death, just as the herringbone wall does when sunlight falls on it at a particular angle. These walls may be a simple piece of practical enterprise, but they are also a perfect example of design that has originated from within.

Pilchards – adult sardines – spend much of their life in shoals. They would come, between July and September, in their millions to feed on plankton. However, the appearance of the shoals was not consistent; their time and location varied. To make sure they were not missed, lookout huts were located along this coast. These huts were manned by huers, who on sighting this molten gleam of silver pass by would signal by crying the Cornish word for fish, hevva, through a trumpet. The boats would then be guided by the huers to the shoal and given instructions as to where to throw their nets.

Each fishing village had cellars where the pilchards were processed. The fish were placed in stone tanks, salted and pressed in straight-sided barrels with weights on top. The oil escaped through a drain hole and was collected. From the sixteenth to the nineteenth century pilchards were a valuable product. As a food they were cured and exported over large distances, mostly to Italy to satisfy a demand for fish during periods of abstention from meat-eating among the Catholic population. Their oil could be used for lighting and heating. One of the causes of the industry's demise in the mid-nineteenth century was greed – the completion of the Great Western Railway in the 1860s brought with it access to a previously untapped urban domestic market. In a couple of decades, the number of pilchard fishing boats rose from a few dozen to nearly three hundred. This extra pressure became too much for the fish to bear and it led to the severe decline of stocks.

No one knew why or where the pilchards went, because the fish jealously guard their routes. There were theories about their disappearance, about the variations in the level of light and the prevailing winds, the influence of geomagnetic fields or the possible shifting of marine isotherms, but none were conclusive. It has not helped that most of the fishermen who went in pursuit of them also left, and with them the traditional knowledge which draws upon much of the history and legend in the area. But there is an uncanny parallel in the story of the fishes' disappearance with that of the residents of Port Quinn, today a small, sheltered inlet with only a few cottages owned by the National Trust. Some time in the nineteenth century, at about the same time the fish disappeared, the village was deserted. Again no one knows quite why; there is no documentary evidence. Some say it happened in a single night, that a violent gale sank the entire fishing fleet, and the widowed wives could not bear to return; others say that when the fish went the people did too, sailing to Canada on vessels out of Padstow. It remains a mystery to this day.

After the Second World War, fishing changed for good. All those family-owned steam-pushed tubs, bobbing out of small harbours as dawn rose, were ruthlessly replaced by more efficient machines and new technologies inspired by the military know-how of the era, such as sonar, which was used to create a sophisticated three-dimensional image of the underwater world. Suddenly huge amounts of fish were being pulled out of the ocean. It would lead to a grossly industrial, non-selective exploitation of our fish resources which is still going on today, most notably with the beam trawlers and their chain nets that literally scoop up everything in their wake, including whole ecologies and their networks.

Nevertheless, there is something of a pilchard renaissance going on in Cornwall. One that relies on sensitive and sustainable methods. Pilchards are once more being caught by smaller day boats, which are mostly skipper-owned and run, using old fashioned ring-netting techniques that prevent the accidental catching of other species. Still, tensions remain between the UK and France, as they try to agree fishing rights after Brexit.

To exceed the rational limits of exploitation is a common theme at the edge. Although there is much beauty in the in-between zone between land and sea, there is also much abuse, much blight. Mining and fishing and even religion aside, think of sewage farms, of car ports such as at Bristol Royal Portbury Docks where eight hundred thousand vehicles a year wait for new owners, and fidgety power stations, retail parks and scrubland. Of iron ore smelting and processing, oil and gas storage and refining, paper mills, vehicle factories, ship building, power plants, food processing. How the throwing down of boulders by large-scale engineering projects interrupts natural processes, leading to sand loss. Residences rising up as blooms. That's before you even look at climate change or water quality and pollution, dredging and dumping at sea, and river runoff.

One of the worst culprits is concrete, the most widely used synthetic material on earth, with three tonnes of it per year used for every person in the world. It accounts for 70 per cent of all coastal and marine infrastructure, such as docks, coastal defence structures and waterfronts; but putting it in place destroys entire ecosystems, its smooth surface making it completely uninhabitable for marine organisms.

It doesn't even have to be this way. Eco-tiles and panels have a greater surface intricacy, with furrows, edges, ridges and crevices which mimic the intertidal zones and offer refuge from predators.

Pocket rock pools can be inserted. There is even bio-cement, in which aggregates such as sand are mixed with bacteria and urine. The urine triggers the bacteria to secrete calcite which binds the mixture together. It's not dissimilar to the way corals have developed their own ability to build reefs and it removes carbon dioxide, a greenhouse gas, from the air. Biomimicry can be quite the treasure trove, if we can be bothered to look for the clues.

So, the edge is where the oppressor and the oppressed go to battle, animal, vegetable and mineral. It is where there is a clash between those who push for freedom and justice, nostalgia even, like me, and those who pull in the opposite direction on their industrial and financial journey. It feels like a test, between two opposing ideas. It doesn't help that we see the coastal edge as being something static and enduring in nature, despite its obvious mobility, including its own erosion. We are forever imposing our own structures on ground that ignores local moods in order to solemnise and bring command to the edge of our land. We are culpable.

Naturally, I would like to see no concrete at all. I would like to see more nature-based solutions for coastal defences such as seagrass meadows, coral reefs, mangrove forests, salt marshes and other forms of wetland. Natural habitats that grow tall as buildings and can retreat inland as sea level rises to provide continuous protection. Is it not the case that building hard concrete structures that are unable to adapt to increasing sea levels means they will just have to be built up again or replaced? Is it really economically viable to keep defending the edge by building on it when nature-based solutions and the huge biodiversity associated with them provides a viable alternative? But I know concrete is here to stay, because it's hard to knock down a wall when you are the one who has put it up to protect yourself.

Living and Dying

Port Quinn to Pentire Point

At the mouth of the Port Quinn inlet, on Doyden Point, there is a truncated Gothic tower built by the wealthy Wadebridge bon viveur Samuel Symons as a pleasure palace; an ideal location where he could entertain his friends, drinking and eating and gambling. If you build your vices in stone you will be remembered, it seems. The tower feels symbolic, not only because it fulfilled Symons's need to create an edge to contain his pleasure but because it represents that hierarchy of the spirit that can be found along the edge. For some this is a place full of rhapsody, for others merely work. Tourists and second home owners bring in the money and a self-assured hubris; the indigenous population, by return, serve them. It is the blood that keeps this edge alive, but for many it runs cold.

The trail from here is generally smooth and the land is bald. My husband Hugo is with me on this section of the walk, and together we drop down with the path into Lundy Bay and find ourselves in a sheltered valley where light woodland and scrub lead down to a rocky bay. There are deep thickets of blackthorn and willow here, interspersed with butterfly glades and wet meadows. The few trees are still green but little patches of autumn are tingeing them here and there, reminding me that our earth is teetering on the point of decline. More noticeable is the absence of birdsong, as if the willow warblers, the blackcaps and the whitethroats have already left.

Near the path, I notice a dead shrew. He is all velvety brown with a little pointed bristly spout, and no sign of injury. It seems the intensity of seeking out insects and slugs by day and night, pausing to rest for just a few minutes every hour, has quite clearly finished this little creature off. It somehow touched me, the exhaustion of its labours, just lying down one sunny afternoon by the side of the road to die. There was poetry in it.

It makes me think about our bodies' end: where and when they come to be touched and seen as giving out. But it also put me in mind of the kind farewells for all the lonely people of this land, and of pauper funerals. In some strange way, there I was, in a chapel before the funeral service begins. There are no pallbearers bringing in the coffin and setting it down on the catafalque, but there are no family members here to see it anyway. I *am* the congregation. A vicar would begin reading but the information is scant; he just lived, worked and died. They say thousands of people in Britain die like this each year, with no one to arrange or pay for their funeral, who are cremated courtesy of their local council on quiet weekday afternoons when no one is looking. The officials no longer call it a pauper funeral; they use the less-stigmatising label 'public health funeral', and over the past five years it has got much worse; a combination of poverty, homelessness, the rise in single-person households and an increased tendency for families to disperse geographically have all caused the number of these types of funeral to rise. In a recession, and when even a simple internment can run into thousands of pounds, it is no surprise families refuse to pay for relatives they have lost touch with or hardly know; they might not even have been alerted to the death. But a lonely death feels like a missing state of mind. Not mere forgetfulness but a breach, a collective mental void we no longer know how to fill. It makes me wonder how my own end will be.

On this path I tread, death is the biggest story; stand almost anywhere and look around, and you will see our preoccupation with it: a hidden church spire, a burial mound, a village war memorial, a coastal bench dedicated to a beloved husband. It has left a deep impression on the physical and psychological of this landscape. Nowadays, death somehow feels less of a preoccupation than it did in the near past. Life and its meaning are where our energy is being spent. We want to build our pleasure palaces on earth rather than in the sky.

I lay a flower down beside the shrew when my husband was not looking; he would have considered it silly romanticism, but I wanted it to replicate an old wayside shrine or a roadside tribute, as with a victim of a road accident.

That flower, like words being written, the ink still shining, was all I could do in that moment of melancholy.

In Lundy Bay I pick up an empty limpet shell. The aquatic snail that once lived here would have clung on to its rock or surface edge with all its might. It would have formed its own small depression, known as a scar, by rubbing against the rock, sometimes using the edge of its shell like a bulldozer to scrape away at the debris and algae; the scar would have ensured a tighter fit for the shell, helping the limpet to avoid desiccation. From here it would have ventured forth to feed on the thin form of algae it found on the rocks and the weeds at low tide before using chemical cues to follow its own mucus track home. We do the same when we choose a site to picnic, a home to build, a place to shelter; we dismiss location after location, as if we are pioneers seeking to settle new territory. This searching out must be something all beings share, that all-important judgement on the terrain, its surface features and general physical character. Will the light warm us? Or the rocks shelter us from the wind? How damp is the ground? Who will disturb us here? We, too,

are most satisfied when we find a hollowed-out shelter in which
to eat our sandwiches. For our bodies and our desires, the homes
we have created are for the tide, ebb, flood and flow. We choose
our rocks carefully and develop a slavish attachment to them.
Removal might just destroy us and all we hold dear; or it might
even advance us.

I pull out the shell from my pocket again when I find myself
sitting on the ground overlooking the narrow isthmus that leads
into the Rumps, a fishtail promontory used as a fortress by Iron
Age man. I'm thinking how many of us have an inherent need
to create an interim edge, something that contains community,
pleasure even. In the case of a perceived external threat, the
first thing we will always do is erect walls to defend ourselves.
Incidentally, limpets also have strong defensive responses, pre-
serving their places of safety. When a whelk attacks, a limpet will
lift the edge of its shell and then slam it down onto the whelk's
foot, slicing it off. If a whelk has the misfortune to find itself
under a limpet's shell it can be attacked so violently its own shell
is seriously chipped. If an intruder enters our home unannounced
our instinct is also to defend. A robbery is forever a violation of
our sacred space.

I try to reset my mental chronometer, to think in Iron Age
time, of their defensive settlements. They were a quiet people,
tinners and farmers, not at all warlike, certainly no match for
the bands of Celtic immigrants who crossed the Channel to join
the descendants who had made the journey years earlier. These
people of the La Tène culture brought with them tipped spears
and long swords and farming implements made of iron, simple
tools from which the hulls of ships and the steel of our bridges
would spring. Bronze had created a privileged culture, a decorative one, but it was iron that would sculpt Britain in to a new
and exciting shape. It was iron and the technology it offered that
would put agriculture and land at its heart. You could indeed
say we still live in an Age of Iron. The principle of burning and

shaping is still behind everything we create; nearly everything we do depends on this act.

The Celts that brought this knowledge were tall and powerful and clannish; they had originated in the area of the Alps, spreading east and west, had appeared in Greek and Roman annals as Keltoi, Galatians and Gauls. They were exotic too, their clothes brightly coloured, with striped and checked patterns. You can see how the women were smitten.

The local people naturally withdrew, tried to secure themselves, but it was no good: they were soon dislodged and subdued, and their conquerors quickly converted their makeshift hilltop refuges into permanent strongholds. Over time they would forgive their agitators, in the main because they were skilled farmers, seamen, craftsmen and warriors, and they had much to learn from them; the La Tène would move the Cornish culture on from one of bronze to one of iron.

By the time the curtain fell on the second century BC, the need for refuges became important again. The Cimbri and other Teutonic wild men were rampaging through northern France; their ships were becoming larger and more seaworthy, and no one quite knew when these swarthy pirates would rock up on a local beach. The sea could no longer be treated like a moat; it was now more of a menace, and Cornwall with its long coastline was particularly vulnerable. The Veneti of Brittany had a similar problem, which they addressed by building clifftop castles. They were already friends with the Cornish across the water, as it was they who shipped most of the tin out of the region. The Veneti taught the Cornish the art of fortifying their headlands. Indeed, the classic cliff castle at Rumps Point is so similar to those in Armorica, Brittany, that it may have been built by refugees from the great sea battle of Morbihan Bay between the Romans and the Veneti in 56 BC.

It is possible to imagine what those early settlers saw on that first scouting party when they came to the Rumps: all that defensive potential, the turf kept short by the salt-laden winds, gullies carved out by geological faults where they could build a series of ditches and ramparts to protect the landward access. The Veneti had explained that in terms of defence it was important to keep the slingers at a distance. They had experienced this latest offensive weapon of hurling stones in the skilful hands of the Balearic islanders in Hannibal's army and it had proved deadly. Increase the number of ramparts in front of the principal fortification, they said. They would start building the innermost rampart first and then, fighting time with sea and wind, add on two more later. There would be facing walls and breastworks leading to a substantial defensive gateway. Through the prehistoric entrance, which leads into a flattish area, they put their sheep in pens and build the circular wooden huts they would call home. Here they could weave their cloth while others were out harvesting the sea and cultivating grain, and others still establishing their trading links as far afield as the Mediterranean. But the problem with walls is that they often weaken the characters of those that build them. We might feel comfort and stability, but it is often a false sense of security because what they also do is incite the hungers of those that wish to come inside and take what is within. The Iron Age would come to an end with the arrival of the Romans in south-east England from AD 43. Resistance lasted decades, but the Romans were successful in introducing an economic and military system that would divide Britain from the rest.

In his lyrical book *The Poetics of Space*, Gaston Bachelard writes, 'A creature that hides and "withdraws into its shell", is preparing a "way out". This is true of the entire scale of metaphors, from the resurrection of a man in his grave, to the sudden outburst of one who has long been silent. If we remain at the heart of the image under consideration, we have the impression that, by staying in the motionlessness of its shell, the creature is preparing temporal explosions, not to say whirlwinds, of being.'

Our hearts of longing don't end when the door is closed and silence surrounds us. We are forever restless, and that is how, and why, dynamism and opportunity occur. It is probably why we keep on moving, as inspiration rarely makes an appointment with the indolent and the housebound. Iron Age men, like Bronze Age men before them, like the limpet, did not stay motionless in their shells for long; they were plotting and planning their next move, their next shelter.

Like picking up a shell from the beach and enjoying holding it in my hands, clasping it to my ear to hear the stories it tells, so I would like a token of this time, a survivor piece: a fragment from a grave maybe, a piece that testifies to all the life that existed here. But I just have to imagine, because there is so little left; bones have crumbled in the damp, sour soil. The same has happened to the tools: iron rusts and dissolves easily in the mists and rains of this land. It somehow contradicts the historical impression that the Iron Age was one of strength. Really, the community here in Lundy Bay was not born out of war, although it had encountered it, but out of the beauty of things, of earth and stone and water and wood and beast and man and woman and sun and moon and stars and fire. Maybe they just weren't interested in 'temporal explosions' or 'whirlwinds of being'. But then iron is like that, like its people; it is a quiet element, probably the most stable of them all, no frenzied tempests occurring in its core. It slowly goes on sustaining life on earth, nourishing plants and moving oxygen around our blood. It takes a lot to disturb its equilibrium.

That day on the Pentire Peninsula, overlooking the Rumps, I had a clear sense of how long we have been travelling to get to the centre of this place, for people to start their empty cities; cities with no lights, churches, roads, bridges. Instead of being motionless in their shell, people travelled so I can be exactly where I was sitting. They travelled to settle me. At last, they are themselves settled and living among us as history. This, our long story of departures and arrivals. And of empty shells.

It is a place for remembering people, where, in the low hums and shakings of the sea, under the deep throws of starry nights, the past somehow forces itself onto the present. It affected the poet Laurence Binyon, who wrote 'For the Fallen' while sitting here too. The poem honoured the British dead of the First World War and would later be claimed as a tribute to all casualties of war, regardless of state. His words feel particularly apt for the moment.

> They shall grow not old, as we that are left grow old:
> Age shall not weary them, nor the years condemn.
> At the going down of the sun and in the morning
> We will remember them.

Burial

Pentire Point to Harlyn Bay

The enigmatic St Enodoc church, overshadowed by Brea Hill, sits on the fairway of a golf course enclosed by hedging. From the sixteenth century to the middle of the nineteenth, wind and sand joined together to bury this church, to stop its spiritual heart from flickering. Known locally as Sinking Neddy or Sinkininny Church, it had been an ancient place of worship, with some of its architecture tracing back to the twelfth century. It is thought to have been built on the site of a monastic cell belonging to St Enodoc, the hermit who in the sixth century baptised his converts at the Jesus Well half a mile away, which now also happens to be stranded inside the golf course. Why it is called the Jesus Well is another question altogether; we can only guess it is another of the places to which Joseph of Arimathea is supposed to have brought the young Jesus.

Like the hermit, who lives in solitude as a religious discipline, it seems somehow appropriate that, because of its burial, the church of St Enodoc managed to avoid all the turmoil of the changing fortunes of Christianity in Cornwall, from the Reformation to the Civil War, the arrival of Methodism and the changing tides of the Industrial Revolution. The fact that it sits in the sand conjures up images of the desert, and its symbolism as a place of profound spiritual struggle. The Chosen People wandered there for a good forty years, and even when they left, God kept calling them back to its silence and solitude for further purification and testing of faith.

The image of a buried St Enodoc lodges in my mind: I think briefly of our own Church of England, in turmoil with its lost congregations and a growing multicultural society bringing their own religions; it also seems to respond by sticking its own head in the sand.

Anyway, the church was finally excavated in 1863–4. Before that, the vicar, in order to keep the church open, had to perform his ecclesiastical duties inside it at least once a year and so was obliged to enter through the roof of the north transept.

Around 1920, Hart Smith Pearce, the son of the vicar, the Reverend Hart Smith, who had led the restoration of the chapel, wrote an account of the work:

> the sands had blown higher than the eastern gable, the wet came in freely, the high pews were mouldy-green and worm-eaten and bats flew about, living in the belfry. The communion table had two short legs to allow for the rock projecting at the foot of the east wall. When the building was restored, the walls were partly rebuilt, on good foundations, the sand removed and the little churchyard cleared and fenced with a stout wall. The roof was renewed and new seats provided. It all cost about £650 and I remember the pains and energy my father spent to raise the money. These works were done by the masons and workmen of the parish with loving care and nothing was destroyed needlessly or removed if it was of use or interest.

Along the clifftop from Polzeath, crossing the beach at Daymar Bay, to catch a ferry at Rock, I am given views over Doom Bar: a huge mass of sand which over the years has shifted from one side of the Camel Estuary to the other. It now stretches from just off the cliffs near Hawker's Cove almost to Trebetherick Point, leaving only a narrow opportunity for boats to travel into the upper parts of the estuary at low tide.

The name Doom Bar is a corruption of the Gaelic word *dunbar* or *dune-bar*, a combination of two words, dun and bar. Both can mean hill or summit, and are associated with sand. The language trail appropriately ends with an interpretation of danger, travel, overcoming hurdles. And it has been certainly that; there have been more than six hundred beachings, wrecks and capsizings here since records began early in the nineteenth century.

I have a moment thinking about the forced diffusion of the sand, about all that sediment from the River Camel and all the sand from the Celtic Sea, and how it sweeps into place as the energy is dispersed. It makes me think of brushstrokes and of the transportation and the laying down of paint from the charged energy of a creator, and how every mark is made by how saturated the brush is with pigment and how much pressure is applied as it moves across the surface; and how many layers of paint will be laid down before that creator stands back and finally feels satisfied that the mystery he is trying to convey has been revealed. Locally, they say that the creator was the Mermaid of Padstow, who cursed the harbour with a 'bar of doom' after being mortally shot by an admirer whose proposal of marriage she had rejected. But it's not the mermaids; something else is definitely at play. Around the coast of Cornwall, an estimated six thousand ships have been wrecked, more than anywhere else in the British Isles.

At Doom Bar, winds, known locally as flaws, can harass, even tyrannise, particularly when they mount Stepper Point and blow down the other side, their force strong enough to thrust unwitting boats towards the sandbank. When that occurs, it is impossible to find anchor in the shifting sand and the boat is indeed doomed. And there are plenty of deposits here in the dark space beneath, not all of them seashells, in this other mysterious dimension below the skin of the sea, layers of history just waiting to be revealed. The coal-carrying *Antoinette*, which sank in 1895, was believed to be the Doom Bar's largest victim. It left so much debris, blocking shipping lanes, the wreck had to be detonated with gelignite to clear the sea; the blast was so forceful windows in Padstow were blown out of their frames. More than a hundred years later, parts of the barque were still coming to the surface.

Shipwrecks are important burial grounds; they give us a window into the study and exposition of our past, they connect us to our cultural heritage and teach us lessons about our relationship with the environment. They are not like graves and shrines in that they are accidental, and when they sink to the bottom they mostly remain untouched, rather like large time capsules.

But scientists are learning how sunken ships influence ecology under the sea. While many of the old wrecks in Cornwall have disintegrated because they were made of wood, the more modern metal wrecks are a perfect place for a sea creature to reside. The wreck becomes like a busy, elevated outpost as soon as it hits the bottom. Rapidly, and slowly, a whole community of sessile creatures will be formed, those moving in including barnacles, tubeworms and hydroids, sea urchins and queen scallops, starfish and solitary sea quirts, dead man's fingers and sea fans. When you think about it, the shipwreck burial is not for grieving: the ship has found a way to come around again; it has lived a life, lived it well, and is now living again through others. It is in a state where it cannot go on or turn back, rather like an old man in his favourite armchair, someone who has at last found a moment of rest upon the sea of life, but who still has the capacity to see the wonderful, the great mysteries at its centre. Something not quite departing, but lingering for what it thinks it can still offer.

Because, really, there is no such thing as a wasteland: something new always moves in.

The small fishing village of Padstow has also been metaphorically buried. In fact, it barely speaks now, the original image all but lost. And yet the illusion is still there; skirmishes as well, between old and new. Its transformation is the result of one man's commercial endeavours: those of the celebrity chef Rick Stein.

Stein inserted himself into this coastal crack, a single tremor that multiplied into a quake. Soon the town lost its old shape. He was as smart a businessman as one can find. He was undoubtedly helped by tourism, which has stolen a great many things along the edge, and Padstow anyway has a history of pillage, most notably by the Vikings, who raided in 981. Stein has restaurants, five hotels, a cookery school, a cottage, a pub, a gift shop, a patisserie, a delicatessen. There is Rick Stein chutney, Rick Stein wine, Rick Stein lobsters, Rick Stein chips. Everywhere I look I am inside the long corridors of Rick's creative mind. There have been costs – mostly jealousy from the locals, and even from visitors uncomfortable about Stein's success. And it comes up too often to dismiss it, this element in the British psyche which is suspicious of ambition and accomplishment, as though it breaches some kind of quiet national cohesion. To flaunt your success is simply an affront to everyone else; it is showing off. When you enter Padstow, it's all around you, the spit and fizz of those envious whisperings.

There have been other skirmishes here, other attempted burials, fishing fleets replaced by yachts. Then there is Mummer's Day, formerly known as Darkie Day, which is part of the pagan heritage of midwinter celebrations. Music is played and gatherers with faces painted black dance down the streets, raising money for charity. The face painting, masks and dark clothing are meant to represent the winter solstice, a contrast to festivals such as the 'Obby 'Oss, when white is worn to celebrate the arrival of spring. Although Mummer's Day is not thought to have any historical connection to people of colour, it has become one of the most controversial festivals in the country. It even prompted the Labour MP Diane Abbott to table a House of Commons motion to have it banned. Her campaign didn't get far; the motion wasn't adopted and there was criticism from Padstow residents, who felt that it was an intrusion in local matters.

How long until this festival is buried once and for all is anyone's guess but judging by the current climate it won't be long.

The harbour of Padstow behind me, I take a tarmac path up to the war memorial above St Saviour's Point. Round Stepper Point before I veer south-west towards Trevone Bay and from there to Harlyn Bay, which was an important prehistoric port owing to its position: comfortably close to the Camel Estuary but also on the vital trade route between France and Ireland.

At the turn of the previous century, in a small inlet between Harlyn Bay and Cataclews Point, a man called Reddie Mallett found a cist grave harbouring human remains while digging foundations for a new house. The relevant authorities were notified and a supervising committee gathered, including the Devonian polymath Sabine Baring-Gould. Further excavations uncovered more than a hundred graves, which were dated to the Iron Age. Of the many skulls found there, some appeared fractured; it was thought this was done after death to release the soul. Many of the bodies had also been buried with a companion: a frog was found next to one, and a little girl had two mice beside her – talismans for the afterlife, perhaps? But there were other relics too, the crumbling trappings of a distant domestic age: spindles, whorls and pottery, needles and flint and slate weapons for acts of survival, Britain's matter.

Some forty years earlier, a labourer was digging a pond for

a Mr Hellyar at nearby Harlyn House when he unearthed two crescent moons of gold. Thinking they were made only of brass, he placed them around his legs and returned to the house wearing what were in fact early Bronze Age lunulae. He had thrown other discoveries over the cliff in the belief they were worthless, including something he described as being 'like a bit of a buckle'. Generous-spirited, the labourer gave the black and tarnished lunulae to children as playthings. It was only when the light seemed to spill out at the edges that Mr Hellyar realised they could be gold. Mr Hellyar then took them along to a local toff, Mr Prideaux Brune, who contacted the Duchy of Cornwall. The finds were claimed as Treasure Trove, and the then Duke of Cornwall (later King Edward VII) ordered they should be deposited at the Royal Institution of Cornwall.

The story fascinates me, and I go off-track for a day to visit Truro's museum.

I walk through the large panelled doors into a square gallery which is dominated by a coach dating from the early eighteenth century, which happens to have come from my family home, Trewinnard. The gallery is dimly lit; skylights have been blocked out to protect the exhibits. Outside, they are moving a bus stop and the drilling, combined with the crashing of china and chattering in the museum café, makes me concerned that I will be distracted from bringing the items I seek back into being.

The museum moves easily between different cultures and historical eras; there are inconsistencies, certainly, but the connections are clear and full of rhyme, and mostly involve sea and stone in their endings. From the door I move to where Cornwall starts. I pass a display case of the Palaeolithic – Chert hand axes, flint blades, a greenstone adze used to fell timber, fragments of a rim from an earthenware object made of Gabbroic clay – and move on towards that for which I have made the special journey to Truro.

Three gold necklaces hang on a sheet of tight grey cotton. Two are those found in Harlyn Bay; they are separated by a copper alloy axe head, also from Harlyn, which sits between them like a nose. The fine and fragile gold of the necklaces is beaten flatter than any natural leaf could be. Less than a millimetre. And on this wafer-thin gold veins are inscribed, each incision glinting threads, so fine you have to press your nose against the glass to catch the complex geometric decorative patterns. The gold is dull, but those scratchings and patterns move as my shadow shifts over them.

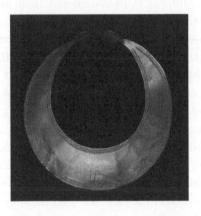

In 1932, not so far from here, in Kerivoa, Brittany, three lunulae were discovered in a disintegrated wooden box. With them was some sheet gold, broken into four pieces, and a rod of gold with flattened ends like the terminals of a lunulae. This rod was probably the beginning of a necklace. A stylus – perhaps one made from bone, bronze or wood, given the style and tool marks – had been used to decorate the necklaces. The thickness, patterns and similarity of style raised suspicions that the lunulae from the Kerivoa hoard and those from Harlyn Bay, as well as two others found at Saint-Pôtan in Brittany, were all made by the same hand: that of a craftsman working both sides of the Channel, someone who may have travelled or traded across north-western France and Cornwall. The contents of the wooden box must have been the tools of his trade from some four thousand years ago.

I am now seeing this same expert goldsmith, this itinerant craftsman, bent over his workbench, applying himself to this object. He is working diligently with all the deceit of his art, hammering the rod of gold, turning it into the slightest of things. He must be young, because his eyes would have to be razor sharp. It has taken him many hours and days, fashioning this shape into the crescent horns of the moon; he needs to turn it into an object of great ritual and ceremonial significance, grand enough for the burial of a local chief or spiritual leader, Shiny enough to illuminate the journey onwards, Gentle enough to caress the nape. Or was he simply turning it into an exclusive piece of clan property? Who knows, except him. While applying the stylus he needs to make sure the decoration is free of blemishes, there must be no indication of the workings of his rough hands; beauty, after all, has its own constitution, to which all artists must apply their obedience. And yet, is this piece not a story about the craftsman's obsessions? His yearnings? Is it not the source from which the river of his mind first issues itself from within himself? Maybe he is not even concerned with he or she that wears it; they are merely temporal, they will reside in the sunken regions of the dark earth, yet he, who creates such beauty, will live for ever. He is the one who will dig into the souls of the men and women that follow him, not God. He is the one I want to dig up. He is a true artist.

I suspect what really lies at the core of these lunulae is not actually gold, but that age-old human desire to suppress a knowledge of death – objects suitably multifaceted and mesmeric that can distract us from our own mortality. Like a plant rooted in the ground offers proof of life, so a necklace offers proof of life after death.

When I got married many moons ago, my husband rather

romantically wanted our wedding rings to be made out of Cornish gold and he went on an exhaustive and unsuccessful search for this precious metal. Thwarted in his attempts at every turn, he did not give up; his investigations continued over the years, as he looked for gifts for birthdays, anniversaries, Christmases. What was unknown became a mystery to him, one that needed to be solved. His fascination eventually led to the Nebra sky disc, the oldest material depiction of the night sky in the world.

Dating from around 1750 BC and now in the State Museum of Prehistory in Halle, the disc is extraordinary in that it exhibits the night sky as seen through pure observation, as opposed to anything religious or mythic. Its purpose to determine the correct seasons for sowing and harvesting. The green patina of its surface – originally a deep black – bears thirty-two gold stars, including the Pleiades, a gold orb representing the sun or a full moon, and a crescent moon. Later, two golden arcs were added to the sides of the disc, hiding two original stars. After that, a stylised ship was attached at the bottommost point, an allegorical symbol of the sun's journey across the sky.

But the most fascinating aspect, for both my husband and me, was not the beauty of the disc itself nor the interesting story behind its burial and discovery, but that the sun, moon and stars were cut out of gold and tin that came from Cornwall. The very same gold, in fact, as used for the lunulae from Harlyn. What these objects tell us is that a lot of long-distance travel was undertaken during this time; that tin streaming, metallurgy and trading practices were a critical catalyst in the cultural and technological shifts between the early to middle Bronze Age, right across north-western Europe. And that instead of the straight capitalist system that we know today, trade was done through exchange, and during those transactions beliefs about the cosmos and the role and origin of the sun itself came into play. Gold was a metal not only carrying the colour of the sun but containing its light-reflecting properties. It was a metal that could be taken beyond the horizon and returned as necklaces and discs; objects that not only had the ability to reflect the sun but harness its power.

It took a treasure hunt that ran across centuries and whole continents to find the true source of this Cornish gold. A chase that ended in 2011, with the discovery of a cache of thirty unlabelled and uncatalogued gold nuggets stuffed away in a dusty drawer in Caerhays Castle, overlooking Porthluney Cove. The Williams family, who owned the castle, had made their fortune from mining and smelting works through several generations during the Industrial Revolution. The gold found in the drawer was part of a mineral collection created by John Williams in the nineteenth century, but much of it had been given away to the Natural History Museum by his son Michael in 1893, with only a small amount retained at Caerhays.

The modern-day curator of the collection, Courtenay Smale, was trying to put together a display of the minerals for house tours at the castle when he stumbled across the hoard. He worked out that the heaviest nuggets contained tin oxide and that the combination of gold and tin in an alluvial deposit probably came from the Carnon River, where the Williams family had had a mining lease. In 2017, the nuggets were analysed by Professor Gregor Borg of the Martin-Luther University in Halle-Wittenberg, who was trying to trace the source of the gold in the Nebra sky disc. After much research and 'fingerprinting', it was concluded that the gold in the disc did indeed originate in the Carnon Valley.

On one of our many trips to Cornwall, my husband and I went to walk the Carnon Valley. Described in the nineteenth century as 'the richest square mile anywhere on earth', we wanted to see for ourselves where the gold and tin came from.

But what we discovered was disappointing. The river's voice

was low and sick, in the places we looked. It wasn't fat with rain, it didn't curve a frothing white as healthy rivers do; in fact, the threads of it we saw were barely writhing at all, and some of the pools were even a rusty red from acid mine drainage. It was as if the river god had left it completely. We subsequently learned that the Carnon is, subjectively, the most polluted river in England, its entire length affected by historic mining. That even as late as 1992 it was hit heavily by a major pollution scandal, when more than forty-five million litres of poisoned water from the closed Wheal Jane mine were released by the collapse of an adit. Suddenly the land over which the water ran became bloodshot. Veins of vile, thick sludge containing mercury, cadmium, tin, arsenic and zinc poured down the Carnon at the rate of about two million gallons a day until the mudflats at Devoran, an exclusive riverside village, were completely stained orange and red, as were all the creeks downriver to the sea. The oyster beds were particularly afflicted, the water so befouled no one would eat the oysters any more, and so strong were the levels of arsenic fishermen deliberately brought their boats to the poisoned waters to have their bottoms stripped clean.

When the river doesn't reflect the sky, it reflects the end. This was the colour of the end, the colour of a bloody accident. We spoke to a few locals about the ghosts of industry past, in particular a lady riding a horse, who we met on the bridle path; she told us she knows the water is polluted, everyone does, but she still swims in it.

So there was no pot of gold to be had at the end of this particular rainbow. No wedding ring. What we found was the opposite of light. The opposite of why necklaces like the lunulae were ever created: it was the end of light; it was about darkness and burial. It was just another sorry tale of human recklessness and environmental degradation. Which leads me now to think of King Midas, the man who wished for everything he touched to turn to gold – and when it did, he found it to be nothing more than a curse, one that spoke of greed and unhappiness. It's just another of many fables about becoming slaves of our own material desires. After our visit to the Carnon Valley we gave up our search for Cornish gold.

Debris and Deposits

Harlyn Bay to Newquay

A house, known as the Fish Cellars and with a fine view over Harlyn Bay, was once owned by a Squire Peters, who lived in a big house at nearby St Merryn. According to Cornish folk-lore, Peters ran a lucrative pilchard business, and in the sixteenth century a cargo of pilchards was returned to the cellars from Italy unsold. At the time, the residents were poor and starving, and a white witch called Mother Ivey appealed to the family to donate the fish. Squire Peters refused and instead ploughed the pilchards into a field to act as fertiliser. A vengeful Mother Ivey cursed the field, saying if ever its soil was broken, death would soon follow for the oldest son.

The family continued to plough the land, and the eldest Peters son was killed in a fall from his horse. In 1860 the Hellyar family acquired the land, and the field lay untouched until 1941, when air-raid trenches were dug. A week later Harold Hellyar, the eldest son, was killed by a German bomb. There were more incidents: in the 1970s, a group of metal detectorists started digging and within days one suffered a fatal heart attack; more than a decade later, when a water company disturbed the soil to lay pipes, the foreman died the following day. Eventually a priest from St Columb Major was called in to bless the 'cursed field'. It appeared to work, as the accidents from the field stopped happening. But today, the tenant farmer has turned the field over to rewilding. Just to be on the safe side.

Life in old Cornwall would have been hard, poverty and hunger never far away, so as a social mechanism a local curse would have been a way of getting an edge over your superiors. Moreover, a curse never grows lonely or bored, it is no respecter of border lines: rather like plants, it can migrate boundaries by dispersed pollination. A curse may be dependent on winds to carry its seed and drop it on fertile ground, and rain may be needed to encourage the seeds to take root, and the sun might be needed to warm up the earth but if it manages to establish itself it will grow tall and strong enough to send out its whispers in the wind and multiply.

I pass the house on the path west. There is not much to look at except for a few ironic words carved in the lintel: 'Dulcis Lucri Odor' – 'profit smells sweet'. But you might just have to pay for it.

Dogs on the path. Dogs on the beach. Dogs in a waking nightmare in which, walking down to the sea, I am almost knocked off course: by the trot and canter on the sand, the nudging past on the path, the panting, the jingle of collars, the whistles summoning them in, the adoring calls as if they are children, the anger at their ebullience, the congratulations of returned goods, all infecting the calm; and the defecation. Oh! The smell of that defecation!

Is a walk no longer a thing in itself? Does it need a purpose? A dog will pull you towards nature perhaps. No, says Roger Deakin: 'The dog is perceived as a connection with nature, whereas in fact the opposite is true. A dog cuts you off from much of the wildlife you might otherwise encounter by disturbing and alarming things. In the larger picture, dogs are a serious disturbance to, for example, ground-nesting birds and hares.' But try telling a dog owner not to take his or her pet on a walk; these are the most pampered creatures in the entire animal kingdom and often the most anthropomorphised. Read Allen G. Folliott-Stokes's comments after encountering a dog during his own coast path walk in 1912:

On returning from the shore we met a lady carrying a long-haired, goggle-eyed, and dwarfed monstrosity that it would be an insult to a noble race to call a dog. It was swathed in a kind of red coat, and round its neck was a blue ribbon tied in a voluminous bow. As we passed, we heard the lady say to her companion, pointing at the monstrosity, "I make him beef tea every day." What can be said in favour of this mania on the part of some women to devote all their care and attention on a dwarfed and unwholesome freak, swathed in bandages and scarcely able to walk, who follows its owners with dropsical gait and asthmatically wheezing, or lies curled up by the hour in her lap, or in a silk-bound bassinette, where, wrapped in uncertain slumber, its rheumy eyes dispel dyspeptic tears and its limbs twitch convulsively?

And then, dear reader, I got a dog, and I learned how love can stretch, how an animal can join your pack and change your entire way of life; how it can teach you about animals and about yourself and lead you towards social interaction; how it helps bypass all stilted embarrassments and launches you straight in as if you were part of a contact culture like Italy is, or France.

Kate Fox, in *Watching the English*, is convinced we grant our animals 'all the freedoms that we deny ourselves: the most repressed and inhibited people on earth have the most blatantly unreserved, spontaneous and badly behaved pets' in the world. She says they are our alter egos, our 'inner child', but not the doe-eyed ones: rather, the 'snub-nosed, mucky, obnoxious "inner brat"'. When we walk on the wild side, maybe we want to be accompanied by one who comes from the wild side as well, from the fast-running, meat-eating wolf himself, hunting prey on open grasslands, not as a solitary hunter but a social one.

Sometimes I feel like a dog myself, sniffing my way along this path with my tail wagging. My dog, Rocco, is never happier than when he is at a place where all the energies collect, where the wind blows, the sand gathers, the water chases him. A strange exhilaration comes over him, which is thoroughly infectious. Is it a rebellion against confinement and foreclosure? Is that why everything inside him suddenly breaks open? Because he is getting away from humanly imposed edges? That he is returning to the wild? Seascapes offer a coherent and non-stop outward view, but they somehow also offer hope, dreams. A seascape is where the earth retreats, where it goes underwater, where all our perceptual engagements of what we understand are altered, it is our most important elemental exchange. What we also know is that the ground beneath our feet may never move again, but the sea will always carry us.

I enter a nesting area by Mother Ivey's cottage, at the back of Trevose Head; it is part of Cornwall's corn bunting recovery project. The birds nest on this headland between May and September, but are easily trampled on because they nest on the ground. Walkers, and particularly those with dogs, not only disturb the birds but also advertise the nests to predators. The buntings are now so rare it is unusual to find a colony of them anywhere; they have completely gone from the rest of the South West, as well as Northern Ireland, Wales and the Isle of Man, though some can still be found in the lowlands of England and Scotland.

The corn bunting is not much to look at, pale brown with dark stripes, stout of beak and no bigger than a sparrow. It is hefty of appearance, portly even, which is probably why it has come by the name 'bunting', which derives from the Scots *buntin*, meaning plump, short and thick, as in the eighteenth-century lullaby 'Bye, baby Bunting'. This fat and ragged appearance, particularly when its chest is expanded to expel not very pleasant-sounding notes, gives it an almost Dickensian appearance, one of jollity and conviviality. At a stretch it could even be judged as grotesquely comic because of its indolence, except, of course, with regard to its promiscuity: a cock can produce two to three broods between late May and early June.

It's something of a paradox that the corn bunting's promiscuity has not saved him, and a sadness too; they have been around since the land was first cleared by Neolithic farmers and it is a bird steadfastly linked to agriculture, just as the corn crake or the grey partridge is, its song evoking memories of sunny cornfields, threshing machines, balmy meadows and horse-drawn hay floats. Seeking to protect it is to invest in an idea of England, in an enchanted or metaphysical notion of the place itself.

We press our kinship with things through our names of them. It makes us understand its character better. The naming of a genus is also an act of honouring – and a moment of connection; it focuses the world through human eyes, making it a richer and more animated place.

In *Birds Britannica*, written by Mark Cocker and Richard Mabey, we are told that extinction impacts not just the local ecology but our culture and language as well. We learn that in the Shetlands the bird is also known by a rich array of names: 'docken sparrow' and 'trussy laverock', and in Orkney, where the most northerly corn buntings in the world reside, it is still known as the 'skitter-broltie' – one who shits on the braithes, the cross ropes over a corn stack. To find an online image of an old-style corn stack, one of its favoured resting places, is not so easy these days. The struggle for survival is as much a part of the intellectual world as it is of the physical world. To ignore it is to look at a long wearing away of oneself. Sudden absences – whatever they are – must keep us guessing.

*

The Gulf Stream, which takes warm water from the tropics and delivers it to the northern hemisphere, is responsible for giving Cornwall its warm and sunny edges. One of its many branches is the North Atlantic Current, which nudges up against the beach at Porthcothan. This place has become one of the world's greatest collection spots, materials intertwined with human history brought by south-westerly gales and deposited right here, all waiting to be observed and reported on by wreckers and beachcombers.

That role was chiefly assumed by a man whose family has lived for four generations in a house facing this cove. He was Nick Darke, playwright, poet, lobster fisherman, environmentalist, beachcomber, politician, broadcaster, film-maker and parish councillor. No one was to have a more complex and intimate relationship with this stretch of shore than he.

Following a stroke, Darke decided to re-evaluate his life. He turned west and started to watch the tide come in twice a day, and each time it left a strandline he would be out there; for him every item on that strandline had been on a journey and had a story to tell. Some stories he found were local, others from many thousands of miles away. 'When I find something I ask three questions – what is it? Where's it come from and what is it doing on the ocean?'

His wonderful medley of objects disgorged by sand and tide included various hardwoods he would use for building; seeds from the tropics, which he planted in his conservatory; lobster tags; empty 12-gauge cartridge cases from shooting guillemots in Newfoundland, where they are eaten as a delicacy; stone crab traps from the Gulf of Mexico; a marker pole from Nantucket Sound – Darke found the fisherman who had lost it, and discovered it had taken nine months to reach Porthcothan, travelling ten miles a day – not forgetting what he called 'the poetry of fishing': smashed inkwells, buts, bongos, buoys, gate hooks, pot necks, parlour, creels, spinners. For Darke it was not about the thrill of finding something for free, an object that might serve a useful function if recycled, nor was it the fun of collecting objects for creative purposes. In fact, much of it was exchanged for bait with local fishermen. It was about learning about life on the Eastern Seaboard of the Americas, about forming bonds with people across the waters; it was about the lineage and poetry of things, and about compiling data in order to forecast the future. He was often called out for cetacean strandings; recording everything from dead dolphins to hydroids to violet sea snails and sub-tropical triggerfish.

Darke's assiduous investigations would bring attention to the way our planet was slowly being poisoned, and by what. He said, 'In fifty years of wrecking, the biggest change I've noticed is synthetic. There's a whole plastic continent out there, floating.' Of particular horror was plastic sand, or nurdles, tiny microbeads which are used to form plastic products but are often on a journey that culminates in the sea itself. They can be found in their millions on the strandlines of every beach of the world. Fish are killed by them, birds ingest them, and stomachs of dead fulmars are full of them. Nurdles absorb toxic pollutants and in turn are ingested by fish, who think they are plankton, and the fish become infertile or die as a result.

Darke died prematurely, at the age of fifty-six, but we owe him and people like him a debt, for it is their time and their observations that witness the patterns and the correlations between species. They prove to us that nature isn't a machine to be disassembled, but a community to which we, the observers, are inextricably linked. Darke's romantic view of the natural world merged the meticulous observations of a scientist. Every change needs to be documented, and there is nowhere better to seek out these changes than the ocean, because of its continuous movement and free-flowing water. Rising sea levels, warmer waters, the decline of salt, all could ultimately affect the Gulf Stream and thereby this coast. But scientists will always need a subjective response, everything must be precise; people like Nick Darke, on the other hand, judge these changes through feeling, an extension of the senses – be it sight, taste, smell, touch, sound or meditation. It is those feelings, about our own neighbour-hoods, and the events that occur there and the people and the nature that surround them, which is the right and proper place for contemplation, because it influences our relationship with it and our respect for it.

Darke came to the natural world and its great mysteries as an artist and writer, and in doing so constructed something new and long-lasting: 'I make my living writing plays and I have ways of creating a world in which the play can live, wrecking is like following a master playwright at work, the sea decides what you pick up, everything is random, you chase the story, you have to be curious, there is order in the chaos, the sea is telling you something very important but you just never find out quite what it is.'

I walk Darke's strandline on Porthcothan Beach and pick up what looks like a severed arm from a lost Barbie doll. The pink of it is so thick, so utterly impenetrable and so palpable, it rises up like a wall; there can be no dispute with it, as with other debris on this beach, which the tides and currents have reshaped or recoloured; saltwater picking at their bones. It does not feel like just a piece of moulded plastic, another piece of indestructible trash, it feels more than that, a symbol of survival, a provocation, a goading. It does not matter that the doll's head – no doubt still holding that demented frozen smile – has been decapitated onto another shore; it is telling me it is here to stay. It is what Freud would call the uncanny, that instance where something can be familiar, yet foreign at the same time, an uncomfortably strange or uncomfortably familiar moment when you are attracted yet repulsed in the same moment.

Much of our world is in a state of ruin and we live mostly in its own graceful mouldering, but not this arm: this arm won't melt back into earth as ice melts in the sun; this arm is going nowhere fast.

The ten-mile route from Porthcothan to Newquay is along the edge of flat-topped cliffs that hover over coves, caves and stacks. Mostly, it is maritime grassland, which holds and courts a mosaic of life-form jewels: the wind-pruned red fescue, wild thyme, Cornish gentian, autumn squill, western gorse, so that it feels as if you are entering a community or phenomenon of natural vegetation as intruder.

So much of this journey is comparable to walking on a thin carpet through a roped-off stately home, its treats locked away (mainly for survival purposes), a line of passage whose push you cannot feel but whose invitation to follow you cannot ignore. I walk westwards, as one is meant to, and it takes strength of mind, in the very real sense of the phrase, to stop, and not just for the strange, the dreadful, the extravagant, but the ordinary and the common, the daily arrangements, because it is often then, as a kind of inquisitive scholar, you will be led elsewhere. For me, it might be the prodigal chough's high-pitched *kjaa* or *kyeow* from a torn cliff on Park Head, or the mining bees digging their nest burrows, the linnets in the protective gorse, the meadow brown butterflies and the spring squill, the peregrine wheeling in the sky. We are all in too much of a hurry these days. So very much is lost to us.

I am thinking about what John Berger called 'ways of seeing', his unique look at the way we perceive art. 'Seeing comes before words. The child looks and recognizes before it can speak,' he wrote. 'But there is also another sense in which seeing comes before words. It is seeing which establishes our place in the surrounding world; we explain that world with words, but words can never undo the fact that we are surrounded by it. The relation between what we see and what we know is never settled.' And yet most of us, myself included, sometimes lack the energy to see, to seek out that settlement; it is how the path successfully edges us on. It is not until I capture what I see in words that I slow down again.

This is also true of the coast's form. Often one needs to turn one's eyes towards something in order to see. Here, it is with these plain grassy promontories that jut out into the sea, as the path moves gracefully and without fanfare through old time zones. Where the land rises out of the sea at Park Head is the site of yet another Iron Age castle. From Park Head to Carnewas, six Bronze Age barrows push through the ground; three ramparts enclose a small clifftop area at Griffin's Point; there are Iron Age defences at Penhale Point and at Trevelgue Head on the outskirts of Newquay. Time must be sought to conjure up the sum of the parts; to transport oneself to a different time and culture. To look at the swells and bumps and stretches on the land and of it.

Of course, these headlands were where it was at, where everything throbbed and pulsed, not like today's national boundaries where the sea feels just like a white lacy frill at the edge of a busily patterned dress. Think of a spin dryer, mud on a bicycle, uranium enrichment centrifuges, the outward acceleration when something is rotated. It is how the maritime trading network came into being: everything was simply spun to the edge. Land borders almost became irrelevant because a new kingdom had been found, one with seas running through it, where trade lines could be laced up between shores, ports, islands, river mouths, almost like a corset, the threads tugging the edges closer and tighter together. Those same routes channelled other things as well: religious beliefs and values, migrants, languages, beakers and battle-axes, gold, domesticated animals. Whereas on land borders were often flashpoints for social unrest, the sea edges were where they came for economic and cultural exchange; the edge was a place where heroes ventured outwards, not inwards, from Ireland, England, Wales, France, Spain, Portugal. It was where ideas turned into sparks. And so it went on, from the Mesolithic through to the Neolithic, from the Bronze Age to the Middle Ages, jumping to the mid-nineteenth century when seaborne traffic was still of vital importance; there was barely a railway system, other than a few mineral lines from ports to mining and quarrying areas. Then there were smaller ports such as Padstow, which dealt in slate and fertilisers, and after that the railways started trading in people and a modern tourist industry was born. All traders, all linked by an interest in where the land and the sea meet.

Now, as Britain enters a new industrial age, Cornwall is once again out front with its energy and climate innovation. Tourism is still a steadfast companion, but there are also some of the best wind climates in western Europe, contributing clean electricity through wind farms both on shore and off. Not only that, there are rich geothermal and mineral resources and it is in the forefront of aerospace technology with its orbital satellite launches and satellite ground stations; its discreet locations, direct access to the sea, scanty populations making test launches uncomplicated. As ever, Cornwall is exporting its expertise, innovation and ideas to a new world, though one progressively reacting against globalisation – Brexit being a case in point. Without succumbing to liberal apocalyptic thinking, nations are increasingly resisting uniformity and seeking out their own identities. This does not mean they want to stop trading with each other – quite the reverse – it is just about adapting to a new world of old roads: ones that are levitated, tarmacked, digitalised. It is not just hands across the seas any more, but hands across the whole world.

Flying

Newquay to Penhale Sands

Newquay. I stop to look at a portrait of local surfing champion
Ben 'Skindog' Skinner hanging in the window of an art gallery on Fore Street. His figure is partly abstracted, a black shape
seen from a distance off the shore. It contributes to the notion that
he is something of an emblem, that he is 'at the still point of the
turning world'. Skindog is the axis around which the planet spins,
which in turn creates a force that makes the wave he rides.

In the picture he is executing a hang ten, one of the most difficult
manoeuvres to achieve on a surfboard. He is poised, knees bent, all
ten toes hanging over the very tip of his board, as the wave rears
up behind him. He is not trying to ride the wave but to conquer
it, in a triumph of will. The power is personal. Balance is king.
Balance is possession.

Surfers continue to transfix me as I walk along Fistral Beach:
a ballet might do the same, these intricate relationships, these pas
de deux: man and sea, man and universe, man and time, man
and woman ...

    At the still point of the turning world. Neither flesh nor
      fleshless;
    Neither from nor towards; at the still point, there
      the dance is,

But neither arrest nor movement. And do not call it fixity,
Where past and future are gathered. Neither movement
   from nor towards,
Neither ascent nor decline. Except for the point, the
   still point,
There would be no dance, and there is only the dance.

Surfers are gathering for a lesson outside the café; others seem to be chatting almost post-coitally before their next sortie; some are looking out to sea, wondering when they will heave their human will and body onto that fluid ledge and triumph as legend. It can only really happen when there is a low spring tide, a depression in the mid-Atlantic, coupled up with a certain type of wind, and when that swell crashes over the Cribbar Reef just half a mile offshore, they will get their thirty-foot waves.

I speak to a surfer called Patrick, who is having a coffee at the table next to mine in the café above the beach. He explains that surfers know energy as scientists do, they understand that waves are the invisible force that drives the universe: 'For us it's visceral, it's all about power.' Surfers know that a wave is not made of water, that it is not really even a tangible object, it is a process, and water is merely the means by which energy moves from one place to another. He says surfers just want a piece of that energy.

'After all, how else can we appreciate it? In towns and cities, we just flick a switch, we fill up a tank, we have lost our connection to the nature of power and energy, haven't we?'

Patrick, like any artist, spends much of his time waiting for a gathering force in his life to carry him off, one that will enable him to defy the laws of gravity and make him fly. Surfers are no different from the rest of us in that respect: they wait for transformation. It is a truth perhaps not universally acknowledged that transformation comes not always from an idea but a thing.

Transformations, not always good ones, seem to run through Newquay's veins. I pass a sign saying 'Alco Stop'. Newquay is full of designated areas like this, where you are told it is an offence to continue drinking or not surrender the stuff when asked to do so by a police officer. Further on: 'HM Coastguard: Serious Accident. A person jumped from here and was seriously injured. Don't jump in the water.' Is this just a holiday town full of high jinks?

No, Newquay, like many of our British seaside resorts, has a long-term disease; the compulsive and uncontrolled consumption of alcohol and drugs has been and continues to be detrimental not only to its health and personal relationships, but its social standing as well. It also adds to the already depressing brew of deprivation stirring in the town.

Its root causes are complex, and have a lot to do with the decline of tourism in the area; the proliferation of low-cost flying means that families who once would have spent their summers in Cornwall often now travel to France or Spain instead. Other local industries have similarly declined and, in a nutshell, it has lost its economic purpose. Correspondingly, places like Newquay have more often than not been left on the edges of regeneration initiatives, playing second fiddle to inner-city deprivation.

Isolation is another factor; many seaside towns like Newquay are hard to get to, end-of-the-line destinations with poor public transport links, a significant barrier for people who don't drive. That also means they cannot commute to higher-paid jobs. How, then, do you draw highly skilled people from elsewhere to work by the sea; particularly in schools? Nearly 30 per cent of children in Cornwall were living in poverty in 2020/21, and Newquay is the second-worst area. And what of those children? Soon enough they face a stark choice: stay at home and stay poor or 'get on your bike'. Not so easy, if none of your family have before you; it just makes it so much harder to imagine your older self moving away to work or study, and besides, parents might well want to keep children at home because they are fearful of the physical isolation they themselves would experience if they left. Then, those who do manage it are draining the town of its talent. At the other end of the spectrum is the inward migration of older people looking to idle out their final years.

Seaside towns are relatively ethnically homogenous; this is mainly a 'white' working-class problem during the period of my walk, but why is this? It's widely thought that it's not about personal but social ambition. Unlike middle-class children and those children of first-, second- and third-generation immigrant groups, poor white coastal children tend not to grow up surrounded by role models. Sometimes it is the middle classes that move into the town who become those new role models, such as Rick Stein in Padstow and Jamie Oliver's non-profit Fifteen restaurant in nearby Watergate Bay, now sadly closed, which ran apprenticeships for young people from disadvantaged backgrounds under a franchise run by the Cornwall Food Foundation. Stein himself is not only a big employer in the area but brings in the tourists via cookbooks and television programmes. These incomers might breed resentment on arrival, but it is indisputable that they are a force for good when it comes to the local economy.

I take a walk off-track, down these streets, and it's like walking through a colour chart, at the start and at the end, from the vivid blues of the skies and yellows sands, the holiday destination of prime ministers, models, comedians and actors, into the greys and whites of bedsit living. Row upon row of what would have been guest houses or small hotels are now subdivided into flats. Rubbish is strewn everywhere, seagulls scavenging. What were once front gardens, lovingly planted by their owners, are now soulless paved yards. A couple brush past me at a hounded, edgy pace, so that you can almost hear their hearts trying to jump out of their chests. White-faced voyagers to drugs and disappointments, moving from the monochrome of their lives to the colour of a dream-like state. Most of the occupants of these streets, according to locals, either work part time or are on benefits struggling with the bureaucracy of late payments, some are in lives dictated to by drugs, rejecting ego and possessions, as close to the point of vagrancy as one can be, but there are also students, hospitality workers, surfers and skaters stacked up on top of each other, playing the hand that has been dealt them.

I walk on to the railway station, the terminus of the Atlantic Coast Line that operates from Par. Trains that arrive here end their journey, or reverse out of the station. For me, the word terminus implies a common dream, that it is a one-way journey to something better. But in reality, arriving at Newquay, like many end-of-the-line stations, can often be going nowhere. Or coming to a dead end. To another edge.

I'm quick to notice the drug paraphernalia here, from scrunched-up silver foil to the occasional needle; there are huddles of addicts around Burger King, dealers openly offering their wares. I turn around and head back to the coastal path so very grateful for my lot in life. We often refer to 'being on edge' as describing a psychological state, but it could equally apply to a bodily state, a time when we have reached the limit of our available energy. Addiction does that, it finds its harbour in people whose lives are intolerably painful or in those suffering from the extreme monotony of their daily lives who do not have strong motivations to channel their energies elsewhere. It comes to people who have fallen over the line they have themselves drawn and are travelling further and further away, until they are at the end of the line, in a town like Newquay. Surely this place will be better. But it seldom is; there is no light at the end of the tunnel, just a blockade, and they soon learn they have nowhere else to go, other than smashing through it (again), or with God's will and their own, reversing back up out of there.

Urban edges can be sharp as a knife; places where tensions simmer between rich and poor, where anger and resentment build up on both sides. These boundaries are always highly porous, with traffic in both directions, friend and foe. It puts me in mind of Robert Frost's poem 'Mending Wall', which explores the nature of human relationships through two neighbouring farmers, who meet each spring to repair the stone wall that separates their properties. The farmers try to work out why the wall is necessary, when even nature makes gaps in it, with boulders falling for no reason: 'Something there is that doesn't love a wall / That wants it down.' Although there is a barrier in communication between the farmers, other things, they know not what, find gateways through the wall. Man-made barriers have always existed between peoples and groups, and walls often symbolise national, racial, religious and political differences. This is why holes in walls, gateways, are so vital to community: they make open passage possible, movement possible. This recognition animates the edges, it allows things to happen. It's a creative space.

Nansledan is an extension to Newquay town, sited on Duchy of Cornwall land. It was based on principles of architecture and urban planning championed by the then Prince of Wales. The ethos is simple: break down walls and create entryways, with walkable routes between shops, offices, leisure facilities. It connects to the sense of place as well: in traditional styles, the use of local materials and craftmanship, language and folklore. The streets and roads bear Cornish names, many from the legend of King Arthur, the pearl-story in the necklace of Cornwall's civilisation, inscribed on signs made from local Delabole slate. By reaffirming these stories, not just as simple entertainment, you yield to the history and experience of place rather than skimming over the surface in all your haste. Simple features such as signage can remind us who we are and where we came from; they introduce a commonality between neighbours.

They are bringing back the skylarks at Penhale Sands.

I came to romanticise this bird through Vaughan Williams's

The Lark Ascending. Unusually, it was the music that led me to the bird, not the bird to the music.

Even now, those first few bars, and the romance of that solo violin within them, take me out every time. I take a deep breath. I shut my eyes. I cannot hear a change in the bow, it is just a seamless flow of pure sound, played close to the fingerboard; it is light and fast and transparent and full of feather and blue sky. The white trailing edge of the wing tip is starting to go up and I am in an English field where the grass is long with poppies and scented mayweed, there is a snowing of white butterflies and all the other sound-sensations of a world in its turning, and here is this solitary creature, this skylark, with all its hollering, still climbing, using its neat torpedo-chest and arrowhead to fight the centre, as if some propellant has entered its combustion chambers, as if it can't get away from this rotten world soon enough. Rapidly, it passes the low dancing wheatear, and the parachuting descent to ground of a meadow pipit before it drops a little to rest, hovering in its station, then off again over a woodlark, higher now than all of them, on and up into the gleaming ceilings of days, up into the moon, up into some ecstatic ether, where it is drawn into the infinite, before it disappears altogether leaving nothing behind but this continuous fountain of song; fallen as if from heaven. Beautiful.

When we glance into the enormity of the sky we are not looking into an abyss; there are birds and treetops, cloud formations, the colours of the atmosphere, there is rain and snow, stars and the moon, there are things and events, each of them with their own edges, there are places we can go to and come back from. Small signs that everyday something has tried to stop us, and failed. Because really, 'Hope is the thing with feathers / That perches in the soul, / And sings the tune without the words, / And never stops at all.' Because, really, Icarus is lodged somewhere in all our souls. We just need to find him.

Sacred Space

Penhale Sands to Porth Joke

I walk along the western edge of the dunes, through Ministry of Defence land. These are the tallest sand dunes in Britain, around three hundred feet above sea level at their highest and so extensive that if it wasn't for military activity restricting access it would be easy to get lost.

The dunes were formed some five thousand years ago, when sand built up on an exposed rocky plateau and then went on to form their own character. The shifting dunes soon got rid of their human inhabitants and their structures, replacing them with shelter for new congregations of species in the constantly changing wet and dry hollows; they were helped by the marram grass which binds the sand with the thin soil. Early gentians, shore dock, petalwort and scrambled-egg lichen can all be found here, alongside more common species such as sea campion and bird's-foot trefoil.

There is a lot of flying going on around here. Touchdowns, and take-offs as well. Sand for one: it lands, then blows off again. And butterflies, also looking to find a place to settle. This place is famous for them, rare ones, such as the grizzled skipper with its *taras* aberration, which means they have more white patches on their upper forewings than other butterflies in their species.

This attractive pigmentation only occurs in a handful of places in Britain, and Penhale Sands is one of them. There are other rare beauties, with fabulous names: robber fly, silver-studded blue, brown argus, small copper, wall browns. Each name a commemorative act, a tick, a mark of respect – they denote a cheerfulness, that moment when the butterfly became something of value to the human eye. Why are the butterflies so busy here? They are probably trying to avoid their own extinction: butterflies are now thought to be one of our most threatened species.

An area that excludes the general population becomes a place of conservation, because it develops a new and rare ecology. Unusual butterflies are brought back, which helps to halt the deterioration of suitable habitats. All those seemingly minor, almost subconscious, actions in everyday life have a gross and widespread effect. This is one of those sites where the idea holds that an action or change that seems on the surface unimportant has a very large effect, that it can bring on a widening of the world.

It gets me thinking about the butterfly effect, the idea that the world is deeply interlocked and that one small creature can influence a much larger, complex system. The beating wings of a butterfly could, hypothetically, cause a storm in the upper air. A typhoon.

The movement of sand in the dunes, a small, seemingly insignificant event over a long period, moves out humans and provides shelter in which new species can thrive. The same dunes are the training ground for a soldier learning to aim a weapon that will produce tremendous consequences in a war on the other side of the world.

The butterfly effect surely then has to be: *Me! Yes, little old me! How do I actually make a difference?* 'Do I dare disturb the universe?' With my smallness, can I actually bend history? The butterfly effect tells us that with a single energy-diverse act of courage, often unintended, great change can be born.

These thoughts take hold of me as I search the dunes for evidence of St Piran, Cornwall's patron saint. It's not such an easy task; sand is the perfect collaborator: it erases everything, the way a veil is thrown over a beautiful face. As here, sand can reverse a whole surge of history, so that even as time marches on it can also move backwards. Only when the wind turns informer can we catch an occasional glimpse of the treasures within. Alternatively, we may need to use a shovel.

In St Piran's case, the seemingly insignificant event that produced far-reaching consequences came after he had performed a miracle. He was in Ireland at the time, in the late fifth century, and already quite old when a group of disgruntled local leaders, tired of his piety, threw him into a stormy sea with a millstone round his neck. Luckily for St Piran, the millstone turned out to be lighter than water and floated, allowing the wind and the waves to wash him up here at Penhale Sands. Taking it as a sign from the Lord that he should settle close to this shore, he established himself, with singular energy, as a hermit in a simple chapel hut built out of wattle and daub. His sanctity and seriousness, and gift for miracles, drew in many admirers, who happily forsook Celtic gods of sun and rain to follow him. Together they founded an Oratory in the Irish style; the Domesday Book records the existence of a small monastery at Lanpiran, but it is not clear whether this was the Oratory, the church that came after it, or both.

St Piran had something of an ignominious end: he drunkenly fell into a deep well, of which there were many in Cornwall. He was buried in his Oratory and there he lay until his remains were exhumed and redistributed, to be venerated in different locations. In the Middle Ages the Church liked to parade its relics, these included a reliquary, bound with iron holding St Piran's skull. One of his arms was fabled to have ended up at Exeter Cathedral.

By around 1150, the Oratory itself, which had been built

simply – a layering of rough stones without mortar – became so sand-beaten and buried it was difficult to enter the building, so another was built two hundred yards away. St Piran's headless skeleton, found under the altar at the Oratory, was moved to the new church. This second church, which became known as St Piran's Old Church, was protected from the shifting dunes by a stream. It flourished until the eighteenth century, but then mine workings caused the waters to dry up and the sand encroached once again. In 1805, much of the fabric of the church – its towers, font, pillars, tracery and other cut stone – was dismantled and used to rebuild a new structure further inland at Perranzabuloe, leaving behind the shell of the building that can be seen today.

After the Oratory was excavated in the late eighteenth century it became a popular tourist attraction, but damage to the buildings and visitors taking stones as souvenirs led to the installation of railings around the site in the 1890s. In 1910, a concrete cover was built to shield the original church, which the archaeologist Dr T. F. G. Dexter later likened to 'a reservoir, a motor garage, an aerodrome, a picture palace, anything except a church'. He lamented: 'If the buried church could speak, she would complain bitterly of the writers who have misunderstood her, of the trippers who have robbed her, of the church that sold her, and of the enthusiasts who have entombed her in that hideous concrete structure.' In any case, that same structure soon became too expensive to maintain, and owing to repeated problems with vandalism and flooding the Oratory was buried by the sand again. In 2014, money was raised for a new excavation and the Oratory once more emerged from the dunes. I revisited it recently and half of the protective concrete structure still remains; someone has graffitied, in purple paint, the word 'smile' on it. The Oratory sits inside it, partially submerged in an aquamarine pool of water, not smiling at all; in fact, looking very down at mouth. In a pathetic attempt to protect the structure

beneath it has been capped by netting and mossy turf. For an
icon of Cornwall, a potent symbol of its culture and heritage, a
place where many people come on pilgrimage, it looks remark-
ably unloved and abandoned.

How many more times will it be buried and revived, I wonder;
exchanging heaven for earth? It's almost as if St Piran and his
church are suffering from a taboo, a prohibition of dying not
dissimilar to that of the Greek island of Delos in the fifth century,
when fading gently away was not permitted, on religious grounds.
Christianity has always been keen on the hereafter; it doesn't like
to stop a story. If anything is to be buried it seems it can only be
with a deep and exemplary gravity.

I walk into a large sandy bowl with the sea on my right and
bear left, to the highest of the gaps on the skyline. As I reach the
top the path dips down and I get a glimpse of St Piran's Cross.
The earliest recorded stone cross in Cornwall, standing proud at
eight feet tall, it is the only three-holed cross in the county. It was
already a well-established landmark by the time it was mentioned
in the charter of King Edgar in AD 906 and it is just a few yards
from the remains of St Piran's Old Church.

The sky has turned that threatening grey which means it will not support new light; the sand is shifting softly on the wind, carrying the dust of dead saints' bones. The ruined graveyard, cross, dunes and sea do their spiritual work well. It is a place where death takes wing but still hovers over you. Where lives go on long after they have left us. The site is highly atmospheric. Standing there, you receive what it offers like a prayer prayed back to one who prays, a poem thrown down on a page coming back in the silence to the head. It affects. In places such as this the submerged histories demand a kind of conversion, back from the veneration of human endeavour to the sacredness of the site itself. You start to question the supernatural force that helped bring the objects to fulfil their purpose.

I walk back through the dunes to the sea's edge. But I can't stop thinking about the sand and its antiquity; the ultimate relic of the leisurely negotiations of earth processes when time felt eternal, not finite like it does today. Sand is such a mysterious substance, with an almost indestructible strength, the final product of the weathering and degeneration of rocks and the carrying of water and waves. Each grain of it, going back to a place where life itself started, each grain a witness. It gets everywhere, it goes everywhere, each particle like a refugee, a nod to strength, courage and victory because a refugee is, on balance, someone – or something, in this case – that has survived.

But sand is in no small measure also a tale about the subjects that find refuge in its dark, clammy coolness, from saints that want to sleep to creatures hiding from their predators. Sand survives in its final form by its tightness to others, and by embracing a film of water, a cushion against more attrition; in this minuscule world, this water film invites others in: single-celled animals and plants, mites, crustacea, the larvae of small worms. Because with such uncertainty and such movement, if you want to survive here, feed, breathe, reproduce, you have to burrow deep below the surface. A beach may have an empty look to it, as if it is uninhabitable, uninhabited, but with sand everything is hidden from view, and never more so than here. At the edge the underworld is not only for the dead.

I pick up a single untenanted razorshell on Perran Beach. It is sharp, open and fragile; its interior lacquered white, with the gentlest of purple tinges. Outside, the markings are divided by an oblique border. Curiously, on one half olive-green lines race downward, while on the other a series of horizontal arcs appear to be mapping the narrative of its burrowing. It uses just one powerful foot to dig to a safe depth under the sand. The foot, which moves in and out of the shell by a valve, can be inflated hydraulically to also act as an anchor. They have a reputation for burrowing deep and fast; at the slightest hint of trouble they upend themselves and cut through wet sand like hot knives through butter, minds commandeering their bodies in an instant survival takeover.

It is this empty shell that makes me order razor clams for the first time, in a seafood café that evening. They are delicious, of course: grilled with garlic butter and parsley, the taste a mixture of cockles and scallops that is sweet and salty all at once. It feels like I am eating a secret.

Nearby, in Holywell Bay, there is another sacred site, a well set in a dark cave on the south-west corner of Kelsey Head. It is only accessible at low tide, through an unprepossessing narrow gash in the rock. If you get inside and manage not to slip on the green algae and iron oxide coatings, adjust your eyes to the darkness and reach the main chamber, you will quickly realise you have entered a supernatural dimension very different from your own. Here lies a spectacular chain of calcareous basins, or rimstone pools, with clear waters cascading down steps lined with creamy white and pink deposits tinted by rocks that carry the deep colours of a rainbow when lit. Drop by drop the water has worked its magic like a master jeweller laying down his precious stones into an ornament that, like all good pieces, has stood the test of time. It is a world of drops, and within every drop a world of slow and sure effort.

On this day, amid the brute fortification of rock, the luminosity and colours of the surfaces are a revelation, the ceaseless welling up and whispering of water connecting one drop with another. You could be, in Cormac McCarthy's words, 'pilgrims in a fable swallowed up and lost among the inward parts of some gigantic beast. Deep stone flues where the water dripped and sang. Tolling in the silence the minutes of the earth and the hours and the days of it and the years without cease.'

At Holy Well the steps, which were carved out hundreds of years earlier, have been worn smooth, this time by a procession of mothers – and it is also a place of the Mother and her mysteries – dipping sickly children in one of the lower pools, before passing them up through the small entranceway into the minute uppermost cave for a final immersion at the water's source. Traditionally, the children were brought here on Ascension Day.

The well itself, however, was said to have been discovered on the Celtic festival of Samhain, which marked the end of summer and the start of winter. If any pagan miracles were to occur, the most auspicious time was always when the boundary between the worlds of the living and of the dead was at its thinnest, allowing the best possible access and communion with the spirits.

The Christians stole Samhain for their own calendar, calling it All Hallows' Eve, or Hallowe'en, a time for the veneration of dead saints. It has now returned somewhat to its Celtic origins, but for the people of the early medieval period the whole of nature was deeply imbued with the special spiritual powers from trees and mountains and water, particularly the last. It would become a kind of elemental battleground between the pagans and the Christians to capture the hearts and minds of the people. The Christians would win this battle with their baptisms, and, because history is written by the conquerors, there is little evidence left of these ancient activities.

I take a slug from my water bottle. It is occurring to me that this yearning for pure and natural water is not only critical for physical life but for our spiritual life as well. Springs became sanctified because they were guaranteed sources of pure water, they were life-giving, health-giving. Despite all technological advances, many of us prefer to drink water from a plastic bottle than from a tap; in that sense we desire exactly what our ancestors held dear, something purer, something life-giving, something that connects us with the inner core.

To come to the Holy Well would have been an act of faith, and buying bottled water is not dissimilar. But *it is* an act of faith, because we have no real understanding of what water actually does to heal us. You could also call it connecting, one act with another, water as rhythm, as pulse, as a pull, it is something that we share in this world, 'like us / with purpose', the poet Philip Gross has written, 'though not one least particle is constant, knows its place, could account, or be held to account for what it is or does'.

Many of our ancient wells have been abandoned, become overgrown, nature reclaiming them as their own. Some were filled in during the Reformation because they were associated with saints and viewed as papist, sources of superstition and even evil. Then cholera arrived, and then taps. The wells were lost, as was the wonder they first inspired.

In a way water in itself is nothing, but the intense desire to control it remains fierce. It might be clear, but in its substance you can see a world reflected in all its angles, not all of them very pretty.

If we reopened many of our ancient wells we would probably find agricultural run-off or industrial effluent: so much of our purity has been lost by progress; we too have been abusing our local environment. But my faith stays with the water; it may appear simple on the surface but, as Philip Gross says, it is the 'most deviously single-minded thing', adept only at being pulled ever downwards by the force of gravity, and in that, he says, 'It makes patterns of endless subtlety and complexity.' Never more so than here in the cave at Holy Well.

Porth Joke next, from the Cornish phrase *poll an chauk*. Meaning 'the chough's cove', it is one of those perfect, rare places that you have to work for to enjoy. A narrow beach deeper than it is wide, which backs onto a shallow valley with a stream running down to it. There are no car parks, therefore no cars, and no commercialism; a cove at its absolute purest. I am always reminded of D. H. Lawrence's words when I come across places like this, and on this walk you do so regularly: 'I like Cornwall very much. It is not England. It is bare and dark and elemental, Tristan's land. I like looking down at a cove where the waves come white under a low, black headland, which slopes up in bare green-brown, bare and sad under a level sky. It is old, Celtic, pre-Christian. Tristan and his boat, and his horn.'

Out of Darkness

Porth Joke to Gwithian

The first sign you are truly entering Cornwall's industrial dimension is the disused mine shafts. Many are capped with conical mesh covers, not only to prevent people plunging down into the depths but to accommodate the bats, who have colonised the mines and require access in and out of these gaping maws.

I suffer from chiroptophobia – the fear of bats. I don't like them because I grew up in an old house where, every night, they would find their way into my bedroom through penny-sized holes in the fabric of the building and muscle through the air above my dreams. I was sure that they would get tangled up in my hair in some nose-diving attack. It would wrap coils of fear around my beating heart and send me streaking, and screaming, down the corridor to sleep in my parents' bed. In the morning my mother would quietly remove the bats from the inside of my curtains, where they were dozing off their night's activities, and try to convince me how sweet they actually were. I was having none of it.

So here I am, peering cautiously over the rim of a shaft, uncertain what I will find. It feels, at first, as if I'm looking guiltily at a body's deep interior, a lung perhaps, black and ravaged by cancer but apparently still alive underneath it all. I know they are in there, in the gloom, growing and dividing as cancer cells do, at an unregulated quickened pace, or so conservationists hope. They are greater horseshoe bats, rare and distinctive because of the horseshoe-shaped piece of skin around their nostrils; the females are in there now giving birth, hanging upside down by one leg, their infants dropping into their overlapped wings for protection; upside-down creatures in what feels like an upside-down world, all along this twelve-mile edge between Perranporth and Portreath, which is best described as Cornwall's Black Country.

The path turns decidedly nasty here, as it takes me through the spoil heaps of numerous abandoned tin and copper mines. In fact, much of the landscape is sobering and oppressive, full of skeletal shapes of an old world. I see the remains of an explosives factory, an abandoned airfield, and the processing works of a mine, and later a chemicals research establishment, all tangled up together in the briar; it is like walking into a future where the world as we know it has been destroyed. The landscape looks ravaged as if an apocalypse has passed, the nature of which is unclear, a portrait of how the world will look when it is sickened.

It looked even worse in Folliott-Stokes's day. In *From Devon to St Ives*, published in 1910, he wrote:

Here the once pellucid brook is almost black, stone walls instead of flowers line its banks, and its befouled waters darken the sand in the cove and discolour the sea for several yards from the shore. Clambering over some rocks we soon reached Trevaunance Cove, where things are still worse. On the beach itself a great over-shot wheel revolves, and discharges dirty water on to the already discoloured sand. On the hill-side above are more wheels, slowly moving chains, mud heaps, and smoking chimneys; while the loud and ceaseless clatter of stamps fills the air with noise. This valley, before man polluted it, must have been a very beautiful.

And yet there are places on this stretch where man and industry have moulded gracefully together, such as with the much-photographed remains of Wheal Coates, with its stamps and whim engine house from its final days. The old trenches and pits are now covered by heather and gorse. We might even be comforted by the fact that nearly all our landscape has been impacted to some degree by humans. In fact, the word landscape, from the Dutch *landschap*, actually means a general situation of activity and its background – in effect the way the land has been shaped – and certainly this coast has been shaped by its fair share of political, economic and social history, from Porlock's sixteenth-century charcoal burners to West Penwith's tin mines, to the silver mines of Combe Martin. Landscaping is all about altering an existing design, a natural one, not only to enhance it but to change its use. So what's the worry? How can a single species that has been crawling all over the earth for less than 1 per cent of its entire history really have any impact?

Except that scientists are using a new word for the period in which we live. No longer, it seems, are we in the Holocene, an abnormally stable era that began only ten thousand years ago; we are living in a new age, one shaped primarily by people. And it seems we are no longer covering our tracks. Humans have become the force of nature that is reshaping our planet on a geological scale.

We are living in one of those moments when we need to come to terms with the science of man's destruction. Our wilderness is gone, and it will not return in the face of this human onslaught. This time, my time, my nature, is becoming governed by an increasingly homogenous and limited group of international crops, livestock and creatures that suit environments dominated by humans. Creatures less precious or malleable will join the extinction figures which are currently running higher than during any other geological period.

W. G. Sebald regards the act of combustion as the root

cause of many of our environmental ills, not in a spontaneous way, but in an intrinsic desire to see everything through the violent glow and mesmerising pulse of a burning flame. In his eyes, the destruction of things can also come about from the making of them:

> Our spread over the earth was fuelled by reducing the higher species of vegetation to charcoal, by incessantly burning whatever would burn ... Combustion is the hidden principle behind every artefact we create. The making of a fish-hook, manufacture of a china cup, or production of a television programme, all depend on the same process of combustion. Like our bodies and our desires, the machines we have devised are possessed of a heart which is slowly reduced to embers.

There are fabulous writers who try to put a positive spin on these changes. *Edgelands*, by the poets Paul Farley and Michael Symmons Roberts, is a beautifully written book that explores the debatable lands of our civilisation, the in-between places of roadside verges and allotments and standing water, of mobile masts and concrete motorway bridges, gravel pits and business parks and landfill sites. The one Sebald rails against. It defines a new landscape and offers it up for worship. As does Cal Flyn, in her brilliant book *Islands of Abandonment*, an adventurous romp through places of human surrender. Flyn looks on the 'post-human landscape' and watches how the natural processes are constantly at work repairing the damage. But I'm a traditionalist at heart. I like the picturesque, and I'm always impressed by the ability some humans have to care for their landscape, to love it, to nurture it, to garden it. Often, we might only see the quality in nature in our own designs. Just as we might only see the degradation of nature in the design of others.

*

South of Porthtowan, the site of a short-lived smelter, the path takes you somewhere altogether more sinister: along the perimeter fence of RAF Portreath, what was once the Nancekuke Chemical Defence Establishment. The path seems hardly permitted here; it is pushed right up to the cliff edge and the wire fence looms over you as you walk; it does not want you to snoop. But peer in and you see more fenced-off areas: strange pools of dirty water, barracks, gateways, a sinister-looking dome, decay; indeed, everything about the place is menacing and intimidating.

Nancekuke had been a sleepy place, consisting of scattered farms and old quarries, and used as an air base in the Second World War. In 1950, when the Cold War arms race kicked off, there was fear that Eastern Bloc countries were forging ahead with chemical warfare and Nancekuke, out of sight, was transformed into a research facility, with plans for a large-scale production plant to follow. Sarin was quickly established as the nerve agent of choice, and tested on animals and servicemen to calculate the lethal dose. Many of the volunteers suffered severe and painful symptoms such as convulsions, paralysis, loss of respiratory function and even death. In the end, the plant was never built and Nancekuke was handed over to the production of chemical fertilisers and then the manufacture of CS gas, better known as tear gas. Declassified government documents have shown that Harold Wilson sold tear gas on a massive scale to countries all around the world, many with poor human rights records. The riot, that most natural of human acts, used to break something that does not work, was controlled by Cornwall's most immoral export.

At Nancekuke, both locals and peace campaigners started to get agitated. They began to worry about the labyrinth of mine shafts: had equipment been dumped down there? Had materials leached into the ground? Every time anyone questioned the goings-on at the base, the government came back with the words 'Top Secret' or 'National Security'. As they do. In 1969 a large number of seals and seabirds were found dead and toxic compounds were said to have been swept up on the beach at Padstow, leaving people burned and suffering the effects of nerve gas. Then, people working at the establishment started to fall ill as well. In 1975, Nancekuke was finally closed and decommissioned; mustard gas incinerated, scrap metal too difficult to bury dumped down old mine shafts, the remaining reserves of nerves gas diluted and pumped out to sea.

Today Nancekuke is an air defence radar station, which concentrates long-range coverage of the south-western approaches to the mainland. The equipment is housed in the rather odd fibreglass golf ball that can be seen from the path.

The saying goes that 'with integrity, you have nothing to fear, since you have nothing to hide', but the ground and the air around Nancekuke feel sequestered, corrupt, heavy with guilt. If I were a bird, I wouldn't be flying over it.

I wonder if nature, in its tolerance of human folly, not only forgives but sees its duty as being to repair the damage. This has certainly been shown to be the case with hyperaccumulating plants, a process known as phytoremediation. What would it say about malevolent places like this? Something like *Here, over here,* whispering to us, through the swaying grass, *Dear God! What evil have you brewed on this ground? Why did you turn all that was green and fair into shame?*

And I do also wonder why ethics don't play a much stronger role in the teaching of science and the practising of it.

Around this time, I had a dream about bats, in which those ugly little imps seemed to come out at me from a black hole as deep and crushing as the vacuum that is the universe. They were relentlessly circling me, just like they did in my childhood bedroom, and the world offered no hiding place, not until the light came back again – if it ever would. At the time I had been reading about a new strain of coronavirus, closely matched to a strain found in bats.

The philosopher Edward S. Casey believes that edges and events run in tandem, that they have a relationship. He cites the Nevada nuclear bomb test site as an example, but it could easily apply to the story behind Nancekuke. It is not simply a facility in Cornwall but a place that 'exfoliates' into a historical event through what went on there: chemical weapons used across the battlefields of the Middle East, most notably in Syria. 'Enclosure gives way to disclosure, obscuration to revelation, the unknown to the known (though sometimes also to a new unknown.)' This happens every day of our lives, but occasionally the edges of an event interacts with all of us who occupy this world, as may well have been the case with a bat and a Chinese laboratory and a global pandemic.

My curiosity about bats, after learning and seeing that they had taken up residence in the old mine shafts, had been piqued; it drove me to a video clip of a cave in Mexico which is home to ten million Mexican free-tailed bats. The piles of their droppings, up to fifty feet deep, produce ammonia as they decompose. In the clip, scientists entered the cave wearing gas masks: without them they would have blacked out in ten minutes, in twenty minutes they would never have woken up. But for bats, this cave, rather like the old mine shafts, with its perfect temperatures and humidity, provided almost total protection, as no predators could stand it down there for long. Indeed, it was at this point that I wondered whether their creation was perfectly evolved to also cope with Nancekuke's abandoned reserves of deadly nerve gases. In the clip, bats were packed into every square foot of the cave, turning the ceiling into a fur-lined mass of bat bodies. It is one of the most overcrowded, disease-ridden, toxic black holes on earth.

No one really knows how the bats can tolerate such high levels of ammonia. Whatever the reason, I kept coming back to this idea of an apocalypse, of the spread of a virus or a biological or chemical war and the subsequent loss of social order, and of the bats and their love of despoiled landscapes, the only creatures able to tough it out, the only creatures able to neutralise the effects.

Would they be the only creatures at the end of the world left standing, or should I say hanging? Would not their loathsomeness match the loathsomeness of the finale? And I thought how appropriate it was that the bats had set up home near the edge of one of Cornwall's great shames. At the very edge of humanity.

Water, Light, Oil

Gwithian to Hayle

At Mutton Cove the grey seals are scattered on the beach like discarded bullets, their fur agleam in the sun. I am in the artist's light, when the air is clean and the colour temperature has been shifted to the blue side by the reflections from the sea and the sand.

I walk on to Godrevy Head, and descend onto Gwithian Sands. It is where the Red River – and it was still red when I was a child, but no longer – discharged its thick and rusty waters poisoned with tin and copper washings from the mining district around Camborne. At its height, when the bowels of this earth were wrenched open in the pursuit of metal ore, when the land was dishonoured and heavy with heaps and wastes of slags and refuse, it ran blood red all the way down to the sea.

Not today; today I am in one of those moments of feeling, the ones that come with a piece of music, or a poem, looking at a photograph of someone you love. It is so beautiful I am completely overcome. I don't know how else to respond – this light, this day, the perfect sweep of St Ives Bay and its sand dunes: maybe it's because I am finally entering the sacred dimension of my childhood; the beaches I played on, the rock pools I trawled, the kites I flew, the sand art I drew, the mussels I cooked, the freezing waves I jumped, and then repeated all of it again with my own children. Like so very many others, this yearning I have for the sea was contracted in childhood, in Cornwall. Any movement towards the monotonous quietude and relative platitude of internal scenery will always result in me looking back over my shoulder. A landscape without sea is a landscape unfinished, one to travel through, rest a while, but not stay for long.

Virginia Woolf, whose *To the Lighthouse* was inspired by Godrevy Lighthouse, felt much the same way as I do about the Bay. In 1881 her father Sir Leslie Stephen took out a lease on Talland House in St Ives, in order to have a holiday home for his growing family. Woolf would say that these memories of childhood came to define her as a person and as a writer, and much more besides. In her autobiographical essay, 'A Sketch of the Past', she wrote:

> To go away to the end of England; to have our own house; our own garden – to have that bay, that sea, and the mount: Clodgy and Halsetown bog; Carbis Bay; Lelant; Zennor, Trevail, the Gurnard's Head; to hear the waves breaking that first night behind the yellow blind; to sail in the lugger; to dig in the sands; to scramble over the pools and see the anemones flourishing their antenna in the pools; now and then to find a small fish flapping there; to look over the lesson book in the dining room and see the lights changing in the waves ...
>
> If life has a base that it stands upon, if it is a bowl that one fills and fills and fills, then my bowl without a doubt stands upon this memory. It is of lying half asleep, half awake, in bed in the nursery at St Ives. It is of hearing the waves breaking, one, two, one, two, and sending a splash of water over the beach; and then breaking, one, two, one, two, behind a yellow blind. It is of hearing the blind draw its little acorn across the floor as the wind blew the blind out. It is of lying and hearing this splash and seeing this light, and feeling, it is almost

impossible that I should be here; of feeling the purest ecstasy
I can conceive.

In his classic book *Art as Experience*, John Dewey wrote: 'at
every moment the living creature is exposed to danger from its
surroundings, and at every moment, it must draw upon something in its surroundings to satisfy its needs'. He believed that all
art is metabolised through experience and our immediate environment, 'not externally but in the most intimate way'. Certainly
for Virginia Woolf her memories of sound and sea in St Ives Bay
permeated every aspect of her work and informed the concep-
tion of her artistic endeavours. Water, vital for all forms of life,
would become vital for Woolf's creative life as well. She would
find inspiration in its lack of solidity, its patience, its persistence,
its softness, its anger; besides, she needed the equivalent of a river
to wash her dams away, her madness, she needed to keep her
mind flowing freely. Even her characters are immersed in water.
In *To the Lighthouse*, her most autobiographical work of fiction,
the sound of water awakens the characters' thoughts, moods
and emotions. Sometimes the sea soothes, sometimes it disturbs,
everything swinging between order and chaos. Mr Ramsay feels
his many children have import beyond his individual life and will
'stem the flood a bit', but you can't control nature, it is like the
sea itself, it remains constant in its deployment; it just carries on
regardless, through time and mortality, in peace and in war. The
sea is uninterested in civilisation. Woolf uses water again in *Mrs
Dalloway*, which details a day in the life of an upper-class London
housewife. On a large scale the book is about the psychological
realities of post-war England, but the book is permeated with a
fear of death that again manifests itself through water.

On Friday 28 March 1941, Virginia Woolf weighted the pock-
ets of her fur coat with rocks and, wearing wellington boots,
waded into the fast-flowing River Ouse near her home in the
village of Rodmell in Sussex. Her husband Leonard had noticed

she was not quite herself that day and told her to go and lie down. Instead she wrote a suicide note and slipped off through the garden gate to her death. Her body was found three weeks later, washed up near Southease. Water had sustained her life; it made sense that it would also sustain her death.

Virginia's ashes were buried beneath an elm tree in the garden at Rodmell and Leonard had a stone engraved with the last lines of *The Waves*: 'Against you I fling myself, unvanquished and unyielding, O Death! The waves broke on the shore.'

Water is something without beginning and without end; it has no shape of its own, but it can take any shape as its own; it is infinite in its possibilities, in its assortment of appearances and moods. In that it is the same as art, as language, the self-repeating possibilities: there might be a finite number of words, but their arrangements are infinite. I truly believe Woolf, met-aphorically so, took to water because water is like language and language is like water.

Woolf's real success derived from a determination to divert herself from the literary mainstream, which for her was too easy, too certain a flow; she disliked language's transparency, so, using the salmon analogy again, she swam upstream. She made the words move in a way that they had not moved before, she sought out the turbulence in the waves, the ripples, the vortices, she watched the light change on its different surfaces.

In the end, just like Leonardo da Vinci's deluge drawings, where the eye gets lost in a maze of lines depicting waves, whirl-pools, eddies, Woolf's mind also started to echo the abstract expressionism of water in a state of crisis. The lines of force in the water, just like the lines of force in her mind, in the end simply overwhelmed her. Leonardo, who at the end of his life could also no longer be subordinated to the laws of perspective and proportion and harmony which had made him famous, came, with Woolf and many other artists and writers before and after them, to a new understanding of nature, one that is full of chaos and complexity, a system that finally exceeds all control. Disequilibrium, forging our way upstream, it seems, is for life and revolution. Equilibrium, death.

In my mind's eye I can see Virginia and her sister Vanessa standing at the window of Talland House, looking out to Godrevy Lighthouse, its bold, flashing white beam sweeping over their bedroom ceiling throughout the night, bringing them a certain security and rhythm away from the unpredictable dangers that lurked in the hugeness of the ocean outside the bay.

Godrevy Lighthouse sits on its own island of slate. Its bright white tower borders one end of the bay's graceful curve holding a sea ever changing in temper and shade. To the north-west are the remains of an ancient sandstone reef commonly known as the Stones, marked by a black buoy with whistle and bell. In the early nineteenth century, when shipping lanes were busy with boats moving to and from St Ives, sailors would live in dread of the reef taking morsels out their ships' undersides until nothing was left of it but the silence of the dead. For the sailors, the reef lay in wait for them like a steel trap.

Although it's difficult to tell how many ships were wrecked upon the Stones, one of the earliest recorded was on 30 January 1649, when the *Garland*, bound for France, dragged her anchor while sheltering in the bay. She was carrying the possessions of Charles I, who was executed on the same day, and his wife Henrietta Maria, as well as the wardrobe of their son, the Prince of Wales. According to the Arundel manuscripts, the correspondence and collections of Thomas Howard, Earl of Arundel, which now reside in the British Library, various royal valuables were washed ashore, including a scarlet coat with gold buttons.

In 1854, when the SS *Nile*, an iron screw steamer, hit the rocks with the loss of everyone on board, the lobbying for a lighthouse grew in force and urgency, most notably on the part of Richard Short, a St Ives master mariner, who wrote to the *Shipping and Mercantile Gazette* the day after the news of the sinking broke:

Had there been a light on Godrevy Island, which the inhabitants of this town have often applied for, it would not doubt have been the means of warning the ill-fated ship of the dangerous rocks she was approaching. Many applications have been made from time to time concerning the erection of a light to warn mariners against this dangerous reef, but it has never been attended to, and to that account may be attributed the destruction of hundreds of lives and a mass of property . . . Scarcely a month passes by in the winter season without some vessel striking on these rocks, and hundreds of poor fellows have perished there in dark dreary nights without one being left to tell the tale.

Short's appeal was followed by a petition raised by local clergyman, the Reverend J. W. Murray, to Trinity House, who by 1856 had agreed to build Godrevy Lighthouse.

The lighthouse began operating in 1859, with a keeper and two others in residence; supplies were ferried over from St Ives every couple of months, and remained in service until 2012. The warning signal is now on a steel construction on an adjacent rock, but is still managed, albeit remotely, by Trinity House.

Godrevy stands on the edge, not only of the land but of our consciousness. It is and always has been an important feature in artistic representations of St Ives; it marks its boundary, its geographical limits, acts as a signpost to the St Ives story and scoops up all its creators into its bay. Many of them gave it prominence in their work, from Alfred Wallis and Ben Nicholson to Sven Berlin, Tom Early and Patrick Heron. The lighthouse has been used in photographs to locate the sculptures of Brian Wall and most dramatically alongside Barbara Hepworth's work in the famous 1954 film *Figures in a Landscape*.

Why is it so symbolic, aside from its obvious lifesaving functions and position in the landscape? For me its inferences are multiple: mostly, it presents itself as an emblem, a masculine,

almost phallic image resisting the forces of nature. It is a symbol
of resilience and constancy, and just as in *To the Lighthouse*, has
an air of resolution. At the same time, it represents a series of
paradoxes and uncertainties in that it stands between land and
sea, strength and fragility. It embodies a vulnerability against
those same forces, comparable to the fragility of a single fishing
boat tossed on the waves over which it watches. It is the mythical
and the real, undefined and defined. It speaks of isolation and
a disinterestedness and individualism sitting on the edge of the
social. It can act as the impetus to draw the participant in, be it
walker or artist. It reveals the relationship between time and the
moving shoreline, a complex set of negotiations between the individual and the environment. But most of all, and on a personal
level, in a world where nothing stays on course for long, it towers
over my patch of ground, my corner of the earth, the one I need
to return to. It guides me down the Hayle Estuary into harbour;
it brings me to Trewinnard, my family home.

I take the air, deeply, into my lungs, exhale again. I want to share
the impact of this place with my body, share the physicality of
the breeze with the physicality of my breath. Connect them. It
helps me understand how we are all one on this earth. But also,
because there is an absolute cleanliness to it, a purity that is difficult to find in our combustible world. The smell, like taking in the
hair-scent of someone you love. And then the sound, how it oblit-
erates everything else, in all the upheaving and the subsiding; in
my mind as well. The light, in the way it shifts and changes at
the edge; how it dramatises the space as if it is an animate force
in its own right, a character all of its own. All these textures and
this materiality and its flexibility give me a more than satisfying
emotional response; they teach me how to communicate with
the surroundings.

Why is it so utterly pleasant here? This edgeland walk on

the beach? I think it's because all the boundaries between land and sea become blurred, everything is interconnected, cliff face and sea, gull and wind, seal shifting between sea and sand, the grazers and the grazed. It is the in-between nature of the place that makes it so special. It is neither land nor sea. It is a different world entirely, one that is in perpetual motion, being worked and reworked in movements regular, rhythmic and continuous, be it the light, the sound, the surface, the depth. Everything finely balanced in the crossing over. When you walk this path even time is cancelled, because all the motion feels ongoing, feels for ever.

Nothing is for ever, though. The light left the bay on a March day in 1967. And the balance. It was the day a catastrophe turned the sea black, the day the oil supertanker the *Torrey Canyon*, with a captain asleep on the job and a first officer making bad navigational decisions, smashed onto Pollard's Rock on Seven Stones reef, between Land's End and the Isles of Scilly. By sundown an eight-mile slick of crude oil had made its way out of the torn hulk, stretching to a good twenty miles by the following day. The dense, foul-smelling yellowish-black liquid would go on to sequester some 270 square miles of sea; it would wrestle and writhe not only along the north coast of Cornwall but that of Brittany, which had to withstand the heaviest part of the slick's assault. All 119,328 tonnes of oil borne by the *Torrey Canyon* would eventually seep into the Atlantic. Almost instantaneously the edge became a place of wild danger and oscillations. It became a deregulated world.

As is often the case with these disaster events, what follows was a catalogue of missteps. After the crew were brought on shore it was decided that the marooned tanker be bombed, to burn off the oil and scuttle the vessel.

An eyewitness account of the bombing comes from Les Hosking from Marazion. 'We saw the Buccaneer bombers coming in. They dropped bombs and that didn't do anything.' Foam containment booms and attempts to use aviation fuel to burn off the oil both failed. Then, napalm was released on the slick. 'When that came in there was a sheet of flames,' remembers Hosking. 'I've never seen anything like it. The smoke went up into the sky for what seemed like miles.'

Eventually the tanker did break up, but it would take a whole twelve days and even then it did nothing to mitigate the destruction the spillage had already caused. Fifteen thousand seabirds would come into contact with the crude oil, causing them to become smothered and later suffocate to death. Birds' feathers are precisely designed for waterproofing and insulation; if oil reaches them, they become matted and the barbs that keep the feathers in place are misaligned, which makes the bird lose important body heat. Birds will preen to remove the oil from their feathers, but when it lies like a thick gloopy black blanket over them, as it did here, they haven't a hope in the lifting of their wings, the weight just too heavy.

It would take decades for certain species to recover, and the effects of the spill went on for years afterwards. It would alter the entire food chain, from small organisms such as plankton to molluscs to fish; all those creatures that lived a shore life, all the interrelationships and mobility destroyed by one colossal human event. The balance tilted. Everything becoming unstable.

I was only a four-year-old child at the time, but I remember a deep sense of mourning descending on the land. Writing about it even now, I can recall the foul and pungent stench. My father, who was MP for St Ives, the constituency most affected by the oil pollution, had given ample warning in the House of Commons that such a disaster might occur. After all, the Japanese super-tanker *Tokyo Maru* had leaked large quantities of oil off the Isles of Scilly just a year before.

After the *Torrey Canyon* hit the rock, he took it upon himself to alert the government to the seriousness of the situation. He had been on his way back to Penzance from Helston after conducting his surgery and had dropped into a pub in Newbridge for a glass of beer and some lunch. Someone there asked if he had heard about the tanker that was pumping out oil. He hadn't. Those in the pub didn't seem to think much of it. When he got home, he received a call from his political agent, Derek Tovey, who drew a more accurate picture of the situation, and when the leader of the District Council said he couldn't raise anyone in Whitehall my father got straight on the phone, informing the Foreign Office, the Ministry of Defence, the Board of Trade, the US embassy and British Petroleum. No easy task when you are a novice MP, sitting on the opposition benches. After the grounding he would become frustrated again by the then Prime Minister Harold Wilson, who also happened to be his constituent, who was dithering over whether to bomb the grounded ship.

I remember we all headed down to Marazion Beach, including my heavily pregnant mother, where the oil lay six inches thick. Whole families, in response to an appeal, had turned out in a 'King Canute' operation. There must have been a hundred or so residents there, spraying the incoming tide with detergent from garden watering cans. I vaguely remember the oil being brown, like melted chocolate, not a black tide as has been suggested. It was thick and it made the sea shine like a mirror, the waves all changed as they slid the slum water onto the beach. The oil had spread itself on those usually troubled waters and eerily calmed them, drugged them, if you like. My family wanted to join the locals in solidarity, with their buckets and mops which my father now says was completely pointless but what a jobbing MP does: look active, get his picture in the paper. Devasted by the scene, he became proactive in other ways: 'I knew the chairman of BP from my days as a banker and he was far more accessible and helpful than the government. He sent oil dispersants which, I would learn later, did more long-term damage to the marine environment than the oil.'

They certainly did. In contrast, recovery occurred much more quickly here at Godrevy, a site where dispersants were not applied due to concerns about the impact it would have on the seal population. The limpets also helped with the clean-up operation by licking the oil off the rocks.

The *Torrey Canyon* disaster was the worst and most expensive in UK waters. But it also came out of an era when the sea was a huge dumping ground for our waste, the attitude being that the environment was there to be exploited. The disaster therefore did have some positive effects, including the creation of maritime regulations on pollution and the start of ethical conservation, but also changes to the way oil tankers were built and emergency responses to similar disasters were dispatched. More importantly, it is now identified as a key event in the making of modern British environmental consciousness.

Looking back all these years, reading some of the oral histories and listening to my father, it is clear that the disaster very much defined the differences in politics between the centre and the edge. When the government took charge, it arrogantly saw the locals as incompetents and as a result they were progressively sidelined. It was a mistake, because those who live and work the edge are much more familiar with their surroundings; they know when the winds blow and tides change, they understand the coast and its moods and how the wildlife adapt. Particularly the fishermen, who know each gully, each cove, using knowledge passed on, as well as superstition and ancient folklore. It's the classic tension between a metropolitan elite dependent on science and technology and insider knowledge based upon everyday experience working the sea; it happened during the 2001 foot and mouth crisis as well, which resulted in the unnecessary slaughter of more than six million cows and sheep.

The *Torrey Canyon* has become just another element in the shipwreck narrative of Cornish memory. Today, the ship rests in peace at the bottom of the ocean as new generations of marine life weave in and out of its cavities, no doubt blissfully unaware that its broken-up carcass represents such a colossal symbol of human error. But history constantly shows that our exposure to man-made and natural perils is largely rooted in our own negligence and that we forever stand at the edge of potential disaster.

I walk on, and the path pushes me inland among wooden chalets and spiny sea buckthorn bushes and marram grass and this beautiful day feels over.

Saints

Hayle to St Ives

Compared to other estuaries, the Hayle only extends a short way inland, and the coast path runs around its outer edge. Although suburban in places, it is a pleasing hour's amble, and one with which I am intimately familiar; Hayle is the nearest town to my family home. When I was growing up, we called it Hell, because it always looked so down at heel, unloved, its people struggling to make a living this far west.

Hayle's industrial life started as a coal importing and exporting harbour, but by the start of the nineteenth century it would be crowned not only the top mining port but the steam engine manufacturing centre in the world. It happened because it was perfectly positioned to transport vast quantities of copper concentrate to South Wales for smelting in Swansea and to import coal and timber for use in the local mines. Two of the largest foundries in the South West were located here: Sandys, Carne & Vivian at Copperhouse, and Harvey & Company in Foundry Square, in the building with the twin clock tower that now houses the Hayle Heritage Centre. There were huge rivalries between the two companies, occasionally dubbed the 'thirty-year war', as both became engaged in protracted legal disputes. Harvey's helped to produce the largest steam engines ever built, and more mine engines left Hayle than from anywhere else. Until 1819 copper smelting was also undertaken here, which created a lot of waste slag. This was cast into blocks (called scoria) to be used for building, which were given away free to the workforce. Many of the workers' cottages in the town are made of these distinctive dark-coloured blocks.

I walk under the viaduct and into Foundry Square, then go back through the viaduct and the path takes me along the mud-flats of the estuary, a renowned refuge for migratory wading birds and wildfowl. More than 270 species, many of them rarities, have been recorded here.

In fact, what flares out of the river mouth is pure festival. A festival of birds. Like a religious holiday. Like a non-stop music event. It has a vibe. Different acts coming and going during the seasons: widgeon, teal shelduck and swans, goldeneye, little grebe and coot in the autumn. Sometimes a chorus, thousands strong, of golden plover, dunlin, oystercatchers and redshank, sitting in low water, poolside. The low bass frequencies of the ocean behind them a counterpoint to the treble of their cries. There are visitors from the moors, flocks of curlew, and vagrant ring-billed gulls from North America. Overhead peregrines and kestrels drop their heads between their shoulders, looking to pick off the weak. It is busy, chatty, a collective emotional dimension. It is a place where friends turn into family as tides roll back.

From the Saltings I look upstream to the river. The Hayle is only a trickle, but it is my trickle; it ran through my child-hood and far beyond. It is an often-repeated line, from the poet Czesław Miłosz, that 'when it hurts we return to the banks of certain rivers', but it somehow feels appropriate here, for this is the river I return to regularly, to smooth and wash away the difficulties of the world.

Only twelve miles long, the Hayle rises in mining country near Camborne and then courses west, arriving just three miles short of Marazion. After that it flows through a steep wooded valley at

Trescowe Common, another area of mineral extraction, before
swerving sharply north near Relubbus. For its last six miles it
passes below my family home, Trewinnard Manor, which was
built near the top of a hill on its west bank. The river then passes
through the village of St Erth before it reaches the estuary at
Hayle and flows out to sea.

The Hayle was not always such a quiet backwater. It was once
a navigable estuary. My family home owes its importance to
its site and position on the river, not least because it was the
highest tidal landing place, and because it controlled the short-
cut to the Red River and Mount's Bay, an ancient trade route
which avoided the long and often treacherous boat trip around
Land's End.

The old sea paths, which came long before any roads, and by
their very nature are mostly dissolved, always had to be the most
advantageous; they were never based on a whim, everything
was determined by limits and opportunities. On a good sea tide,
a tradesman's boat might ride the river up to Relubbus, where
there was a ford and the river turned east, but mostly he would
decide it was not necessary to go that far, since there was a large
pool and good landing place at Trewinnard. From here it was just
a short portage to the top of the Red River, which would allow
boats to float down with the tide to Mount's Bay. The location
also provided a natural boundary, with Trewinnard at its centre.
The history of the house does not extend to a few hundred years
but a few thousand.

All this happened long before Cornwall became a holiday
destination or even before Arthur was king, or Tristan seduced
Iseult or the arrival of the Romans and the Saxons. As far back as
2500 BC, these explorers came here, to this ground, from all over
the Mediterranean and Germany to trade their pottery and wine
and tin. Any traffic to Ireland, Wales and the Severn Estuary or

to the Midlands would take a sea route and would pass through here for ease and safety.

I often think of the boat traffic below the house. It must have been busy; the boat was the only means of long-distance travel. In the right conditions and with the wind and tide on your side, you could travel and trade in a matter of days. Bronze Age boats in particular were big, often sixty feet, with sewn planks that were capable of carrying considerable weight and a crew of paddlers on board as well. Flat-bottomed, the boats could slip up a muddy estuary with ease.

A boat was found here in 1946, in Trewinnard Pool, when the river had to be diverted in order to dredge and pump for tin. The Pool, the remains of which is now in my ownership, was, and I think still is, very deep in parts. At the bottom, in the deep mud some eighty feet down, in the soft stack of centuries, they found a large wooden barge. In the hull were some black coal-like lumps and a wooden pump made from a hollowed-out tree trunk. Near the boat were two mooring posts. The find was not properly recorded, so it was difficult to verify its date; it was left in its grave and reburied, but for me the mud, size and description support the theory it was a barge from the Bronze Age, and that this site is one of great importance for early trade. A port. A station.

This route continued through the Iron Age where forts and rounds have been found all across the Hayle valley. Then, in Roman times, ancient trackways were built to connect signal stations or marching camps, dispelling the notion that the Romans did not come this far west. By the thirteenth century, silting and sand had reduced the viability of the route and with a decrease in activity its pulse slowed, it concealed its secrets and started to live off its inner reserves, which is how it can be seen today. Only the energy of historical geographers and early historians revive this water memory, follow its turns, seek out its DNA. Had they not been awake we would have all but missed it.

My river, this river, that I have walked along so often, is now a weedy, reedy, unimpressive thing, too small to swim in; it is can-alised in parts by the church in St Erth and is fairly slow flowing, but the fauna is rich, birds in particular, with the sounds of song thrush and linnets and bullfinches and reed buntings as well as warblers. And the vegetation is luxuriant and diverse, with tall water-loving plants including wild angelica and hemlock water dropwort. In the summer the meadowsweet exudes its syrupy-sweet smells into the air.

As for the estuary, it has been dramatically altered from those long-ago days. Lelant lost its town and port and a second church. Three hundred years of sand invasion and coastal movement have only momentarily been reduced by the introduction of elephant grasses. At Gwithian, three chapels and all the buried bones have gone, as well as several farms. The estuary at Hayle has changed its shape and position. And the bridge at St Erth has altered the appearance and use of the river as mining waste has changed the contours of the landscape. The same has happened to the Red River at Marazion, where another lost village lies off the mouth.

It should come as no surprise that the legends of Cornwall have often been wrapped up with the underworld side of the water, where everything can be dark and uncertain; about lost lands such as that of Lyonesse, Tristan's country, which sank beneath the waves between Land's End and Scilly, the 'land of old upheaven from the abyss'.

The lost land of Lyonesse might be a legend, but it still plays into modern fears with its local population who ultimately believe they are beyond salvation; that the sea does, and will, swallow them whole. And we are now being told it could happen by the end of the century. A recent climate assessment report for Cornwall says changes will include high-impact flooding, stronger storms and higher wind speeds, faster coastal erosion, more heatwaves and droughts. The long coastline means a greater hammering from bigger waves than anywhere else in the country. Just walking the path, one is aware how often the edge is crumbling by all the diversions one has to take, away from the edge. If sea levels rise as high as four metres it would have major implications for Cornwall's coast and towns and ultimately the disappearance of the land itself.

According to a gauge in Newlyn's Tidal Observatory, used for recording the rise in sea levels for the whole country, there has been an increase of twenty centimetres over the past sixty years. The trend of a rise of three to four centimetres each year is likely to continue for the next two decades, after which it would start to increase exponentially. Certainly, at nearby St Michael's Mount something is up: the window in which people can walk across the causeway to the island at low tide has shrunk from three hours two centuries ago to around two hours today. Based on current models, the time slot will be down to an hour in forty years' time.

The Cornish are right to be pessimistic. Those on the eastern coastal edges of Britain, who suffer from the same hopeless struggle against the sea and its greed, have always been able to build westwards, but in Cornwall there is nowhere else to go but into the sea.

The myth of Lyonesse also represents an enduring folk memory of another sinking: the flooding of the Isles of Scilly and Mount's Bay. Even today those living in Penzance say they get occasional glimpses of a drowned forest in the bay, when petrified tree stumps are revealed at extreme low water. Submerged ruins have been found off the Isles of Scilly as well, including sunken roads, the foundations of houses, tombs and cairns.

Just as some events are predetermined – decay, death, the seasons, the recurring rhythms of life – the Cornish know they are ultimately fated to sink below the ocean to a place where nereids play lyres and 'green translucency beats', and where they can be gently 'lapped by the moon-guiled tide'. The isolation in which they stand, and the threats faced, have made them probably the most resilient people on our island. The wildness of the

sea has bred a race of seamen and smugglers, and their mineral
wealth has dragged thousands of them underground. Through
some strange principle of being they stay, and they stay because
they have made themselves a tribe out of the affections for their
obstacles. They are ordained by the cause of fate, one that can
be temporarily mastered but never conquered. In the words of
Marcus Aurelius, 'Whatever may happen to thee; it was prepared
for thee from all eternity; and the implication of causes was from
eternity spinning the thread of thy being ... it is all part of the
great web.'

Trewinnard Pool was given to me by my mother, Miloska Nott,
more than a decade ago. It caused something of a row between
my brother and me as he was all set to inherit the entire estate.
But our mother, who was born in Maribor in Slovenia, ten miles
from the Austrian border, had been defined by her experiences
of living through the Second World War. Her gift to me was to
do with her survival as a woman, of losing her own land, not
to the sea but to the rising tides of fascism in early twentieth-
century Europe.

Abandoned by her teenage mother at two months old, my
mother's father, who became a fighter with the anti-Nazi
National Liberation Army and Partisan Detachments of
Yugoslavia, placed his daughter, for her own protection, with
a farming family up in the hills. She remembers those days as
some of her happiest; the only thing she ever recalls buying was
coffee and sugar. On the farm they killed all their own pigs and
cattle, and preserved meat for the winter in pigs' fat. There was
a small plum orchard from which they made their own slivovitz.

You'd think we are mostly influenced by the landscapes that
contain us, like the Cornish are, the ones we feel and touch, that
are nearby, but this is not always the case. Often everything
that lived previously somehow arrives back again: a smell, an

understanding, methods and procedures, a fear. My mother gave me this patch of ground because of her days spent on the Slovenian farm. She is of the belief that anyone can survive if they go back to subsistence agriculture; and her daughter will survive also if she has to, but only if she has some ground. In her heart that farm was where she lived the longest; it does not matter that it has been twisted by time or removed by distance: she has lived in that gap between one world and another, and like all exiles she has spent a lifetime reconciling the two.

My mother first came to England to study English at Cambridge, and met my father at her engagement party to another man. Raised a communist, she switched smoothly between fiancés, then on into the life of a political spouse of an arch-capitalist. She had three children, and after the purchase of Trewinnard, which lay in the heart of my father's constituency, resulted in a dire shortage of money she turned once more to the soil. She delivered her first sheep with a book in her hand and built up a herd of pedigree Hereford Cattle to a hundred head:

'I remember delivering my first calf; it was a breech birth and I was alone in the field at night with the mother but I didn't have the strength for it. I tied a cord around the legs of the calf and lay down on my tummy and yanked it out. Usually they are easy-calving cattle, but not this one. I loved the Herefords, they were single-sucklers and made lovely mothers; they have nice, docile natures, but in the end we didn't make any money from them. The bulls lost size because the land was too rich and they became fat.'

My mother switched her attentions to her daffodil-growing business. She took back some fields she had let to a farmer in Newlyn, thinking, 'if he could do it, I can do it as well'. She started with seven rows of plants and finished up with seventy-two acres of them; at its height the business employed more than sixty flower-pickers paid on piece rates, with about three hundred boxes of daffodils dispatched to markets around the country every day. Back then there was no imported European labour, it was still a cut-off place where locals usually laboured as agricultural workers or in the tourism industry; there wasn't much in between. 'I got on very well with the pickers, they accepted me as a real foreigner – not the sort of foreigner from over Plymouth bridge.'

Cornwall, because of its extreme south-westerly position, has a unique situation for the growing of the narcissus tribe. The mild maritime climate helps it crop the earliest open-ground flowers in the country. In fact, early growers even planted their daffodils in very small fields as near to the sea edge as possible to benefit from the sea's warming influence and some still do, particularly on the Isles of Scilly, which sit dead centre in the Gulf Stream's warm whispers.

The British love of daffodils, which is perhaps to do with respect for the flower's determination to defy the weather and push cheerily through the hard ground of deep winter, also helps. The flower can be untended, undemanding but flirtatious, brightening the landscape long before spring arrives, offering an optimistic signal that change is on its way. For a small industry, Cornwall's production of daffodils is also culturally important: it has become part of its identity, an indicator of its independent will. It may not be the centre of production – the Netherlands produces more, and Lincolnshire's acreage is larger – but in Cornwall it is more than just another commercial crop. Here, it is like an original thought rather than a copied one.

I still have a vivid picture of my mother picking in yellow oil-skins, her straining rump among the tight-fisted yellow buds, her legs bestriding the rows; the movement is rhythmic and similar to milking, except this procedure ends in a snap. The sticky sap to which she is allergic is drooling into her rubber-gloved hands. Ten to a bunch; she straightens up to band it, then falls back again to the earth, every bit the peasant. It is Bruegel's *Landscape with the Fall of Icarus*, the labourer's indifference to the suffering of others. This is the ordinary event that continues to occur, like the Flemish proverb, 'And the farmer continued to plough ...' (*En de boer ... hij ploegde voort*). I interpret it slightly differently, a mother's indifference to her husband's glittering political career in Westminster. It is the energy of the earth my mother responds to, not the politics, and the Gulf Stream, bringing the flowers early at the edge. But it was a hard life, starting at four in the morning, packing boxes in cold sheds, treating her hands with antihistamine cream, her allergy swelling up her face and hands. I remember her saying to me at the time, 'If anyone puts daffodils on my grave, I will come out of it and haunt them.'

When my mother hit her fifties, she began a furious search for what preceded her life in this country; it was as if she had become trapped in another person's dream. Her memory left England and returned to Slovenia, 'an emigrant / wandering in a place, / where love dissembles itself as landscape: / Where the hills / are the colours of a child's eyes, / where my children are distances, horizons'. Slowly she put the jigsaw pieces of her early life back together; she discovered half-brothers and -sisters, aunts, nieces, surviving members of her foster family; she obtained pictures of her mysterious heroic father, even a copy of a letter he sent from Dachau, where he died with other partisans. After that she returned time and time again to the farm, supporting the family and its descendants to survive as they had supported her.

Then, while watching moving images of people trying to defend their lives against an aggressor, she became immersed in the Bosnian conflict. She had found parallels with her early life, of what life was like at the edge, when the ordinary suddenly becomes the extraordinary. In 1992, when more than eighty-six thousand refugees came into Slovenia, she set up a charity to help with the schooling of the children. A year later, she started to go over the mountains in Bosnia, delivering medicine on the front line at considerable personal risk. Tired and emotional, she would come home, collect some more cash from wherever she could source it and then go off again. The conflict entered its gruesome endgame at Srebrenica in July 1995, when more than eight thousand Muslims were killed after the town fell to Serb forces. NATO responded with a three-week bombing campaign in August. Three months later, the Dayton Peace Agreement ended the war. My mother started working in Srebrenica in 2002. Since then she has built over three hundred houses, three schools and a clinic. She raised money for sheep and cattle, and planted a fruit orchard. With dogged determination, and helped by local, national and international contributions, she raised four million pounds for her charity. The hollow-cheeked old men and grieving mothers still greet her in the villages as if she is some sort of saint. She was awarded the OBE for her efforts.

Is my mother a saint? No, of course not. For one, she hasn't ended up dead because of her valiant exertions, but if you think of saints as those who want to correct the world, without restraint and with exuberance, that come, argue the case, leave behind truths, then she certainly falls into that category.

When I look at my mother's life, the whole pattern of it, its shape, the way it was informed, I know it has left its mark, not least on me or my family and those she has helped in Bosnia. There are physical marks too, on the soil there and here, the one she ploughed, planted, nurtured livestock, grew trees, passed over. She is Slovene by birth, but she is Cornish and Bosnian also, in that she invested in those places, in their conditions and their character and history and people and their soil. Above all, in their soil.

In many ways, she is the living embodiment of the daffodil she so hates. A symbol of spring, of new beginnings and rebirth. She is a positive, life-affirming individual whatever the winds chuck at her, and as anyone who knows her will tell you, the holder of a permanently sunny disposition.

The piece of ground that comes to me, the one I say is mine – the one on which a granite house sits overlooking a small river, the one that can protect me, and which I come back to always to find my peace – is in my life because my mother responded gravely to the sad penalties of conflict, knowing that land might be the cause of war, but that it can also be its cure.

There are eight ancient stone crosses in Lelant, whose movement from their original locations have slightly confused their history. What matters is that they are scattered about here, and they originate from a time when this was a feral and inhospitable heather-levelled moorland, strewn with granite intrusions through which single struggling streams interlaced; when there were no landmarks and no fences and no wheel tracks, just the soft incursions of angels' feet bringing a new worship. For the wayfaring palmers and pilgrims arriving from Ireland or Wales, it was better to disembark here and walk the twelve and a half miles cross-country to St Michael's Mount than negotiate the wild winds and waters around Land's End. These crosses would have been welcoming beacons, soothing signals in the solitude of their faith, guardians of their westward course. And not always statements about the dead, but exhortations, an asking of those who walk by to read or pray. To touch these stones today is to touch the rough language of saints and their excitements to holy feeling.

It is these early missionaries, now commemorated as saints, who have lent their names to many of Cornwall's churches and religious sites. And the route they took is now known as St Michael's Way. Some of the arrivals were emigrants building on trade links, others were escaping famine and conflict in their own countries, and the devout among them were responsible for Cornwall's conversion to Christianity.

I stand in the enchanting graveyard of the church of St Uny looking at some of the crosses which would have led these wandering devouts from hermitage to chapel, from cave to sacred spring; standing in solemn stone to honour an old Syria, a lost battle, a wayfarer's grave. In those long-forgotten days men on the eastern flanks of our land would make vows to each other to make pilgrimage to St Michael's in the west; this route, after all, is as old as the hills, and is part of a network of trails leading to Santiago de Compostela.

The church, far removed from the village, sits on a chunk of headland with commanding views over the medieval harbour and the estuary. It probably originates from the arrival of St Uny at the end of the fifth century, but like many of the churches I have visited on this edge, St Uny has been overwhelmed by the movement of sand and rescued twice, in the thirteenth century and again in the seventeenth.

Uny had navigated his small boat up the estuary on an incoming tide to reach here. With him were his brother Ercus (now known as St Erth), who was the bishop of Slaine in Ireland and said to have been baptised by the great St Patrick himself, and his two sisters, Ia and Anta. Ercus promptly moved downriver to where the bridge now crosses the River Hayle at St Erth and there began his work converting the Cornish heathen. It was thought Trewinnard was another up-country cell, or small chapel, serving part of the area that was controlled by St Uny. Ia went west towards St Ives, which was to be named after her, the name travelling through Sancte Ye, Seynt Ya, Seynt Iysse, Seynt Iees and other variants before reaching its modern form. Here, she built her oratory on the site of the present parish church and gained her martyrdom at the hands of Thedric, King of Cornwall. Anta, meanwhile, created a cell up on the point opposite the black rock where Godrevy Lighthouse now stands. Uny, who remained in Lelant, was also martyred during a local skirmish but the remains of his chapel are said to be on the sixth green of the golf course ...

Despite the golf course, one does feel an extra dimension here, otherworldly, not only geographically but spiritually. There is a real sense of an added energy, one that seems to rise up from layers of early Christian history; layers piled one on top of another. This is combined with a mysterious kind of interplay between the intangible and the material. Landscape knows how to mess with the human soul.

Such surges of faith, as experienced by these early pilgrims, are now rare and sporadic in our sceptical secular society, even when the temperature rises in the liturgical calendar, such as with Lent and Christmas. Faith practitioners are viewed as oddities and healing happens in hospitals. God-hater Richard Dawkins has built a career on this cynicism. In *The God Delusion* he writes, 'I suspect that alleged miracles provide the strongest reason many believers have for their faith; and miracles, by definition, violate the principles of science ... I imagine the whole business is an embarrassment to more sophisticated circles within the Church. Why any circles worthy of the name sophisticated remain within the Church is a mystery.' You can almost hear him hissing as he says it.

And yet here I am, back at St Uny's Church, thinking about these things. Yes, I too, am a member of this new secular society that he taps into, a non-believer. But I look at the stunted, single-eyed benign cross that is to the left of the church door, and follow the raised cross with my finger. And I am feeling – most definitely feeling – a disorder of perception through a hidden religious pulse. I think the reason why that is the case is because this is an object of exchange. While the sacred past projects onto me, I in turn project my own spiritual longings back onto this cross; it has the capacity, unlike so many other objects, to make me step out of time and out of myself. Put simply, there are objects that can move you unusually, that come from the minds of others, that come from better truths.

Magnet

St Ives to Zennor

S t Ives. The quality of the light is ephemeral and ever-changing; it is something to do with the climate of the region and the situation of the town and its surroundings, and the interplay of its components: the clarity of the air, cloud, sea, sand, diffused light, reflection, mist. These combined qualities act as an invisible force on the imagination, an attraction, it is why the artists came here to work, why they still come; to the wide-windowed lofts and the old-fashioned wooden studios, in houses overlooking the lighthouse where great Atlantic swells, on a windy day, ride like white horsemen onto the rocks. St Ives acts like the earth itself, like a giant bar magnet. As if it has some sort of molten iron running through its core, something that brings everything in.

Here in St Ives the artists respond like compasses, they are able to move freely, respond to what surrounds them and what a variety it is, from fishing boats far out in the bay, turbulent seas, moorland pathways, ancient stones, the width of Lelant Downs, the loneliness of Hayle Towans, the lighthouse, the dark chimneys of industry against a blue sky. Of course, there are other lovely parts of Britain to paint, but nowhere else have they come in such large numbers, nowhere else have they settled and created such an evolving and long-lasting colony.

I believe painters also came here because of the edge influence, the fundamental human movement westwards. They were attracted to a place towards which the sun appears to constantly progress, and where it eventually sets. To where it all ends in drama. To where the land gives out. Artists have always followed the light's trajectory. Moreover, the nearing of the edge offers abundant inspiration: it gathers, collects, assembles, and in so doing creates its own community of like-minded people. These are often those from a 'disparate farness', people who want to break down barriers, the accepted order; people who want to rebuild in their own likeness. The edge is something they inherently understand because a painting is full of different limits and ends: moving from one object to another, from one colour to another, one plane or face to another face within a frame. Here in St Ives they will be inspired by the natural edges.

I stroll through the narrow cobbled streets to pick up the coast path through Porthmeor Beach and past the Tate Gallery, and out towards the open heathland of Clodgy Point. Tourists are crawling through the back streets like army ants, battalions several thousand strong; moving in streams and slipstreams. It is easy to do: the town runs down hills, the buildings rising and falling in light and shadow, they are whitewashed and built over cavernous cellars with external staircases. Everything is dropping to the sea, into a harbour embracing a colourful riot of small boats and seaside sounds that stack in layers high above your head, including clouds of gulls, swooping, swirling, thieving.

St Ives sits in a time warp, the fishermen drying their nets on the green slopes of The Island may have gone, and the smell of pilchards also, but it remains gloriously unspoilt. It somehow always reminds me of walking the Cinque Terre in Italy, the coastal area within Liguria and its five villages. St Ives has a definite continental feel about it, particularly at night or if viewed from the sea.

I still have to pinch myself that this small reeking pilchard port, far from anywhere, came to be the centre of a post-war art movement and rivalled even the grand metropolis of New York. How it successfully brewed up a common philosophy that was not only closely connected with the raw elements of the rocks, the soil and the ocean and the influence of the weather around it, but also, and far more decisively, with the idea that life in abstract can convey an even clearer meaning than is possible in visual language. It was the abstract painters who translated this end of Cornwall into sombre geographical patterns and movements, as in the case of Ben Nicholson, considered by many to be the founder of the modern movement. But it would create tensions as well; before the 1940s most of the artists were members of the St Ives Society of Artists, but by the end of that decade disputes started to arise between the abstract and the figurative, until the abstract faction broke away to form a different society, the Penwith Society of Arts, led by Hepworth and Nicholson.

Hepworth, St Ives's most famous daughter, the first great woman sculptor, would never change her outlook. Besides, she saw the world differently: in shapes, size, texture, in colour, in forms. She wanted to simplify what she saw, be sovereign over the visual. Her imagery wouldn't have slight or partial references to other things, it would be large in size, bold and confrontational, and different from what preceded it. That independence would entirely mirror her own life in St Ives and establish her fame.

Hepworth's philosophy, which lay behind much of her sculpture, was that 'there is an inside and an outside to every form. When they are in special accord, as for instance a nut in its shell or a child in the womb, or in the structure of shells or crystals, or when one senses the architecture of bones in the human figure, then I am most drawn to the effect of light.' And light is everything for Hepworth: 'Light gives full play to our tactile perceptions through the experience of our eyes, and the vitality of forms is revealed by the interplay between space and volume.' If you follow her wisdom, the inside of this town, with its primeval outside and every ray cast by a sun from ever-changing angles, gives St Ives not only its translucent, beautiful light but also its harmony.

And St Ives, this town on the edge, was positively brimming with form, colour and meaning:

> The sea, a flat diminishing plane, held within itself the capacity to radiate an infinitude of blues, greys, greens and even pinks of strange hues, the lighthouse and its strange rocky island was the eye: the island of St Ives an arm, a hand, a face. The rock formation of the great bay had a withinness of form that led my imagination straight to the country of West Penwith behind me – although the visual thrust was straight out to sea. The incoming and receding tides made strange and wonderful calligraphy on the pale granite sand that sparkled with felspar and mica. The rich mineral deposits of Cornwall were apparent on the very surface of things; geology and prehistory – a thousand facts induced a thousand fantasies of form and purpose, structure and life which have gone into the making of what I saw and what I was.

As a woman, what I find most fascinating about Hepworth is how she, despite being a mother of four in a male-dominated era, managed, through a gruff but determined personality, to take on the cosy traditions of the British art world. Even then she had to play second fiddle to that other great sculptor Henry Moore. As her critical status grew so did the resentment and jealousy. Even in St Ives there was pub talk of artists urinating against her garden wall or couples making love behind the statues in her garden. The artist Peter Lanyon was said to be 'obsessional' about Hepworth. However dissident Lanyon's call for revolution in all matters art-political may have been, he and the St Ives avant-garde were not prepared to approve equality of gender as one of them; in their view women were better equipped to be artists' wives and muses than artists in their own right. Women of the era were also negative; they decided Hepworth had only been able to succeed as a career artist by being a dysfunctional parent.

When Ben Nicholson separated from Hepworth – they had married in 1938 and divorced in 1951 – she retreated to Trewyn, her studio-garden in St Ives. It was as if she was trying to exist in one of her own sculptures, work out her own enclosure of space. Trewyn – now the Barbara Hepworth Museum, and possibly my most favourite museum in the world – was hidden behind a high stone wall. Outside, they would continue to compare her to the moon – distant, cold and sterile – but inside was an entirely different story: landscaped walks and subtropical greenery dotted with installations that conveyed her deeply creative engagement in ideas about relationships.

It became increasingly apparent Hepworth was at the top of her game. Her achievements, always meticulously and proudly recorded in the local press, included an increasing tally of international exhibitions, commissions and prizes. Hepworth had become the magnet to which everyone wanted to cling, she was the star; around her was an invisible force field, drawing everyone to the town. This was much easier for the non-art community to celebrate; local politicians, including my father, came to see her as a civic institution, a secular patron saint, a reliable feature of the town's artistic heritage compared to other artists that had come and gone before her.

But the truth runs deeper than that: when an artist is elevated over the heads of other artists, it is often because she or he is the one that connects with the people on the ground, the ones looking up to the sky for clarity. For those less able to express or understand themselves, Hepworth explained to them, through stone, marble, wood and bronze, how all sensitivity to landscape lies in one's ability to feel within one's body a primitive humility, a response to life and location, a response to form, texture and rhythm, and a response to the magic of light from an

ever-changing sun and moon. Hepworth interactively involved
her community with material substance and in doing so she gave
them context.

I am thinking about Hepworth as I prepare to enter the strange
dimension of West Penwith, keeper of some of the finest Neolithic
tombs, stone circles, standing stones, hill forts, fogous holy wells
and stone crosses known to this land. I am thinking about the
properties of stone as material, how measurable it is. Material
is the matter from which something can be made, and it can
be built upon by our imagination; the stoniness does not have
to be constant or brutal, a formless lump of geological matter,
but something that can be endlessly variable in relation to light
or shade, wetness or dryness and the position of the onlooker.
Something in which we can find accord. When I come to look
at the stone here, I no longer see it as just part of the landscape,
as something that merely exists between earth and air, but as a
connection between nature and civilisation, the physical world

and the world of ideas; Hepworth taught me that. And the stones
in West Penwith are most definitely the ones that have become
entangled with human life, in their social and historical frame-
work. Here the stones are not about the characteristics of their
materials but in the emotions expressed making them. If we feel
an emotive charge from the atmosphere in a place like West
Penwith, or from a thing such as an ancient stone tomb, a religious cross, a circle, it is because something real and important
is still residing there to connect us.

Nowhere does Cornwall express its terrestrial rawness better
than on the path from St Ives to Zennor as it pulls you into
West Penwith. Nowhere is the impatience of age more ignored.
Nowhere has a god made himself less felt. I have done this walk
many times in my life and I never feel as alone as I do out here.
It is a place that makes its own laws, finds its own justice, employs
its own guards. You are its prisoner until you turn inland, and it
is entirely inhospitable: it erupts stones in odd places, it damages
your knees and makes your ankles slide, it chucks weather at you
in grand gestures. And yet its sway over us is somehow what we
are seeking; it has the power to stimulate the mystical faculties of
human nature, those so commonly crushed to earth by the cold
details and criticisms of civilisation and its gods. It offers all the
elemental, cosmological themes of fire, water, stone, birth, death
and the regeneration of life. It brings you back to the start of
things. 'The sea on the wild coast is like the dawn of the world,'
wrote D. H. Lawrence, who lived here. 'Oh, it is good, there are
no more Englands, no nations, only the dark strong rocks and
the strong sea washing up out of the dawn of the sky. It is the
beginning, the beginning only.'

The name Penwith stems from two Cornish words, *penn*,
meaning 'headland', and *wydh*, meaning 'at the end'. And there
is an end-of-the-world feeling here, lodged between a promise
of attachment at one end and its termination on the other. That
separateness is helped by the fact that it is almost an island,

surrounded by sea on three sides: the Atlantic Ocean to the north and the English Channel to the south, with just four miles between them, and the Land's End peninsula forming its westernmost tip. In fact, to the east, almost running from coast to coast, lies the River Tamar, so in geographical terms Cornwall is almost completely surrounded by water, like a proper island.

It is also one of the longest successively occupied and managed landscapes on the planet. A land full of the debris of stone-based lives. The left-behinds of our old Celtic and pre-Celtic ancestors. They sit in the landscape in a lumpy, grounded defiance, like muscles flexing. Some of the dolemens, or as they are called in Cornwall 'quoits', the slabs of rock standing like giant stone tables in the landscape, could be up to four thousand years old. When these tombs were built, they were once covered over with earth and were known as barrows; West Penwith is full of them.

I sit for a moment and follow these necklaces of granite boulders with my eyes, and say to myself, yes, this is where it all began, where civilisation took hold, here, under raptor pinions, on a lonely moor, at a south-westerly point. But it's not like a house where somebody dies and someone else moves in; no one has ever moved in here. This is a left-behind land, one that exists on the edges of ignition. It never seems to flinch with modernisation. Nowhere else in Britain seems so closed, so ancient, yet contains so much.

Geography matters here; the arrangement of things matters: the elemental clash where the granite outcrop reaches the sea gives it its rugged coastline, the fabric of the air that sculpts the tors on the rock-strewn ridges of its moorland hills already rich in tin and copper, the running water chiselling its channels, the sea theatres gorged into the basalt, the blue Atlantic glistening in the sunlight, a solar calendar that allows the sun to have a spectacular watery birth and death. Everything perfectly ordered, in the same way that dancers move together in harmony and in narrative. It is as if it has perfected the art of mystery all by itself.

D. H. Lawrence had a true sense of its character when he came to live here in 1916, in the parish of Zennor. He recognised early its inner aloofness and despondency in its relationship to the rest of the country. It somehow matched the despair he already felt for the Great War, which had been exacerbated by being attached to a German wife and the banning of his latest novel, *The Rainbow*. Lawrence by now wanted to be 'out of England', he wanted to be rid of the war, rid of the degradation created by the forces of industrialisation, rid of working men who only thought of 'wages and money and machinery'. He needed to find a place that would offer him romantic excitement, a place where he could create an alternative utopian community of like-minded spirits. West Penwith would be that place; it would be his '*Rananim*' – a quirky, idealistic name of Hebrew derivation which he had borrowed from one of the lyrical songs of his Ukrainian émigré friend Samuel Koteliansky. Lawrence had fled west, into the sun, just as many have done before and many will continue to do after him.

'I do like Cornwall,' he wrote. 'It is something like King Arthur and Tristan. It has never taken the Anglo-Saxon civilisation, the Anglo-Saxon sort of Christianity. One can feel free here, for that reason – feel the world as it was in that flicker of pre-Christian Celtic civilisation, when humanity was really young – like the Mabinogion – not like Beowulf and the ridiculous Malory.'

Other like-minded souls felt this Celtic pull as well: Katherine Mansfield and her husband John Middleton Murry, and the composer Philip Heseltine, then a budding Celticist obsessed with pagan and pre-Christian Cornwall. As is the way with intensively creative people, and despite having shared interests and goals, these relationships would ebb and flow; newcomers would be introduced, and some dismissed. Then the thumping beat of politics would disrupt Lawrence's *Rananim*; he and his wife Frieda would be expelled from the county by military authorities, as part of what he called a 'war-wave'. The writer who had come to live at the edge, their edge, represented the end of history, politics and change, and anti-utopians do not like perfection or any of its forms. Lawrence would leave feeling Cornwall had at last been submerged by the English spirit, by its war spirit, and that this was contrary to its stubborn character.

And yet the relationship between utopias and politics is not quite so clear cut; politics might reject utopias, but policies are often built from them. The dreams and nightmares that concerned Lawrence originated from the way he saw others arrange their lives; his *Rananim* was an expression of this, it stemmed from a discontent with his 'now'. It was, in effect, his social dream, and the writings that followed provided a route into the debates of his time. And politics needs *Rananims*; it needs to have access to people's fears and desires because politics and utopias after all have parallel and overlapping concerns, each feeds the other, each sustains the other.

I walk off the coast path and up a tarmacked track into the last parish of Britain, which includes the village of Zennor. The village sits some 360 feet above the sea and consists of a few houses, a pub and a church; it has a wonderful end-of-the-world charm to it. A place so remote it has managed to anchor down its old traditions and beliefs. I am here to see the famous mermaid that resides in St Senara's Church; she is carved into an oak panel, on the end of a church bench. Zennor's hidden treasure.

The story of the Mermaid of Zennor is a folk tale centred on a beautiful and richly dressed woman who occasionally attends services in this church. So enchanted are the parishioners by her beauty and her voice that she becomes a source of intense gossip. The fact that no one knows where she has come from, and that she appears so infrequently over the years and never seems to age, only adds to the mystery. After many years, she does, however become interested in a young man named Mathey Trewella, who is known as the best singer in the parish. One day he follows her home and disappears; neither is ever seen again. The belief being he has been taken to her home under the blue-green waters off Zennor Head. The parishioners at St Senara's subsequently commemorated the story by having one end of a bench carved in the shape of a mermaid with some believing later that the famed 'mermaid chair' was actually the same bench on which the mermaid had sat and sung, opposite Trewella in the singing loft.

The mermaid is a symbolic edgeland creature. As the artist and writer Alex Woodcock explains: 'In the medieval period to which she belongs, extremes of form and place were closely linked. On the old maps the monsters frolic at the edges, warning the unwary of where the known world thins out. In the church too the mermaid is a portent, a sign that this is not a normal space but a place of overlap, from time to time, a supernatural tide might roll in.' It is why the mermaid is the most common paranormal creature to be found around Cornwall's coast, and the county has almost twice as many legends about individual mermaids as the next closest location, the Hebrides. A close study of the Zennor mermaid appears in the *Ordinalia*, the medieval mystery plays written primarily in Middle Cornish, where she is portrayed as an androgynous figure. But mermaids crop up elsewhere as well: from the Mermaid's Rock at Lamorna to that well-known Cornish sailor's song, 'The Mermaid'. Seaton, near Looe, is said to have lost its standing as a major port when a mermaid blocked up the harbour after being insulted by a local man. Mermaid emblems are frequently found in Cornish churches, which were built by and for fishermen and their families, and are mainly negative symbols of diabolical temptations though lust: 'We have lingered in the chambers of the sea / By sea-girls wreathed with seaweed red and brown / Till human voices wake us, and we drown.'

These strange tales of mermaids take place in the littoral zone, where land and sea meet, between the high and low tide zones. Today it is an area mostly used for leisure, but it still inspires, it still intoxicates; artists, from writers to painters, still hear the siren song and are drawn to it. Marc Quinn's *The Zone* and the *Before and After Humans* series depict the ocean as a washing machine of churning blue-green water full of light and beauty. Through his depictions he tells us water can exist without us, but we cannot exist without it. More than that, we are spellbound by it: we see this through scenes populated by swimmers – Mathey Trewella might as well be one of them – this is our built-in life support system. But in later works, there is no human content;

Quinn goes back to the beginning, 'as the planet was billions of years ago before the emergence of life on land or like it will be in billions of years of time when the planet has destroyed itself and is finding a new equilibrium'. When you look at these pictures you see the space from which we have come: swimming, crawling, walking from the mermaid's world. You understand how water haunts us.

The mermaid story is a story about the sea, and in Mathey Trewella we have our response to it; our longing, our memory, our origins, our returns. Our relationship with the oceans is not just about economics, food, survival, it is about so much more; in its science our bodies share its density, our blood has a similar composition to that of seawater, and both are enriched by salts. When we are just beginning, we have gill slit structures and for nine months we are contained in amniotic fluid. But it also drives our decisions and desires, even our grief: the salt in seawater is in our sweat, our blood, our tears. Truly, we are drawn by the sea, haunted by it, as if we have lost our place and can't quite work out how we can ever go back. How do we come to terms with the truth that, many millions of years before this one, we scrambled up a beach and over a rock without even a by your leave? Is that why melancholia can descend upon us when we come to the end of landscape? As if what we are really doing is looking for repatriation with the great mother of life, the seas. Is that why it keeps accepting us, taking us back into its shiny blue-green emptiness?

Into the Sacrifice Zones

Zennor to Cape Cornwall

At Wicca Cove I am on the lookout for the royal fern, *Osmunda regalis*. I had been alerted to this plant once again by Allen G. Folliott-Stokes who, in his *The Cornish Coast and Moors*, said it grew plentifully along these cliffs. What was intriguing was that he refused to mention the exact spots where this occurred. He goes on to explain that this is on account of the 'extraordinary infatuation some people have of tearing up by the roots any flowers or ferns they imagine to be at all rare, quite regardless of whether they have in their gardens suitable soil to put them in, which in nine cases out of ten they have not. The result is that some localities have been almost denuded of their most interesting plants.'

Folliott-Stokes was living in the aftermath of the Victorian pteridomania, or 'fern fever', which swept through the South West. It was an obsession not confined to a few professional botanists or amateur gardeners, but which affected men women and children of all classes. Cornwall and (most notably) Devon were to become a rich seam for the fern fanatics on account of the mild oceanic climate and diversity of topography, geology and soils which for millennia had provided ideal conditions for many species of the British fern flora to live and thrive.

The cult started with a general interest about the plant, but as soon as new discoveries and localities were documented in journals, it became the plant equivalent of the Gold Rush. This enthusiasm spawned a group of collectors who fuelled a new interest in including the plant in garden design, scientific research and more gentle pastimes such as pressing the fronds into albums. Others would start to deal in the plants themselves, making it a profession.

Areas that were previously remote became accessible to visitors through the opening up of the railways, and accidents also became more common, as did fatalities, while over-collecting and fern-stealing became endemic. Before long, ruthless collectors, working on behalf of fern vendors, would clear whole locations of their ferns, which they would then ship off to the cities, where they would be mood-boosters among the bricks and smoke. Meanwhile, fern nurseries grew up in Ilfracombe and Lynton, with a mail-order service for those who could not make the long hike west.

Folliott-Stokes was not the only one to take offence, and to attempt to conceal the location of prize ferns. The botanist Frederick Hamilton Davey commented that the 'continued depredations on the part of local and itinerant fern-vendors render it undesirable to give a list of localities for this handsome species. In some of the districts with which I am acquainted such shameful plundering has gone on that I now hesitate to speak or write about localities where the royal fern grows. A collector once boasted to me that he had recently dispatched a truck-load of roots, weighing over five tons, from one of our railway stations.'

The art of collecting can often be an unfaithful act when overcome by greed. Folliott-Stokes clearly saw it this way, as a hobby stemming from a terrible desire to possess that which we cannot own or control. He would also have seen it, and rightly so, as a violation of our heritage. By tearing up these living fossils, collectors were in effect removing the long memory of eyewitnesses to the earth's dance. Looting a plant is just as bad as looting a grave; it divorces it from its location and therefore its history and context, making it meaningless.

Wild plant legislation was introduced in 1902, but what saved the ferns was not a law but a loss of interest; by 1891 most of the earlier motivators of the craze had died and their followers moved on to new pastures of obsession. From being the most wanted of plants, ferns fell to being the most despised.

I confess I didn't initially get the fern. I didn't get it at all. It stands in its strangeness, unfurling on tides of sea-sprayed cliffs, faint wet stains in the air, its green luminous. But with rocks fragile and a sea anxious around, these plants have an undeniable confidence in their spread and staying power. They are, after all, descendants of some of the oldest traditions found on earth, older than any mountain or sea or continent. They have outlived dynasties of animals; they have seen continents drown;

they have printed their form into fossils when mass extinctions occurred. They have survived it all. With them you can wander into a theatre of time, touching ages and forms in a delirium of immensities where units are not measured by minutes but by millions. Here is a plant so utterly oblivious to deep time, to the anarchy and energy of the universe, you simply cannot help but become intrigued.

So how did they spread? For a long time, no one really knew. A plant so secret, so unshowy. Where were the flowers, to produce seeds? Early beliefs centred on them coming into being on Midsummer's Eve, with a fleeting spray of flowers, before vanishing again. It was not until late in the eighteenth century that the basic details of ferns' complicated reproductive process were known.

The actual secret of the fern's success derives from the start of its 'colonisation' or 'journey' from its protective parental stem, which is ballistic, cannon-like, firing on all cylinders. After that initial burst, drag will slow it down, causing it to plunge more sharply than it climbs. From there the long draught of dispersal takes over, pushing the spore several hundred miles into other damp and friendly vacancies. With a little luck the spores – and millions perish for every triumph – will find suitable moisture and light. The spore will grow by cell division; sex occurs between male and female cells and an independent plant will flourish with its own roots hairs and storage systems to give it sustenance and fluids. It will take up to three years for a bud to develop and a frond to start growing. And it is this hereditary principle that has let the plant renew itself, producing endless new offspring and generations, each one renewing the vigour of the species and each in turn passing on the secret formula to the next generation. It is essentially a story of family loyalty and of the love it carries inside. Of radiation.

*

The time I love best is in the autumn, on these same West Penwith moors, when the fronds begin to scrunch towards their own decay, the sun ignites that turning and the whole land goes up in orange smoke before it settles back into a dark copper patina for the winter months. This is bracken, *Pteridium*, the most successful and widely distributed member of the fern family. It is also the oldest, fossils some fifty-five million years old having been found. Moorland is where it mostly likes to set down its roots. And like history, nothing will hold it back from coming forward.

The plant's architecture, caught in sunlight, feels redolent with imaginary objects – things far older than modern human thoughts, ideas and emotions, something beyond them. The trampling migrations of extinct and mythical creatures; the seismic tremors of delinquent gods; the atmospheric pressure of the sky carrying spores of ancient story; the gravity of eco-logical webs tying them to the earth; the crushing indifference of a world that doesn't care: history is not weightless.

After my interest in ferns had been piqued, it soon developed into my own version of fern fever, so much so that my husband gave me a long Coalbrookdale fern and blackberry-pattern garden seat for Christmas. He said it was for a wife who had become infected with pteridomania. In his card he wrote:

Come sit you wench
On this garden bench
Come sit and rest your feet
Come view your garden of earthly delight
And your happiness will be complete.

The inky sky is a warning I have ignored. Besides, those quick monsoon-type squalls that glide east to west on this coast I can take; it's the persistent face slapping of a north-westerly gale that is less bearable, and this is shaping up to be one of those. With everything already bleared I turn into my shell, huddle under my hat, turn my face landward, but the rain is so solid, between Zennor and Gurnard's Head, I am forced to shelter in one of those gourmet pubs, where I ruefully admit to my cowardice and let the rain march on. It is a defeat of which I am not proud.

The next day I am walking Gurnard's Head to Cape Cornwall, via Bosigran Cliff where the granite crags rise sheer from the sea four hundred feet below. I can just make out two climbers scrambling up the rocks and can only wonder at the exhilaration they draw from this barren challenge. This was where commandos trained in the Second World War, and in 1963 Sir John Hunt and Tenzing Norgay climbed Bosigran Cliff to celebrate their team's conquest of Everest ten years earlier. It was the first time Tenzing had ever climbed sea cliffs.

The landscape is beautiful and wild all around, but soon enough I enter another one of those dystopian areas connected with mining. The sacrifice zone. This is mining country and metal extraction has been a feature here for at least two thousand years. At first, primarily in the Bronze Age, it was all surface: tin extracted from metal-encrusted stones found in running streams; but when mineworkers discovered how to pump out after digging holes in the ground, they soon started to hack away at the rich veins running under their feet. Then it became like a game of cat's cradle, a warren of dark galleries deep below the ocean floor pushed along by shafts, platforms and ladders. It was not until they went underground that the tinners became miners in the modern sense.

Keith Russ, an engineer, spent twenty-five years creating extraordinary three-dimensional maps of more than 350 abandoned mines around the world, including the ones here at Levant. The heritage left behind, the underland. Russ acquired the mine abandonment plans, digitised them and overlaid them on Ordnance Survey maps. He then animated the tunnels, creating a fly-through. The results are, quite simply, beautiful. Russ has joined a band of modern 'desktop' explorers, entering brave and dark new worlds, condensing them, humanising them, decodifying their meaning through high-precision accurate graphics and animation technology, and in doing so has not only bared the physical geography and often miraculous master-pieces of engineering but the irregular topography of the human soul, the long-gone landscapes of memory, the strange world of human dreams.

By its very nature mining is a hidden activity, but Russ has brought the occupation to the surface; he has archived it and he has visualised it, not only for the curious like me, but for those who worked the seams: 'I once gave a talk and a group of retired miners came along,' he says.

> They had created some of the passages that are on the model. It was really good for them to see where they had spent the majority of their working life. They said it gave them some idea of perspective and told me they had worked in many different parts of the mine but only saw for the first time on the model how the levels related to each other.
>
> This gave me an enormous sense of satisfaction. The models are abstract but they are based on something that's real – the holes are actually there, under the ground, and these miners created them. I was told about three generations of the same family who had worked in his mine. To think of the number of hours that have gone into creating these passages is just phenomenal. Mining is unseen but it's one of the world's oldest and most dangerous professions. Many lives were lost down those mines and it is not something we should forget.

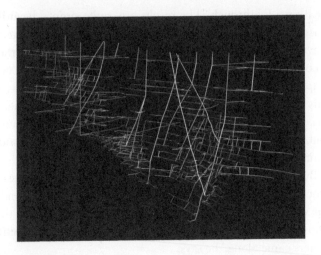

The actual view of this landscape first comes after Boat Cove, and then more clearly after Pendeen: tall chimneys, sheds, the remains of the tin dressing floors where they crushed the ores and separated the waste using water and gravity – hence building them on sloping ground. On those slopes the weeping blues, reds and browns of the minerals, caused by the distress of having their faces cut in the side of the cliffs, can also be seen.

I follow the path which scratches through this desolation, through a silty waste stained red by the iron oxide once intimately mixed with the ore – it is how I imagine a stroll over Mars. Then on to the Levant Engine House, which is perched high on the cliff edge as if it might at any moment topple over into the sea having lost its footing but in not quite as savage an aspect as Botallack Mine slightly further west, clinging to the dark rocks. It is an historically important industrial building because it houses the restored beam engine in its original position, the oldest surviving one in Britain still worked by steam. The Engine House itself sits on the site of the former Levant mine, which closed in 1930, the seams having been worked for

110 years. It ran a mile under the sea and was worked for tin, copper and arsenic.

The shafts that this complex of separate mines catered for had to be sunk as close to the Levant Zawn and the rich undersea workings as was possible – 'zawn' being Cornish dialect for the word chasm. It is incredible to think that the miners extracted copper and tin for a mile distant from these cliffs and more than 350 fathoms below the seabed. It is said they could often hear the sea thunderously pushing the ocean's boulders above them. The best account of this sensation is probably by Wilkie Collins, who once went down Botallack Mine:

> We are now four hundred yards out, *under the bottom of the sea*; and twenty fathoms, or a hundred and twenty feet below the sea level. Coast-trade vessels are sailing over our heads. Two hundred and forty feet below us men are at work, and there are galleries deeper yet, even below that! ...
>
> After listening for a few moments, a distant, unearthly noise becomes faintly audible – a long, low mysterious moaning, which never changes, which is *felt* on the ear as well as *heard* by it – a sound that might proceed from some incalculable distance, from some invisible height – a sound so unlike anything that is heard on the upper ground, in the free air of heaven; so sublimely mournful and still; so ghostly and impressive when listened to in the subterranean recesses of the earth, that we continue instinctively to hold our peace, as if enchanted by it, and think of not communicating to each other the awe and astonishment which it has inspired in us from the very first.
>
> At last, the miner speaks ... and tells us that what we hear is the sound of the surf lashing the rocks a hundred and twenty feet above us, and of the waves that are breaking on the beach beyond. The tide is now at the flow, and the sea is in no extraordinary state of agitation: so the sound is low and distant ... But, when storms are at their height, when the

ocean hurls mountain after mountain of water on the cliffs, then the noise is terrific; the roaring heard down here in the mine is so expressively fierce and awful, that the boldest men at work are afraid to continue their labour. All ascend to the surface, to breathe the upper air and stand on the firm earth: dreading, though no such catastrophe has ever happened yet, that the sea will break in on them if they remain in the caverns below.

You can get a feel of this dark, grim, mineral obstinacy when you buy a ticket at Geevor mine and descend into the tunnel. It's not quite the same sensation Collins would have experienced, that of being a stone dropped into a well, but you can get close to the silent shadows of men as they worked in an underworld deeper and more intense than any grave, where the only light was pinpricks far above where their brothers were at work; and the noises, those of drilling and blasting and of rocks trembling, and the air hot and smoky and wet from water trickling down these dark walls of granite and red.

Here at Geevor retired miners now show you around; mine is implacable, politically angry, throwing out comments about how Guy Fawkes had the right idea when it came to politicians. Even my taxi driver bemoans the fact the mines have closed when there is so much mineral wealth still to be had. What they need around here is jobs: he means mining jobs, real jobs, manly jobs, not fluffy jobs that cater for a seasonal tourist trade upon which they barely survive. These Cornishmen are caught in their history but not yet released from it; as if they are still standing at the top of the shaft, waiting to go down in their red-stained, tattered underground clothes; as if nothing has ever matched that excitement of drilling holes and filling them with blasting gelignite and running alongside the fuse; as if nothing matches the music that comes from the rock's roar of pain as it breaks up. Time will not take away their story, because of the wreckage it has left behind, but the story has moved on, moved elsewhere, as it always does.

Copper or clay, or coal, or soil – it sometimes feels as if the earth is all woman and a muscular male nurse is coming around, tapping her arm, saying the time has come to express a little more milk, for you have spawned a creature with a voracious hunger, and you must devote your flesh to his survival. *Wake up, my dear, the time has come again.*

And it always happens the same way: politicians speaking about our children's future. On the ground locally, talk of investment, jobs, community projects; the entrepreneurs involved will attempt to seduce those directly affected but only those truly at the top will get rich, as they always do. Environmental studies will be published, with safety procedures probably sponsored by self-interested parties and ring-fenced by lawyers. Advisers will be appointed by the government and are set to profit from the venture; they will ensure that there are no obstacles and that licences are handed out liberally. In turn, the politicians, who think they have come up with an easy solution to energy supply and jobs, will offer tax-free incentives and no rent for factories or mines, as if the land belongs to them and not to the people who live above it. They will scoff at the notion of a common law that claims ownership of your plot reaches up to Heaven and down to Hades. If that was the case, we would not have any aeroplanes in the sky, they snort. Parliament will amend the laws on property rights. Placards will be waved as the bill is rushed through.

And then it starts, the drilling and the consequences: headaches, contaminated ground water, toxic waste, because when you loot the earth there are always consequences. And then it ends: the people who have exploited the ground move on with their cash and all that is left behind are bleeding open wounds. The community will retreat to a quiet corner and watch as that slow set of complex biochemical events begins to repair the damage. Just as with a cut, with its lunar white flap of skin and outpouring of red blood, nature's busy compounds will start to constrict the vessels and promote the clotting. Plants, rivers, air, all will find their right of way through the carnage. They will come like white knights or angels, migrating to the area, to clean up the debris and they will stay until things are growing and covering and producing by a multiplication of parts and the wound, although still raw-looking, is improved. And that is the time that the miners start mourning its loss, mourning the camaraderie they shared; that is the time they sit in the pub after their taxi shift or tour at the local museum, when they grieve for a lost identity, when they share the mystery of those huge hidden depths. For more than two hundred years the mining industry of Cornwall and West Devon dominated the landscape. It fuelled the Industrial Revolution and influenced every aspect of the modern world. It has now all but gone.

But has it? Like all things, there is a cyclical nature to the exploitation of resources and Cornwall's identity as an energy producer is difficult to shift; it's genetic, it pumps through its veins in more ways than one.

Cornwall is indeed about to find itself back at the centre of Britain's extraction industry. Natural heat from granite found under the ground is now being tapped to drive turbines at the country's first deep geothermal power station, and there are large reserves of lithium, a rare earth metal vital to the electric car and mobile phone industries. The presence of lithium is not even a revelation: miners of eras past recorded how they had stumbled on hot underground springs whose water was laden with lithium-rich salts. It's thanks to their poorly drawn, aged maps that today's mining companies know where to dig. It seems this shiny metal may well trigger something of a new gold rush.

Cornwall will always be ready for the next big energy adventure. It was a pioneer in solar and wind, and it will probably be the same for lithium mining and geothermal energy. And what of the consequences? The promise of a revived mining industry may well be perceived as conflicting with the other great modern money-spinner: tourism. Some of the lithium-rich and 'hot rock' areas lie close to renowned resorts such as Porthtowan and St Ives. Jeremy Wrathall, chief executive of Cornish Lithium, which hopes to exploit the county's reserves, is reported as saying: 'We could create up to three hundred jobs but we also have to convince people we can be good neighbours.'

And so, the wheels start turning again. To the abyss we return. For those who are uncertain, as I certainly am, all we can do is ask questions. What ecosystems are spoiled to bring these minerals to the surface? Isn't it true to say that much of what we are digging up isn't the stuff that we actually want, but just aggregate, rock? How many people are displaced? How are these raw materials converted into usable components? Don't they require fossil fuels? How are they transported? To make a single wind turbine, hundreds and thousands of tonnes of steel, concrete and plastic are required, the production of which emits even more tonnes of carbon dioxide. Doesn't the manufacturing of solar panels release greenhouse gases, which stay in the upper air for centuries? Isn't recycling also an energy-intensive activity, which only salvages a small fraction of anything that is reusable? Don't we, as a country, just send our plastic waste overseas for other countries to deal with anyway? Are we not caught up in a brutal global race for natural resources?

Does green technology ease our conscience? Is that why we push it? What purpose does it perform for us – does it help the real world, the physical world, or does it help industry?

So many people in this new revolution think they have angels on their shoulders directing them, but do they? Really? As C. S. Lewis wrote, 'Of all tyrannies, a tyranny sincerely exercised for the good of its victims may be the most oppressive. It would be better to live under robber barons than under omnipotent moral busybodies. The robber baron's cruelty may sometimes sleep, his cupidity may at some point be satiated; but those who torment us for our own good will torment us without end, for they do so with the approval for their own conscience.'

And so it goes on. What happens when it wears out? What happens to the materials? How toxic are they? What happens to the site? Will it damage and poison everything left behind? Is technology ever really neutral? Are humans just governed by an acquisitive and destructive spirit? Is avarice the spark that keeps the human soul aflame? If there was no greed would human civilisation even exist? And actually, who are these guardians of ours?

Aldo Leopold, in *Think Like a Mountain*, writes: 'It is inconceivable to me that an ethical relation to land can exist without love, respect and admiration for land, and a high regard for its value. By value, I of course mean something far broader than mere economic value; I mean value in the philosophical sense.'

Even with the green revolution the land is still seen as something of economic value rather than something we should attempt to understand or be connected to. We should not be deceived into believing that a new ethic has been placed on it; what we are seeing out there is very much an old ethic.

Entrances and Exits

Cape Cornwall to Land's End

Porthledden House, a mysterious Gothic monstrosity, stands defiantly on the bald edge like a large mythical beast that has escaped the fold. Ever since I can remember I have been spooked by its appearance. It always felt like a house of horrors, a place where forked lightning lived permanently in the clouds above. Adding to the eerie atmosphere was the barren and windswept moorland, peaked by Carn Kenidjack, known locally as the carn of the howling wind. It stands 650 feet above sea level and the astringent sound is indeed unnerving, like blowing across the top of a bottle – that's if the wind comes from the right direction and is of sufficient strength, and travels through the thin vertical strip that cuts through the formation. It's no wonder that this was feared to be a special domain of evil spirits, a place where demons wrestled on disturbed ground. It feels like King Lear's blasted heath.

What Porthledden really represents, however, is *faith*; a defiant bastion standing proud at the world's end with waves breaking all around it, crying the sea's salty tears but letting nothing pierce its skin. A chosen view that looks out across the pilgrim route, out to the New World, out to paradise, a view that would make a man walk on water. But to build a house here, at the very edge, also says something about detachment; although still connected to England, it somehow lies apart. It exists in between. Between home and the away. Which exactly reflects the character of the person who erected it.

That man, the man who built Porthledden, was Francis Oats, a true Cornishman. Born in 1848, in Golant, he came to the mining town of St Just, which sits above Cape Cornwall, and like all young men of that place and time went underground. Unlike other miners, he bettered himself by walking the seven miles to Penzance to take evening classes in mining engineering. He was so adept at his subject, having practised it as well as studied it, that by the age of seventeen he was ranked second in the whole country in his mineralogy test. He was given the opportunity to further his studies, for free, at the London School of Mines, but couldn't afford living costs so he decided to become a mine manager at Botallack instead.

It was not to last. Captain Frank, as he became known, would, like others, fall victim to the flood of Malaysian tin, which was found much more easily and cheaply, which soon swamped the market. St Just's mining community was particularly hard hit as Cornwall fell from prominence. Doom and gloom spread as men left for mines overseas in ever-swelling numbers. In November 1877 the *West Briton* newspaper reported: 'The present depression has probably been felt more heavily in St Just than anywhere else. At the last census it had a population of 9,000 souls but that this has very much decreased is shown by the fact that at the last poor rate assessment, no less than 289 houses were struck off the list as unoccupied.'

Oats metaphorically 'got on his bike', having been accepted for a job as a mining engineer by the Colonial Office and leaving for South Africa. He would go alone, leaving his wife and children back home in Cornwall. The Colonial Office subsequently appointed him Inspector of Mines. After that he became manager of the Victoria Diamond Mine at Kimberley, and later reached the lofty heights of chairman of De Beers, the famous diamond company.

Oats walked the line between miners and authorities and bridged the differences. There were many Cornish miners at Kimberley, and Captain Frank did his best for these men. After all, his entire career was based on an understanding of a life lived underground, his popularity founded on a desire to make improvements for the diggers with whom he went into regular conference. He forced the adoption of water hydrants to lay the dust created by mining drills, the main cause of silicosis. And he insisted that De Beers give each Cornish miner a yearly paid holiday at home. For all his time there he represented and honoured the Cornish, supporting them from a political perspective when he was elected to represent Namaqualand in the South African Parliament, where he held office until 1907.

Oats would base himself in South Africa for the rest of his life. He was the archetypal colonial pioneer, from the strongest breed this country has to offer, the ones built like trees. When he first got to Kimberley, it was not the town it is today; the climate was stifling, dusty and flyblown, water was scarce and disease was rife. But Oats stuck it out: to men like him everything was young; the land, the wind, the sky, the sun, even the dust. He was of a stock that craved independence, one that could look after themselves, the ones that forced forests back and shaped tracks and dug holes, men of courage blazing their way where lesser mortals would later follow. Men who looked ahead to something they could not see.

But Cornwall was never far from his romantic heart; whenever he came back he bought shares in the local mines, and he even tried to modernise the tin mine at St Just by sinking a new vertical shaft so that ore could be raised direct from the lower levels to the surface, though it proved to be an extravagant waste of money. Most of his endeavours at home were misguided, probably even the building of Porthledden, which he suspected – correctly, as it happens – would eventually be turned into a hotel.

I suspect Porthledden was not built to crown Oats's ascent to a higher social bracket, even though it did eclipse every other house in the area. Surely what must be understood about him is that he lived the life of a human mole; everything about him was suited to a subterranean lifestyle. Even his body was cylindrical, small, stocky with short and powerful limbs perfect for digging. His head was pointed. Porthledden is where Oats sporadically came up for air, on the highest piece of land he could find, a place where he could look out from the great bow window past the chimney stack above the cape to the sea stretching out either side, and on to America. He barely lived in this house, but it represents everything he was: sturdy, ambitious, successful, and it offered everything he dreamed of: light, air, sea, adventure. But it is also a building heavily emblematic of the strength and courage of the miners of this ground. It is in many ways their monument, their gravestone.

*

From Cape Cornwall I pass by Ballowall Barrow, a large and chambered Bronze Age cairn which was excavated in 1878 by the Cornish antiquarian William Borlase. I'm then waved on by the rich sub-tropical plants of Cot Valley, over which birds, newly arrived from America, spread their wings. There are tin streaming works and shafts in this area, so one has to be mindful of sticking to the path. Also present are those do-gooding plants, the ones that help clean up contaminated environments, the ones that come in like an army of cleaners after a big event to remove different types of pollutants and restore balance, sometimes without any need to excavate or dispose of the offending material. *Silene vulgaris*, or bladder campion, is one such plant, able to mop up zinc from the soil. I find it here, rushing its white flowers over the edges of old shaft walls like virginal bridesmaids peering over a balcony at a wedding party. On each stem, a small propeller of white petals hangs over a vase-like calyx. So large is this vase that the layer of air inside it apparently insulates the flower's more delicate inner parts from heat, keeping its petals fresh, but it is such an odd-looking part, it makes me think of a cauldron, and I ponder that maybe this is what is needed to contain the toxic poisons of this place. By dusk, the work is apparently done; alchemy has taken place and the flower starts to secrete a pleasant, clove-like fragrance, a smell so sweet it tells the night butterflies to clamber into its cup. And then you begin to question its innocence; maybe it is not such a votary of whiteness, maybe it is a Lolita or a Lady Macbeth. Flowers are often deceitful, seducing, cheating and even killing insects in their efforts to have them perform pollination.

There is a view that, for phytoremediation to occur, *Silene vulgaris* should be harvested and disposed of safely elsewhere, and the whole cycle repeated over several seasons to bring con-tamination down to safe levels, but I wonder if this is the case. Sometimes I feel we are over-manipulating plant life in the nat-ural world – I suspect mostly out of guilt for our destruction of it – that we are altering their natural clocks, taking away the time they need to perform their spells. Sometimes we just need to sur-render control and let them get on with it. Maybe we should focus more on the absence of interventions that may cause adverse outcomes, just like doctors do with the Hippocratic oath when they pledge to 'first do no harm'. I am no botanist, but I never doubt the intelligence of flowers. I never doubt that they possess the power of thought without knowledge, a capacity that consti-tutes a form of intelligence. What we perceive as being a serene and peaceful entity is in fact something completely different. A flower is in a constant state of mutiny against its destiny, which is to be forever rooted. Its entire spectacle is based on a single plan: to avoid the dark incarceration that has it chained below, because, like all captives, it dreams of breaking its bounds, it dreams of having wings, of conquering the space where it is held captive. A polluted soil like this one will not break its spirit; in fact, it will activate it, and that is how the flower inspires. Apart from its obvious beauty, it sets a towering example of dissension and non-compliance, recklessness and resourcefulness.

In his essay 'The Intelligence of Flowers', the Belgian Nobel Prize-winner Maurice Maeterlinck tries to break down the barriers between the animal and plant kingdoms. His belief is that the psychology of flowers is not that different from our own psychology because we all have one thing in common: a scattered general intelligence, 'a kind of universal fluid that penetrates diversely the organisms it encounters, depending on whether they are good or bad conductors of consciousness' with mankind offering the least resistance to this so-called fluid. He assumes that both bodies carry this same spirit and that it reveals itself when we try to reproduce, when we try to survive, when we attempt to maintain perfection and happiness. that, ultimately, we react and long for the same outcomes.

> We could truly say that ideas come to flowers in the same way they come to us. Flowers grope in the same darkness, encounter the same obstacles and the same ill will, in the same unknown. They know the same laws, same disappointments, same slow and difficult triumphs. It seems they have our patience, our perseverance, our self-love; the same finely tuned and diversified intelligence, almost the same hopes and the same ideals. Like ourselves, they struggle against a vast indifferent force that ends by helping them.

Maeterlinck was writing more than a hundred years ago, when less was known about plants than today, but that is unimportant to his philosophy. What he was trying to do was bridge the gap between literature and science with metaphoric reasoning. He wanted to reconcile the two, so that a more personal experience with nature can be sought. He might overly attribute human sensibility to botanical forms but in doing so he brings us closer not only to our similarities but to the mystical in science and the poetry that can be found there. When we talk to our plants to make them grow quicker – and yes, I do that – perhaps, we are doing the same.

The colour change is creeping upon the moor, fewer russets and purple browns of winter and more greens from the grass and the bracken and the purple of heather and the yellow of gorse.

On the beach at Porth Nanven ultra-smooth ovoid boulders are littered across the shore and lodged into the cliff base. So striking are they that the site, known as the dinosaur-egg beach, has been denoted a Site of Special Scientific Interest to prevent the theft of the rocks. The boulders were smoothed by being bashed against each other in violent seas about 120,000 years ago, and are, in rock terms, quite beautiful as a result. For all that has passed – all the violence, the geological turmoil, the encounters, the pain, the clashes – they must be enjoying this passive moment, lounging around the beach until deep time enacts another plan for them, or maybe place for them.

At Gwynver Beach, I notice there is a fenced-off adder conservation area. Folliott-Stokes was also very keen on adders, if not their preservation. He tells us: 'I once killed four in as many minutes, just below the boulders to the westward of the stream. They came out of a hole in a stone hedge one after the other.' And the purpose of this? Apparently, they make an 'extremely handsome' belt. Men are so much better than us when it comes to holding and killing a wild thing. They are what the American poet Ada Limón would call, 'the hurting kind'.

Folliott-Stokes goes on to tell us the process involved in making said belt. The first skill is to catch the blighter, which involves 'a little patient observation', because they live 'in the interstices of stone hedges': 'A careful perambulation of a few of these hedges, in the vicinity of the cliffs, on a sunny day in April or May, before the bracken and flowers have grown to their full height, will probably discover one or more adders crawling along the stones, or coiled up asleep in the sun. They are very timid creatures, so you must be quick, or they will escape you disappearing between the stones.' The weapon of choice is a stick, he writes, striking as near to the head as possible to avoid damaging the scales.

'When disabled,' he continues, 'place the sole of your boot on its head, and, with a sharp knife, sever the head from the body. You can now take the body in your hands. Never mind the writhing, it is purely muscular; the creature is as dead as a door nail. Cut the skin for about an inch down the under part of the neck; then turn it back, exposing the stump of the body. Give this stump to a friend to hold, or, if you are alone, place it under the sole of your boot. With your two hands you can now peel off the skin, as easily as you can peel off a glove. It will not peel to the extreme end of the tail, so you cut off the last six or seven inches.'

Once home, Folliott-Stokes tells us he pins down the skin on a board and sprinkles it with pepper to absorb the moisture. When dry, it is dispatched to a leather merchant in London where it will be shaped and sewn into a belt, and the buckle attached.

'Two full-grown adder skins will make a belt large enough for the average maiden's waist,' but he advises: 'The male's skin is the handsomer, being black and silver. The female's is of a reddish hue, and not so distinctly marked.'

It's beyond imagination that anyone would be permitted to commit such a gross act against one of God's shyest creatures today, or if anyone would even have the courage to do it.

Lady Macbeth's line, 'Look like the innocent flower but be the serpent under't', makes me thinks about the thread that connects these three disparate subjects, miner, flower and snake. It occurs to me that what they share is a concentration of activities below the surface, and when they leave that place they are reaching the very outwardness of something, the place where everything comes to a definite end, or to a new beginning.

We know how much of a flower's work occurs underground, and how it draws insects over its rim and into its cup. Then there is the adder, a cold-blooded creature which passes the winter months in hibernation, usually in some form of a burrow, curled together in a tight ball with other snakes. When it emerges, lethargically so, over the rim again, it goes out to select surface dens in tussocks of grass, hollows or old tree stumps. Here he stays, waiting for its reproductive organs and skin to grow into a new coat of colours that will dazzle female adders in the area. Deaf and with restricted vision, he cannot travel far and relies on scent and the gathering of adder populations to find his mate. There will be fights as he selects and defends his queen among other males, raising his head and swaying it from side to side in a challenge, locking himself in a wrestling match, throwing coils around the other until the opponent flees and he is left free to bask, flicking his forked tongue along the side of his sweetheart's body before encircling her in coils, to mate in the long grass. After that the population will move to summer feeding areas before finding their way back to the strict enclosure of their ancestral hibernating burrows as autumn approaches. Not exactly hitting your woman over the head with a club but certainly dragging her back to his cave.

When Francis Oats stood at the entrance of a mine shaft, he too was standing at a rim, an opening, at a threshold, a place where everything conjoins, between the inner space of the burrow, the mine, and the outer one of land and sky. Inside there will be seams, folds, margins, where the minerals rise and fall, but these are mere walls, they don't mark the end or start of an activity. A rim, however, is a point of turning: between worlds, in and out, to and from, where the exhausted miner leaves the shaft, passing fresh-faced colleagues going in for a new shift. Where an adder takes his new mate over the threshold of his hibernating burrow. A rim encapsulates the idea of passing through to a new opportunity. The direction of travel is irrelevant. From Cornwall to South Africa, from South Africa to Cornwall.

Our worlds are full of entrances and exits: a door, a window, an arch, eating, drinking. With sex one is always hovering over fleshy gateways to corporeal depths. In every example, the edge, the rim, comes into play, as does the threshold we need to cross; in erotic pleasure, in the world of work, in life and death, good and evil, for the adder and the miner, and the insect landing on a flower petal, every exit is an entrance, every entrance an exit. As if all we are ever looking for on this earth are doors.

Lost Lands

Land's End

I am coming to the end. Land's End. Here, two large seas collide and battle for supremacy: one from the west – the stream connecting the Irish Sea and the Celtic Sea – the other from the English Channel – coming from the east. It is not a happy place for fishermen: winds can veer unexpectedly, pushing boats onto the rocks or chasing them around the arm of the Lizard Peninsula. A summer fog can blind them as well. They have named this treacherous and notorious province the Throes, and its temperamental character the Pooks.

Land's End itself is just a protuberant block of granite, lower than nearby headlands such as Pedn-men-du or Pordenack, but what it loses in size it wins in sentiment; there are few other locations in England that carry such weighty mythology, that can change perspectives and emotions. What happens here is pure theatre; it is a place of performance, natural, supernatural and unnatural. A stage set. There is the scenery of faraway islands sitting like clouds in the midst; music from the orchestra pits, the roar of an angry sea ascending from the caverns below; the purple light show of a storm; wings full of winds; live performers in the form of wheeling seabirds. It is the last of the land, a place where we have to stop running, where we are forced to break our journey, to watch, to listen, to feel, to clap, to cry.

Just before Land's End, by that I also mean where the land starts to reach its conclusion, I pass a model pirate ship and zip wires, and the old Padstow Severn Series lifeboat, marooned in the Wreckreation Area, before coming across the Land's End Landmark, the main draw. I am at one of our nation's major tourist attractions, bringing hundreds of thousands of visitors a year. One that is in competition with the natural surroundings. It feels like a blockage on my path.

When I was younger, there was not much here, just some undisciplined parking and a hotel that had seen better days. Back then, the average visitor stayed no more than twenty minutes, spending most of that time in the car, so uninviting were the winds and weather. A quick look at the Atlantic rollers breaking in clouds of spray over the Longships, the line of rocks a mile offshore, then the key was straight back in the ignition and they were off again. In 1987 the businessman Peter de Savary outbid the National Trust and commercialised the site through an irresponsible and profligate planning decision. His original footprint was developed by owners that followed after him.

It always makes me depressed to think of it. The clifftops and ground around Land's End became worn through the tread of tyres and feet. Large parts of heath needed darning. Cornish heath is the most important and extensive habitat at Land's End. It is a dense but low-level community consisting of heather and gorse scrub that hosts a rich variety of flowers, including yellow bartsia, nodding scirpus and bog pimpernel. The plants are vital for the topsoil, because if they are removed erosion soon follows. The solution, if you can call it that, was to create gravel walkways with commanding signs instructing visitors to keep to the path. Turves were laid on the most eroded slopes, but that just introduced alien species of grass and flowers. Anyway, it was too much too late, the land was lost, it no longer ran wild all the way to the sea. It still doesn't.

The main entrance to the attraction is large, and shields a complex that represents everything that is loathsome about the commercial world. It even manages, in its core, to avoid the views which should be the main attraction. In an inner courtyard I am expected to be 'seduced' by a *ewe-nique* and *baa-rilliant* attraction for the 'young and the young at heart', before venturing into the state-of-the-art 4D cinema to immerse myself in a cutting-edge showing of *The Lost World*, an adventure forty million years in the making. Fierce raptors, pterodactyls and the mighty T-Rex all roam this hostile world, so be afraid, be very afraid. But there are other options too: Arthur's Quest, for example, an 'interactive world of discovery', where you can 'accept Merlin's terrifying challenge' and discover 'plenty of spine-chilling surprises as you seek the terrible lair of the dragon'. And so, the language goes on, like emergency sirens, amid bands of children who appear to be in states of extreme exaltation, as if induced by drugs or dance or drumming, and on through the canteen of smells, and the flogging of gifts and souvenirs, but mostly through a severe violation of how topography should be interpreted. A case of how the outside can disguise the inside of a place, by which I mean its soul.

There are ways to handle all this sadness. To reverse this spell. The first and most obvious is to get away as soon as it is physically possible, because this place is clearly the complete antithesis of why anyone ever sets out on a walk like this one. The second is to behave as dolphins do: they shut down half of their brain to sleep; the other side remains at a low level of alertness to prevent it from drowning. That alert half watches for predators and obstacles, and after two hours, sometimes even two weeks, the brain's hemispheres switch to give the other side a rest. It's all you can do until you get to the other side of the Land's End Landmark set-up, and a stretch of path that is simply exquisite, and of which I am very fond.

On that other side, I do indeed stop, the 'attraction' shrinking away to my right side, and from the granite cliffs that rise out of the Atlantic Ocean I look out in studious attention to the Longships Lighthouse, and into a space that contains the Isles of Scilly, twenty-eight miles away, and beyond that, North America. Somewhere out there is also that mythical land of milk and honey, the lost land of Lyonesse. The place where the tragic love and loss of Tristan and Iseult played out. I have written about these lost lands in earlier chapters, and how inundation stories were widespread among Celtic peoples, but standing here I think how relevant and modern this legend has become, with climate change and rising sea levels.

Lyonesse – the Cornish know it as Lethowsow – was a truly beautiful land, stretching from here to the Isles of Scilly and colonised by a race of strong and fine-looking people who worked its lush and abundant plains. Here they built many churches, 140 of them, and its beating heart was the City of Lions, which had the biggest church of them all, a great cathedral which sat atop what is now Seven Stones reef. Then one night, in a Cornish version of Sodom and Gomorrah, the sea overtook the land in anger for some dreadful unknown crime people had committed, killing every living thing in one night, bar a single man by the name of Trevelyan. He had, after a day's hunting, fallen asleep under a tree, only to be woken again by a horrendous sound. Trevelyan escaped, riding his white horse ahead of the wave, and managed to get to higher ground. So vivid was this legend, and the fear that the waters would rise again, that for many years old Cornish families always kept horses saddled in their stable in case an evacuation was called for. The Vyvyan family, whose ancestral home is on the Lizard at Trelowarren, and who claim to be descended from Trevelyan, maintain that this character was the last governor of the lost kingdom before it was swallowed up by God's wrath. Other myths have bubbled to the surface, mostly from fishermen, who say that on calm days, they can hear the bells toll from the many churches.

Lyonesse is without doubt an extraordinary survivor of folk memory, but it was Alfred, Lord Tennyson's *Idylls of the King* that truly salvaged this sinking land from the depths of the sea, rescuing its precious cargo and its crew from the peril of oblivion. He writes of 'A land of old upheaven from the abyss / By fire, to sink into the abyss again; / Where fragments of forgotten peoples dwelt, / And the long mountains ended in a coat / Of ever-shifting sand'. Lyonesse is raised on the day that King Arthur fights his last battle, with the traitor Modred. Mortally wounded, Arthur is seen lurching through the mist, a tragic symbol of power lost. His last knight standing, Bedivere, will place him on a barge which will take him, in all his last loneliness, further west, to 'the island-valley of Avilion'. In versions older than this one, Arthur's soul will then migrate into the body of a chough, with glossy black plumage and blood-red talons, residing on the cliff edges of Cornwall acting as a mediator between the living and the dead, only to return in England's hour of greatest need.

The myth plays into some of our deepest insecurities, those associated with the loss of lands, and is part of a tradition that stretches across the seas from Cornwall. Sunken kingdoms appear in Breton legends as well, in the tale of the Cité d'Ys or Ker Ys, similarly drowned as a result of its depravity with a single moral and upright survivor also escaping on a horse, in this case King Gradlon. The Welsh equivalent is the drowned kingdom of Cantre'r Gwaelod, which once settled where Cardigan Bay stretches today. Not too dissimilarly, the Gaelic otherworld of Tír na nÓg was a sacred and mysterious land that required a boat trip, although not one swallowed up by water.

But those traditions of Arthur and other lost territories are not just folklore and the hollow imaginings of a poetic people. Britain itself is an emergent mass of land rising from a submarine platform attached to continental Europe. It has an absorptive capacity of understanding about changing sea levels. Its physical history has always been one of continents coming together and being wrenched apart. Of seas rising and falling. The formation of channels by waves. Of ice cutting through. And of shallow waters. Flood myths, perhaps unlike a creation myth or a paradise myth, often originate in real events. Indeed, the Lyonesse Project proves this. Commissioned by English Heritage, it studied the impact of rising sea levels on the Isles of Scilly over the past twelve thousand years and in 2013, after seven years of work, concluded that the Isles had once been a much larger island, but were separated into smaller ones due to rising sea levels. Further research also found that rather than abandon the area following coastal flooding, communities adapted to the changes in their environment. Bronze Age communities remained on Scilly despite the islands shrinking, hunting and foraging on the newly exposed intertidal zones, as well as keeping animals and growing crops. The islands have a large number of sacred monuments from that time, and the building of them went on longer than on the mainland. In fact, their concentration here is greater than anywhere else in the country. Archaeological remains, including stone walls, have been discovered below high water, and fragments brought up from the depths sometimes appear in fishermen's nets. In geographic terms, Lyonesse might have disappeared but its people remained behind. It is a classic tale of lost and found.

If you visit the Isles of Scilly today, so numerous and low-lying are the islands in this archipelago, island-hopping feels almost like walking over stepping stones in a river; you are grateful to be hoisted onto solid ground to keep your feet dry. These stony isles, the last upward thrust of the granite backbone that runs down from Dartmoor and through Land's End, arriving here in shallow waters, come across as small hymns to resistance. Because if Scilly demonstrates one thing, it is this: sea-level rises do not always lead to a predictable human response. For many coastal communities, migration is the absolute last resort, and this has been the case for millennia, for edge communities all around the world. In islands, we see a mirror of ourselves, an absolute determination to remain relevant.

It also highlights how 'submergence' has always been at the forefront of people's minds. It is why the flood myths are so resonant, not just in the Christian tradition, with Noah's Ark in Genesis, but all around the world. These stories arise not only because they are based on actual events but because they come from a universal condition, of enduring the bad and delivering the good; it is how we make sense of things, separating one from the other. Floods happen when communities get above themselves, when they represent man's wickedness, vanity and conceit, when they presume they are above the laws of nature, and God, it is then that the waters, the most destructive force of all, will be sent to destroy that civilisation, in a supreme act of divine retribution.

And in this deluge, in this cleansing of humanity, a spark of hope might be introduced, a folk hero: a Trevelyan, a Noah, a young girl called Greta. Most of us live without gods these days. But we still listen to the messengers – scientists, campaigners, politicians – who speak of divine retribution, building their doomsday cases on peer-reviewed papers that paint a near-dystopian future of ice caps melted, floods, famine, mass migrations and war. Supervolcanoes that erupt with such fierceness they decimate whole populations. It's so much easier to imagine the end of the world than the saving of it, I suppose. But there is almost a perverse thrill out there, that this is our destiny, to return to a previous geological epoch. Young people certainly seem to believe the Four Horsemen of the Apocalypse have ridden out of the Book of Revelation and are coming our way. Projecting into the future with such certainty exudes an extraordinary confidence in their own visionary powers. I am less confident; I think I see deep time as its own master.

*

I am standing here still, at the end of all the land, on the tip of this bulky peninsula, the Bolerion of Ptolemy, the Penwith of the Celts, knowing many a travelling pilgrim has done the same, waiting for the sun to set in a great orange flare, burning everything to a watery end. For many, there is no other spot where the falling sun seems so resolute with meaning than at Land's End. I look to this end, this edge, where the cliffs are precipitous and the granite forms prismatic and cubical at low water. For me, there is nothing here that says much about the social, economic, technical and political aspects of our time on earth. It is more a view. A feeling. White horses. Aquamarine waters. Drowned lands. Voids. Hope. Death. Reaching an extremity. It can feel like the first day of a new world, or the last.

Today, however, at the end of my journey, I seem to be stalled, arrested, metaphorically so, on the Land's End clifftop, having some sort of internal dialogue. Kierkegaard would call it a classic example of existential angst; the type he ascribes to that familiar urge we sometimes feel to jump off something high – a cliff, a building, a bridge – a feeling that is so completely at odds with our most powerful instinct, that of survival. Kierkegaard explains this emotion as 'the dizziness of freedom'. He thinks it is all bound up with us having to make moral decisions as a consequence of us being in possession of free will. I see that same angst among many of the politicians I know, at least the ones that take politics seriously. I even know one who did indeed throw himself under a train, or at least tried to. When I started this walk it was to avoid the land of political decision-making, to enjoy the unencompassability of places, to be somewhere where there was no time, no limit, no choices, and yet all I see around me is politics still. Walking the edge has, in places, put me on edge as well. Floods, new mining, the disappearance of species; I am seeing environmental doom everywhere I look, and not only here but abroad: in droughts, in fires, in aridity, in plumes of radioactivity from nuclear power stations, in the drones that carry dirty bombs, in the pollution of cities.

There is more. I worry that not enough is being done to protect my green and pleasant land. I fear the digital technologies that make mass political engagement possible, but equally impossible, to act on. I fear the removal of political restraints. I worry how the smallest voices make the largest noise, and how the media spreads dissent. I worry how promises made by politicians cannot be delivered. How the old order is on the brink of disintegration and that different versions of civilisation may be collapsing before our eyes, of wars in the Middle East and Europe rising into the sky like spectacular fireworks and falling down as ash and darkness. Of new iron curtains descending. Of authoritarian regimes tightening their grip on their people. Of women being turned into a handmaid's tale. That rage on the right continues to drive populist and nativist movements, leading to racial and religious hate crimes. That the poor keep getting poorer and the rich richer. That the West is becoming impotent as an idea. I worry that through politics we all have the freedom to change everything, but positions of power are full of cowards who shirk great responsibility, and I'm anxious that as an individual I'm not up to the task of changing minds. How can I be? I am a nobody. All I really want to do is run away, go on a long walk, shut down half my brain, take a leap into the unknown.

I'm finishing this book long after I started this walk, almost a decade in fact. Brexit has happened, so has a global pandemic which killed more than six million people; Donald J. Trump has been and gone. President Biden is unsteady on his feet. The Queen is dead. Hairline cracks continue to appear in the very foundations of the European project. All the electoral playbooks have been abandoned. Questions are being raised about the merits of democracy. Every generation, I suppose, has considered itself to be the most turbulent, aggressive and imperilled, but the capacity for this anxiety to be shared at the touch of a button is something quite unique to our times. One cannot go without news any more; it is everywhere, it pings on our phones, it comes at us in comment and counter-comment, it comes as urban myths and fake news. It feels like poison is entering our veins, is a rush of blood to our heads. My dread, if you can call it that, now seems to encompass edge-like feelings as well. I return to Kierkegaard, and find he is surprisingly positive about my anxiety, he tells me the condition is not such a bad thing after all, that it can actually mobilise us, spur us on, that it should be used to inform our options, our self-awareness. Only when an individual is standing at the edge can he or she become aware of his or her potential, take action, pursue risks, explore the unknown, determine the limits of their capabilities. If we flee our freedom in an attempt to avoid anxiety, we ignore the possibilities that lie before us, and we will ultimately succumb to despair.

'Learning to know anxiety is an adventure which every man has to affront ... He therefore who has learned rightly to be in anxiety has learned the most important thing.'

To know this anxiety and break away involves small, significant, revolutionary acts; acts that will change the order of things. And I think of the revolutionary acts I have encountered on my journey, acts committed for survival, money, empire and religion: of a plant that receives the sea with a hero's welcome; a woman of science finding fulfilment from a mathematical discovery, from breaking things up; a group of poets exhausting words as weapons; an invasive plant that overcomes indigenous populations; a man crossing oceans carrying the rudiments of a living organism; a new religion that will multiply and occupy; a writer observing nature and slowing it down for others to look; an island people refusing to leave their sinking lands. The stories of smugglers and wreckers, lesbians, parasites, witches, pagans, eccentrics, myths, cults, preachers, conscientious objectors, beachcombers, surfers, miners, conservationists, hermits, saints, emigrants, environmentalists. All of these revolutionary acts, many borne out of anxiety, disrupting the order, pulling them and us back from the precipice by the scruffs of our necks.

The world I inhabit is indeed a world on the edge – some would say on the edge of its own annihilation. Though how that will come about is anyone's guess. Rising oceans? Climate change? Nuclear fission? An impact event? Edward S. Casey knows it will be difficult, we all do, but asks: 'Can we think the world on edge by occupying the edges of thinking more effectively? Can we have the courage to think on the edge by bringing us to the edge of our own thought?' I believe we can, that we are a resilient force, individually and collectively and naturally. Because dreams are as vivid as nightmares, faith stronger than mistrust; if the road darkens our instinct is to stay on it. We, and nature, know how to hang on, to stay connected, to repair, to recover; we are not ones to walk away, we will think and then we will fight on. It is, after all, in the hardest of moments that we are at our strongest. What comes next occurs far from the realms we occupy, it comes from a curious depth, where only the dream matters.

And then, by perfect chance, it appears, the creature of the far Atlantic edge, the Cornish chough, searing past my ears with its *kjaa* cries, cries that come from the deep disused mines, cliffs and crevices it inhabits. Its tipped wing feathers are splayed out like porcupine quills, its colour black as a starless night, its feet and down-curved beak dipped in the brilliant vermilion of King Arthur's blood. It is now the keeper of his spirit. His winged messenger. It is such an extraordinary and important moment I think I might have imagined the encounter, that it was a romantic dream, but no, the choughs have definitely returned. They have defied their own extinction. In fact, so lost was the bird, so missed, the only ones to be found were those preserved in heraldry on Cornwall's coat of arms, alongside other lost symbols of the county, the fisherman and the tin miner, left standing in anticipation of some great return. 'Man is in love and loves what vanishes.'

It's quiet now. I shut my eyes. Will I make a leap into the

unknown, give in to my anxieties? Or will I turn inland and carry on? And I know almost immediately that I will carry on, just like all the others that occupy the edge, for that is all we know.

The sun is no longer falling at Land's End, it is rising, and I am heading east, back into the fray. Because really there is no escape, no beyond. If there ever was, it was only a short dream.

Notes

3   *As the American philosopher Edward S. Casey states:* Edward S. Casey, *The World on Edge* (Bloomington: Indiana University Press, 2017).

1: Home and Away

10   *'If I were reincarnated':* Interview by Jean Stein, 'William Faulkner, The Art of Fiction No. 12', *Paris Review*, 12, spring 1956.

10   *'every drop of me trembles':* D. H. Lawrence, 'Indians and an Englishman', *The Dial*, February 1923.

12   *'iodine-and-ozone tang', 'chimera', 'like bowling greens':* Richard Mabey, *The Cabaret of Plants: Botany and Imagination* (London: Profile, 2015).

13   *'Samphire taught me':* Ibid.

2: Contagions

16   *'over hills, valleys, moors', 'unseen worlds':* Betty A. Toole (ed.), *Ada, the Enchantress of Numbers: A Selection from the Letters of Lord Byron's Daughter and Her Description of the First Computer* (Mill Valley: Strawberry Press, 1992).

18   *'the Khan Kubla':* Samuel Taylor Coleridge, 'Kubla Khan', preliminary note (1816).

21   *'His tongue spools':* Jen Hadfield, 'Canis Minor', in *Nigh-No-Place* (Hexham: Bloodaxe, 2008).

3: Devils and Gods

28   *'covered with huge stones'*: Robert Southey, letter to John May, August 1799.

28   *There is a place:* William Hazlitt, 'My First Acquaintance with Poets', *The Liberal*, April 1823.

30   *'Well satisfied to be his own'*: William Cowper, 'The Snail' (1799).

33   *'charged sanctity'*: Colin Thubron, *To a Mountain in Tibet* (London: Chatto & Windus, 2011).

35   *'This is a real energy'*: 'The Aetherius Society and Holdstone Down', *North Devon Journal*, 11 July 2009.

35   *'vulgar mistake of dreaming'*: A. W. Plumstead and Harrison Hayford (eds), *The Journals and Miscellaneous Notebooks of Ralph Waldo Emerson, Volume VII: 1838–1842* (Cambridge, MA: Belknap Press of Harvard University Press, 1969).

4: Silver

39   *'a glorious intense victory'*: Damien Hirst, Rudi Fuchs and White Cube (Gallery), *For the Love of God: The Making of the Diamon Skull* (London: Other Criteria and White Cube Gallery, 2007).

40   *'high country of the winds'*, *'eve-star shining' etc.*: Henry Williamson, *Tarka the Otter: His Joyful Water-Life and Death in the Country of the Two Rivers* (London: G. P. Putnam's Sons, 1927).

42   *'barbarous conduct'*: Charles Collins Crump, *The Morte Stone: A Tale of the Coast* (London: Simpkin, Marshall, 1850).

42   *'its massive masonry'*: Henry Wadsworth Longfellow, 'The Lighthouse' (1849)

44   *The amazing thing:* Laurence Krauss, 'Cosmic Connections', YouTube talk, https://www.youtube.com/watch?v=7ImvlS8PLIo, 21 October 2009.

5: Water

47 *'I'm told every kind of English wildflower':* Henry Williamson,
   The Pathway (London: Jonathan Cape, 1928).

47 *'A heaven in a wild flower':* William Blake, 'Auguries of
   Innocence' (*c.* 1803).

48 *'You can get off alcohol':* Quoted in William Langley, '"You
   can get off alcohol and drugs, but you never get off orchids.
   Never"', *Daily Telegraph*, 22 January 2006.

48 *'even on the stillest day':* Henry Williamson, *From a Country
   Hilltop* (London: Henry Williamson Society, 1988).

52 *'How goes on the Northam Burrows scheme':* Charles Kingsley,
   letter to Dr W. H. Ackland, 1864.

6: Barriers and Breaks

59 *Mary Stella's diary:* See the Ackland and Edwards Trust
   website, acklandandedwardstrust.co.uk, and *World of Interiors*
   (August 2013).

63 *'But we haven't time':* Gaston Bachelard (trans. Maria Jolas),
   The Poetics of Space (London: Penguin, 2014).

64 *Sweeter than the odours borne:* Edward Capern, 'To Clotted
   Cream' (1882)

64 *'A straggling village':* Charles Kingsley, quoted in *A Pictorial
   and Descriptive Guide to Bideford, Clovelly, Hartland, Barnstaple,
   Ilfracombe and North-West Devon* (London: Ward, Lock & Co.,
   1900).

64 *'the old established beauty queen':* H. V. Morton, *In Search of
   England* (London: Methuen, 1927).

68 *Underlying the beauty:* Rachel Carson, *The Edge of the Sea*
   (London: Penguin, 1999).

7: In the Beginning

71 *'heaven and hell mixed as they spun':* Dylan Thomas, 'In the
   beginning', in Thomas (ed. Walford Davies and Ralph
   Maud), *Collected Poems 1934–1953* (London: J. M. Dent,
   1998).

73   *'conceived through themselves alone'*: Benjamin Wolstein, 'The Romantic Spinoza in America', *Journal of the History of Ideas*, 14:3 (June 1953).

76   *'one of those men'*: A. L. Rowse, *Robert Stephen Hawker of Morwenstow: A Belated Medieval* (St Germans: Elephant Press, 1975).

76   *'I find that by a sweeping abolition'*: R. S. Hawker, letter to the Reverend H. T. Ellacombe, 25 April 1837.

76   *'Gable on one front'*: R. S. Hawker, letter to the Reverend H. T. Ellacombe, 27 November 1837.

77   *'filled with the thoughts of God's own mind'*: 'A Legend of the Hive', in R. S. Hawker, *Reeds Shaken with the Wind: The Second Cluster* (Derby: Henry Mozley and Sons, 1844).

77   *'fell into a condition of piteous depression'*: Sabine Baring-Gould, *The Vicar of Morwenstow: A Life of Robert Stephen Hawker, MA* (London: King, 1876).

78   *'Mine was a perilous warfare'*: R. S. Hawker, 'Remembrances of a Cornish Vicar', *All the Year Round*, 11 March 1865.

78   *'The earth is an orb of emblems'*: E. R. Appleton (ed.), *Stones Broken from the Rocks: Extracts from the Manuscript Note-books of Robert Hawker, Vicar of Morwenstow, 1834–75* (London: Basil Blackwell, 1922).

79   *'We expect bodies every hour'*: Hawker's account of the wreck of the *Caledonia* is in his *Footprints of Former Men in Far Cornwall* (London: John Russell Smith, 1870).

82   *'pastoral staff'*: C. E. Byles (ed.), *The Life and Letters of R. S. Hawker (sometime Vicar of Morwenstow)* (London: Bodley Head, 1905).

83   *'A human being is part of the whole'*: Albert Einstein, letter to Robert J. Marcus, 12 February 1950. Translation quoted in Walter Sullivan, 'The Einstein Papers. A Man of Many Parts', *New York Times*, 29 March 1972.

84   *'To-day I think'*: Edward Thomas, 'Digging', in *Collected Poems* (London: Faber and Faber, 2004).

84   *five-part poem of epic proportions*: Ronald Duncan, *Man* (Bideford: Rebel Press, 1970–4).

8: Winds, Waves and Windows

87   *'little cat feet'*: Carl Sandburg, 'Fog', in *Chicago Poems* (New York: Henry Holt, 1916).

97   *'the most destructive force'*: George Monbiot, *Regenesis: Feeding the World Without Devouring the Planet* (London: Allen Lane, 2022).

9: Mystics and Mayhem

102   *'The cardinal doctrine'*: Caesar, *The Gallic War* (trans. H. J. Edwards), Loeb Classical Library 72 (Cambridge, MA: Harvard University Press, 1917).

104   *Perhaps then, having heard that silence:* 'A Native Hill', in Wendell Berry (ed. Norman Wirzba), *The Art of the Commonplace: The Agrarian Essays of Wendell Berry* (Berkeley: Counterpoint, 2002).

107   *'The Labyrinth has always been associated'*: Cecil Williamson, information for '318 – Labyrinth', Museum of Witchcraft and Magic, www.museumofwitchcraftandmagic.co.uk.

110   *'London's International Newspaper'*: *The Westminster Independent – Camelot Castle News*, issue 10,178.

10: Exploitation

110   *'the liveliest place in the circuit'*: John Wesley, *The Journal of the Rev. John Wesley, Volume 3* (London: J. Kershaw, 1827).

11: Living and Dying

132   *'For the Fallen'*: First published in *The Times*, 21 September 1914.

12: Burial

139   *'like a bit of a buckle'*: Reginald A. Smith, 'On Some Recent Exhibits', *Antiquaries Journal*, 2:2 (April 1922).

13: Debris and Deposits

148 *'The dog is perceived'*: Roger Deakin (ed. Alison Hastie and Terence Blacker), *Notes from Walnut Tree Farm* (London: Penguin, 2008).

149 *On returning from the shore*: Allen G. Folliott-Stokes, *The Cornish Coast and Moors* (London: Greening & Co., 1912).

149 *'all the freedoms that we deny ourselves'*: Kate Fox, *Watching the English: The Hidden Rules of English Behaviour* (London: Hodder & Stoughton, 2004).

151 *In* Birds Britannica: Mark Cocker and Richard Mabey, *Birds Britannica* (London: Chatto & Windus, 2005).

152 *'When I find something'*: Voiceover for *The Wrecking Season*, BBC Four, 21 June 2004. Available at nickdarke.net.

152 *'the poetry of fishing'*: Ibid.

153 *'In fifty years of wrecking'*: Ibid.

154 *'I make my living'*: Ibid.

155 *'Seeing comes before words'*: John Berger, *Ways of Seeing* (1972; London: Penguin, 2008).

14: Flying

159 *At the still point of the turning world*: T. S. Eliot, *Burnt Norton*, in *Collected Poems 1909–1962* (London: Faber and Faber, 1974).

164 *'Something there is that doesn't love a wall'*: Robert Frost, 'Mending Wall', in *North of Boston* (London: David Nutt, 1914).

165 *"Hope" is the thing with feathers*: Emily Dickinson, '"Hope" is the thing with feathers' (*c.* 1861).

15: Sacred Space

168 *'Do I dare disturb the universe'*: T. S. Eliot, 'The Love Song of J. Alfred Prufrock', in *Collected Poems 1909–1962*.

170 *'a reservoir, a motor garage'*: T. F. G. Dexter, 'St Piran: A Study in Celtic Hagiography and in Cornish Church History', doctoral thesis, University of St Andrews, 1922.

174 *'pilgrims in a fable'*: Cormac McCarthy, *The Road* (New York: Alfred A. Knopf, 2006).

175 *'like us / with purpose'*: Philip Gross, 'Pour', from *The Water Table* (Hexham: Bloodaxe Books, 2009). Reproduced with permission of Bloodaxe Books.

176 *'most deviously single-minded thing'*: Quoted in Stephen Adams, 'Philip Gross speaks about "The Water Table"', *Daily Telegraph*, 20 January 2010.

176 *'I like Cornwall very much'*: D. H. Lawrence, letter to Catherine Carswell, 13 January 1916, in George J. Zytaruk and James T. Boulton (eds), *The Letters of D. H. Lawrence, Volume II, June 1913–October 1916* (Cambridge: Cambridge University Press, 1981).

16: Out of Darkness

178 *Here the once pellucid brook:* Allen G. Folliott-Stokes, *From Devon to St Ives: The Cliffs, the Coves, the Moorland and Some of the Birds and Flowers* (London: Greening & Co., 1910).

180 *Our spread over the earth:* W. G. Sebald, *The Rings of Saturn* (London: Harvill, 1998).

180 *fabulous writers who try to put a positive spin:* See Paul Farley and Michael Symmons Roberts, *Edgelands: Journeys into England's True Wilderness* (London: Jonathan Cape, 2011) and Cal Flynn, *Islands of Abandonment: Life in the Post-Human Landscape* (London: William Collins, 2021).

183 *'Enclosure gives way to disclosure':* Casey, *The World on Edge.*

17: Water, Light, Oil

186 *To go away to the end of England:* 'A Sketch of the Past', in Virginia Woolf (ed. Jeanne Schulkind), *Moments of Being: A Collection of Autobiographical Writing* (London: Harvest, 1985).

187 *'at every moment the living creature':* John Dewey, *Art as Experience* (London: G. Allen & Unwin, 1934).

187 *'stem the flood a bit':* Virginia Woolf, *To the Lighthouse* (London: Hogarth Press, 1927). See also *Mrs Dalloway* (London: Hogarth Press, 1925).

188 *'Against you I fling myself':* Virginia Woolf, *The Waves* (London: Hogarth Press, 1931).

192 *'We saw the Buccaneer bombers'*: Quoted in Patrick Barkham, 'Oil
     spills: Legacy of the Torrey Canyon', *Guardian*, 24 June 2010.

18: Saints

198 *'when it hurts we return'*: Czesław Miłosz, 'I Sleep a Lot', in
     The Collected Poems 1931–1987 (New York: Ecco, 1988).
201 *'land of old upheaven from the abyss'*: Alfred, Lord Tennyson,
     'The Passing of Arthur', in *Idylls of the King* (1859–85).
202 *'green translucency beats'*: Walter de la Mare, 'Sunk Lyonesse',
     in *Collected Poems* (London: Faber and Faber, 1979).
206 *'an emigrant / wandering in a place'*: Eavan Boland, 'The Lost
     Land', in *The Lost Land* (Manchester: Carcanet, 1998).
     Reproduced by permission of Carcanet Press.
210 *'I suspect that alleged miracles'*: Richard Dawkins, *The God
     Delusion* (London: Bantam, 2006).

19: Magnet

215 *'there is an inside and an outside'*: Barbara Hepworth, *Barbara
     Hepworth: Carvings and Drawings* (London: Lund Humphries,
     1952).
215 *'Light gives full play'*: Ibid.
216 *The sea, a flat diminishing plane*: Barbara Hepworth, *A Pictorial
     Autobiography* (1970; London: Tate, 1985).
216 *'obsessional'*: Michael Bird, *The St Ives Artists: A Biograph of
     Place and Time* (London: Lund Humphries, 2016).
219 *'The sea on the wild coast'*: D. H. Lawrence, letter to Lady
     Ottoline Morrell, 24 January 1916, in Zytaruk and Boulton
     (eds), *The Letters of D. H. Lawrence, Volume II*.
221 *'out of England'*: D. H. Lawrence, letter to Katherine
     Mansfield, 27 December 1918, in James T. Boulton and
     Andrew Robertson (eds), *The Letters of D. H. Lawrence,
     Volume III, October 1916–June 1921* (Cambridge: Cambridge
     University Press, 1984).
221 *'wages and money and machinery'*: D. H. Lawrence, letter to
     Lady Ottoline Morrell, 27 December 1915, in Zytaruk and
     Boulton (eds), *The Letters of D. H. Lawrence, Volume II*.

221 *'I do like Cornwall'*: D. H. Lawrence, letter to J. D. Beresford, January 1916, in ibid.

221 *'war-wave'*: D. H. Lawrence, *Kangaroo* (London: Martin Secker, 1923).

223 *'In the medieval period'*: Alex Woodcock, 'Zennor Transformations', *Elementum: A Journal of Nature & Story*, 1 (2016).

224 *'We have lingered'*: Eliot, 'The Love Song of J. Alfred Prufrock'.

225 *'as the plant was billions of years ago'*: Overview, *The Littoral Zone*, markquinn.com.

20: Into the Sacrifice Zones

229 *'continued depredations'*: F. Hamilton Davey, *Flora of Cornwall: Being an Account of the Flowering Plants and Ferns Found in the County of Cornwall including the Scilly Isles* (Penryn: P. Chegwidden, 1909).

231 *The plant's architecture:* Paul Evans, 'Country diary: Nothing can hold back the bracken', *Guardian*, 27 October 2022.

233 *'I once gave a talk'*: Extracts from Jay Armstrong, 'Abandoned Mines: In Conversation with Keith Russ', *Elementum: A Journal of Nature & Story*, 3 (2017).

235 *We are now four hundred yards out:* Wilkie Collins, *Rambles Beyond Railways: or, Notes on Cornwall Taken a-Foot* (London: Richard Bentley, 1851).

239 *'We could create'*: Quoted in Jonathan Leake, 'There's lithium in them thar hills, Poldark: Cornwall set for mining bonanza', *The Times*, 22 July 2018.

239 *'Of all tyrannies'*: C. S. Lewis, 'The Humanitarian Theory of Punishment', in Walter Hooper (ed.), *God in the Dock: Essays on Theology and Ethics* (Grand Rapids: William B. Eerdmans, 1970).

240 *'It is inconceivable to me'*: Aldo Leopold, *Think Like a Mountain: Essays from a Sand County Almanac* (London: Penguin, 2021).

21: Entrances and Exits

247 *In his essay:* Maurice Maeterlinck (trans. Philip Mosley), *The Intelligence of Flowers* (Albany: State University of New York Press, 2008).

248 *'I once killed four', etc.:* Folliott-Stokes, *The Cornish Coast and Moors*.

22: Lost Lands

260 *'the dizziness of freedom':* Søren Kierkegaard (trans. Alastair Hannay), *The Concept of Anxiety: A Simple Psychologically Orientated Deliberation in View of the Dogmatic Problem of Hereditary Sin* (New York: Liveright/Norton, 2014).

262 *'Learning to know anxiety':* Ibid.

263 *'Can we think the world on edge':* Casey, *The World on Edge*.

264 *'Man is in love':* W. B. Yeats, 'Nineteen Hundred and Nineteen' (1920).

Acknowledgements

This walk has indeed been slow. I started it in 2010 in the September equinox and walked it in sections, returning like a migratory bird over the years to the spot I had left off from. I'm ashamed to say I still haven't reached Poole, the end of the South West Coast Path, but I'm getting there, albeit now with knee supports and sticks.

The book itself started out as diary entries, but when my metaphoric pen went off road into areas that encompassed, among other things, astronomy, botany, philosophy, history and poetry, I knew I needed a much larger vehicle to channel my thoughts, hence *Edgeland* was born.

It has been a long journey in other ways, and many people have helped tame my wild, rampaging thoughts and kept me from straying off the path: my treasured agent Caroline Dawnay and her assistant Kat Aitken, and all at Abacus, most notably Richard Beswick and Susan de Soissons, and Zoe Gullen for her skilful editing. I would also like to thank Richard Collins, who was the first to cast his beady eye over it, as well as Marcus May, Angela Stucley and the staff at Morrab Library in Penzance. Lastly, my husband Hugo, and my dog Rocco, who when accompanying me, walked silently and mostly ahead of me, leaving my mind to range freely over all that this varied, complicated but beautiful land offers up.

Credits

Images
Courtesy of the author: 25, 53, 91, 93, 171 (*right*)
Sophie-Ann Steers/Alamy Stock Photo: 62
Epics/Getty Images: 79
Tom Sanderson/Shutterstock: 120
National Museums Scotland: 140
© Anthony Harrison (cc-by-sa/20.0): 171 (*left*)
4 season backpacking/Alamy Stock Photo: 181
Paul Armiger/© *Daily Telegraph*: 208
Ashley Cooper pics/Alamy Stock Photo: 211
Historical Picture Archive/Alamy Stock Photo: 218
The Mermaid of Zennor. Global Warming Images/
    Shutterstock: 223
Fern Gatherers by Henry Woods. From *The Graphic*, 1872: 228
Dr Keith Russ/*Elementum*: 234
Wikipedia: 242
Sendro Serra/Shutterstock: 246

Text
Burnt Norton and 'The Love Song of J. Alfred Prufrock' by T. S.
    Eliot: extracts reproduced with permission of Faber and Faber
'Pour' by Philip Gross: extract reproduced with permission of
    Bloodaxe Books
'The Lost Land' by Eavan Boland: extract reproduced with
    permission of Carcanet Press
'Abandoned Mines: In Conversation with Keith Russ' by
    Jay Armstrong: extract reproduced with permission of Jay
    Armstrong and Dr Keith Russ